EDGARDO FERNANDEZ CLIMENT

Cloud Security Posture Management (CSPM) Demystified

A Complete Handbook for Cloud Security

Copyright © 2024 by Edgardo Fernandez Climent

All rights reserved. No part of this publication may be reproduced, stored or transmitted in any form or by any means, electronic, mechanical, photocopying, recording, scanning, or otherwise without written permission from the publisher. It is illegal to copy this book, post it to a website, or distribute it by any other means without permission.

Edgardo Fernandez Climent has no responsibility for the persistence or accuracy of URLs for external or third-party Internet Websites referred to in this publication and does not guarantee that any content on such Websites is, or will remain, accurate or appropriate.

Designations used by companies to distinguish their products are often claimed as trademarks. All brand names and product names used in this book and on its cover are trade names, service marks, trademarks and registered trademarks of their respective owners. The publishers and the book are not associated with any product or vendor mentioned in this book. None of the companies referenced within the book have endorsed the book.

First edition

This book was professionally typeset on Reedsy.
Find out more at reedsy.com

Contents

I Introduction

Chapter 1: The Importance of Cloud Security … 3
  A. Overview of Cloud Adoption Trends … 3
    A.1 The Rise of Cloud Computing … 3
    A.2 Cloud Service Models … 5
    A.3 Cloud Deployment Models … 5
    A.4 Security Implications of Cloud Adoption … 6
    A.5 Conclusion … 7
  B. Common Security Challenges in Cloud Environments … 7
    B.1 The Shared Responsibility Model … 7
    B.2 Data Breaches and Data Loss … 8
    B.3 Identity and Access Management (IAM) … 9
    B.4 Insecure APIs … 10
    B.5 Compliance and Regulatory Challenges … 11
    B.6 Threat Detection and Incident Response … 11
    B.7 Conclusion … 12
  C. Introduction to Cloud Security Posture Management (CSPM) … 13
    C.1 Understanding CSPM … 13
    C.2 Key Components of CSPM … 14
    C.3 Benefits of Implementing CSPM … 16
    C.4 Real-World Applications of CSPM … 18
    C.5 Conclusion … 18
  D. Benefits of Implementing Cloud Security Posture Management (CSPM) … 19

D.1 Enhanced Security	19
D.2 Improved Compliance	20
D.3 Operational Efficiency	22
D.4 Proactive Risk Management	23
D.5 Conclusion	24

II Understanding CSPM

Chapter 2: Fundamentals of CSPM	29
A. Definition and Core Principles	29
A.1 Definition of CSPM	29
A.2 Core Principles of CSPM	30
A.3 The Role of CSPM in Cloud Security	33
A.4 Conclusion	33
B. Key Components of CSPM	34
B.1 Continuous Monitoring	34
B.2 Risk Assessment and Prioritization	35
B.3 Compliance Management	36
B.4 Automated Remediation	37
B.5 Visibility and Reporting	38
B.6 Integration with Existing Tools and Workflows	39
B.7 Proactive Threat Management	40
B.8 Conclusion	41
C. CSPM vs. Traditional Security Measures	41
C.1 Overview of Traditional Security Measures	42
C.2 Limitations of Traditional Security Measures in Cloud Environments	43
C.3 Advantages of CSPM over Traditional Security Measures	44
C.4 Case Study: CSPM vs. Traditional Security Measures	46
C.5 Conclusion	48
Chapter 3: CSPM Tools and Solutions	49
A. Overview of Leading CSPM Tools	49
A.1 Palo Alto Networks Prisma Cloud	49

A.2 Check Point CloudGuard	50
A.3 AWS Security Hub	51
A.4 Microsoft Azure Security Center	53
A.5 Google Cloud Security Command Center (SCC)	54
A.6 Open Source CSPM Tools	55
A.7 Conclusion	57
B. Criteria for Selecting a CSPM Tool	57
B.1 Comprehensive Coverage	57
B.2 Compliance and Regulatory Support	58
B.3 Automation and Remediation	59
B.4 Integration Capabilities	60
B.5 Usability and Reporting	61
B.7 Vendor Support and Community	63
B.8 Cost and Licensing	64
B.9 Conclusion	65
C. Comparison of CSPM Tools	66
C.1 Palo Alto Networks Prisma Cloud	66
C.2 Check Point CloudGuard	67
C.3 AWS Security Hub	68
C.4 Microsoft Azure Security Center	69
C.5 Google Cloud Security Command Center (SCC)	70
C.6 Open Source CSPM Tools	71
C.7 Comparison Summary	74
C.8 Conclusion	75

III Planning and Preparation

Chapter 4: Assessing Your Cloud Environment	79
A. Inventorying Cloud Resources	79
A.1 Importance of Inventorying Cloud Resources	79
A.2 Steps for Creating a Comprehensive Inventory	81
A.3 Best Practices for Inventorying Cloud Resources	84
A.4 Tools for Inventorying Cloud Resources	85

- A.5 Conclusion — 87
- B. Identifying Security Requirements and Compliance Needs — 87
  - B.1 Understanding Security Requirements — 88
  - B.2 Understanding Compliance Needs — 90
  - B.3 Developing a Security and Compliance Framework — 92
  - B.4 Tools for Identifying Security and Compliance Needs — 94
  - B.5 Conclusion — 95
- C. Conducting a Risk Assessment — 96
  - C.1 Importance of Risk Assessment — 97
  - C.2 Steps in Conducting a Risk Assessment — 97
  - C.3 Best Practices for Risk Assessment — 102
  - C.4 Tools for Conducting Risk Assessments — 104
  - C.5 Conclusion — 106

Chapter 5: Setting Goals and Objectives — 107
- A. Defining Clear Security Goals — 107
  - A.1 Importance of Clear Security Goals — 107
  - A.2 Process of Setting Security Goals — 109
  - A.3 Examples of Effective Security Goals — 111
  - A.4 Monitoring and Revisiting Security Goals — 114
  - A.5 Conclusion — 114
- B. Establishing Key Performance Indicators (KPIs) — 115
  - B.1 Importance of KPIs — 115
  - B.2 Selecting and Defining Relevant KPIs — 116
  - B.3 Examples of Effective KPIs for Cloud Security — 118
  - B.4 Best Practices for Monitoring KPIs — 121
  - B.5 Tools for Monitoring KPIs — 122
  - B.6 Conclusion — 124
- C. Aligning CSPM Goals with Business Objectives — 125
  - C.1 Importance of Aligning CSPM Goals with Business Objectives — 125
  - C.2 Strategies for Aligning CSPM Goals with Business Objectives — 127
  - C.3 Examples of Aligned CSPM Goals — 130

- C.4 Best Practices for Aligning CSPM Goals — 132
- C.5 Conclusion — 133

IV Implementation Steps

Chapter 6: Configuring CSPM Tools — 137
- A. Setting Up the CSPM Environment — 137
  - A.1 Initial Configuration — 137
  - A.2 Integration with Cloud Services — 139
  - A.3 Best Practices for Optimizing CSPM Performance — 141
  - A.4 Tools for Setting Up the CSPM Environment — 143
  - A.5 Conclusion — 145
- B. Integrating CSPM Tools with Existing Systems — 146
  - B.1 Importance of Integrating CSPM Tools — 146
  - B.2 Steps for Integrating CSPM Tools with Existing Systems — 147
  - B.3 Best Practices for Successful Integration — 151
  - B.4 Tools for Integrating CSPM with Existing Systems — 153
  - B.5 Conclusion — 155
- C. Initial Configuration and Setup — 155
  - C.1 Choosing the Right CSPM Tool — 156
  - C.2 Pre-Configuration Planning — 156
  - C.3 Setting Up the CSPM Tool — 158
  - C.4 Integration with Cloud Services — 159
  - C.5 Initial Security Policies and Baselines — 161
  - C.6 Monitoring and Fine-Tuning — 162
  - C.7 Documentation and Training — 163
  - C.8 Conclusion — 164
  - D.1 Step-by-Step Installation Guide — 165
  - D.2 Configuring Prowler for AWS — 167
  - D.3 Running Your First Scan — 170
  - D.4 Best Practices for Using Prowler — 173
  - D.5 Conclusion — 174

Chapter 7: Continuous Monitoring and Assessment — 175

- A. Setting Up Continuous Monitoring — 175
  - A.1 Importance of Continuous Monitoring — 175
  - A.2 Selecting the Right Monitoring Tools — 176
  - A.3 Configuring Monitoring Services — 178
  - A.4 Best Practices for Effective Continuous Monitoring — 184
  - A.5 Conclusion — 185
- B. Automated Scanning and Risk Detection — 186
  - B.1 Importance of Automated Scanning and Risk Detection — 186
  - B.2 Tools and Technologies for Automated Scanning and Risk Detection — 187
  - B.3 Implementing Automated Scanning and Risk Detection — 189
  - B.4 Best Practices for Effective Automated Scanning and Risk Detection — 196
  - B.5 Conclusion — 198
- C. Interpreting CSPM Reports and Dashboards — 198
  - C.1 Importance of CSPM Reports and Dashboards — 198
  - C.2 Key Metrics in CSPM Reports and Dashboards — 200
  - C.3 Recognizing Trends and Patterns — 202
  - C.4 Making Data-Driven Decisions — 203
  - C.5 Best Practices for Interpreting CSPM Reports and Dashboards — 204
  - C.6 Conclusion — 206
- D. Hands-On Exercise: Continuous Monitoring with Prowler — 206
  - D.1 Scheduling Regular Scans — 207
  - D.2 Automating Scan Results to Dashboards — 212
  - D.3 Conclusion — 215
- Chapter 8: Remediation and Response — 216
  - A. Prioritizing Security Issues — 216
    - A.1 Importance of Prioritizing Security Issues — 216
    - A.2 Risk Assessment and Categorization — 217
    - A.3 Using Automated Tools for Prioritization — 220
    - A.4 Best Practices for Prioritizing Security Issues — 221
    - A.5 Conclusion — 223
  - B. Automated and Manual Remediation Strategies — 223

B.1 Importance of Remediation	224
B.2 Automated Remediation Strategies	225
B.3 Manual Remediation Strategies	230
B.4 Combining Automated and Manual Remediation	234
B.5 Conclusion	235
C. Incident Response Planning	236
C.1 Importance of Incident Response Planning	236
C.2 Key Elements of Incident Response Planning	237
C.3 Developing an Incident Response Plan	241
C.4 Best Practices for Incident Response Planning	244
C.5 Conclusion	246
D. Hands-On Exercise: Remediation Strategies with Prowler	246
D.1 Identifying Critical Vulnerabilities	246
D.2 Applying Remediation Steps	248
D.3 Verifying Remediation Effectiveness	251
D.4 Conclusion	256

V Advanced CSPM Strategies

Chapter 9: Integrating CSPM with DevOps	259
A. CSPM in CI/CD Pipelines	259
A.1 Importance of Integrating CSPM with CI/CD Pipelines	259
A.2 Implementing CSPM in CI/CD Pipelines	260
A.3 Example: Integrating CSPM with a CI/CD Pipeline	270
A.4 Conclusion	274
B. Ensuring Security in DevOps Practices	274
B.1 The Need for DevSecOps	275
B.2 Key Principles of DevSecOps	276
B.3 Implementing Security in DevOps Practices	277
B.4 Best Practices for Ensuring Security in DevOps	289
B.5 Conclusion	291
C. Hands-On Exercise: Integrating Prowler in CI/CD Pipelines	291
C.1 Setting up Prowler Scans in Jenkins	291

C.2 Setting up Prowler Scans in GitLab CI	296
C.3 Automating Security Checks in the Deployment Process	300
C.4 Conclusion	307
Chapter 10: Multi-Cloud and Hybrid Environments	**308**
A. Managing Security Across Multiple Cloud Providers	308
A.1 Understanding Multi-Cloud and Hybrid Environments	308
A.2 Security Best Practices for Multi-Cloud and Hybrid Environments	310
A.3 Tools for Managing Security in Multi-Cloud and Hybrid Environments	313
A.4 Implementing a Multi-Cloud Security Strategy	315
A.5 Conclusion	317
B. CSPM Strategies for Hybrid Cloud Setups	317
B.1 Understanding Hybrid Cloud Setups	318
B.2 Key CSPM Strategies for Hybrid Cloud Setups	319
B.3 Implementing CSPM in Hybrid Cloud Setups	322
B.4 Tools for CSPM in Hybrid Cloud Setups	325
B.5 Case Study: Implementing CSPM in a Hybrid Cloud Setup	327
B.6 Conclusion	329
Chapter 11: Compliance and Regulatory Considerations	**330**
A. Understanding Industry-Specific Regulations	330
A.1 Overview of Industry-Specific Regulations	330
A.2 Key Industry-Specific Regulations	331
A.3 Integrating Compliance into CSPM Practices	335
A.4 Tools for Managing Compliance	337
A.5 Case Study: Achieving HIPAA Compliance in a Hybrid Cloud Environment	339
A.6 Conclusion	341
B. Using CSPM for Compliance Management	341
B.1 Importance of Compliance Management	341
B.2 Leveraging CSPM for Compliance Management	342
B.3 Implementing CSPM for Compliance Management	345

B.4 Case Study: Using CSPM for PCI DSS Compliance	348
B.5 Conclusion	350
C. Generating Compliance Reports	350
C.1 Importance of Compliance Reports	350
C.2 Using CSPM Tools to Generate Compliance Reports	352
C.3 Best Practices for Generating Effective Compliance Reports	354
C.4 Tools and Techniques for Effective Compliance Reporting	356
C.5 Case Study: Generating GDPR Compliance Reports with Google Cloud SCC	358
C.6 Conclusion	359
D. Hands-On Exercise: Compliance Reporting with Prowler	360
D.1 Configuring Compliance-Specific Checks	360
D.2 Generating and Interpreting Compliance Reports	362
D.3 Best Practices for Compliance Reporting with Prowler	366
D.4 Conclusion	368

VI Case Studies and Best Practices

Chapter 12: Real-World CSPM Implementations	371
A. Case Studies of Successful CSPM Deployments	371
A.1 Case Study: Financial Services Firm Achieving PCI DSS Compliance	371
A.2 Case Study: Healthcare Organization Ensuring HIPAA Compliance	373
A.3 Case Study: E-commerce Company Ensuring GDPR Compliance	375
A.4 Lessons Learned and Best Practices	377
A.5 Conclusion	379
B. Lessons Learned from Industry Leaders	380
B.1 Key Lessons from Successful CSPM Implementations	380
B.2 Conclusion	383
Chapter 13: Best Practices for CSPM	384

A. Establishing a Security-First Culture	384
A.1 Importance of a Security-First Culture	384
A.2 Strategies for Establishing a Security-First Culture	385
A.2.6 Foster Collaboration Across Teams	389
A.3 Measuring the Success of a Security-First Culture	390
A.4 Conclusion	392
B. Continuous Improvement and Adaptation	392
B.1 Importance of Continuous Improvement and Adaptation	393
B.2 Strategies for Continuous Improvement in CSPM	394
B.3 Adapting to Changing Regulatory Requirements	397
B.4 Tools and Technologies for Continuous Improvement	399
B.5 Case Study: Continuous Improvement in CSPM	400
B.6 Conclusion	403
C. Keeping Up with Evolving Threats	403
C.1 Importance of Staying Ahead of Evolving Threats	403
C.2 Strategies for Keeping Up with Evolving Threats	405
C.3 Adapting to New Threats and Technologies	408
C.4 Case Study: Adapting to Evolving Threats with CSPM	411
C.5 Conclusion	413

VII   Conclusion

Chapter 14: The Future of CSPM	417
A. Emerging Trends in Cloud Security	417
A.1 Increasing Adoption of Multi-Cloud and Hybrid Cloud Environments	417
A.2 Integration of Artificial Intelligence and Machine Learning	419
A.3 Zero Trust Architecture (ZTA)	420
A.4 DevSecOps Integration	421
A.5 Enhanced Compliance and Governance	423
A.6 Conclusion	424
B. The Role of AI and Machine Learning in CSPM	425

B.1 Enhancing Threat Detection and Response	425
B.2 Improving Compliance and Governance	427
B.3 Enhancing Security Operations	428
B.4 Future Trends in AI and ML for CSPM	429
B.5 Conclusion	431
C. Preparing for Future Challenges	432
C.1 Anticipating Emerging Threats	432
C.2 Adapting to Regulatory Changes	434
C.3 Leveraging Advanced Technologies	435
C.4 Enhancing Security Posture Management	437
C.5 Building a Security-First Culture	438
C.6 Conclusion	440

VIII Appendices

Appendix A: Glossary of Terms	443
Appendix B: CSPM Tool Comparison Matrix	450
Appendix C: Additional Resources and Reading	457
Appendix D: Templates and Checklists	463
D.1 Security Policy Template	463
D.2 Risk Assessment Checklist	465
D.3 Compliance Checklist	466
D.4 Incident Response Plan Template	467
D.5 Cloud Security Audit Checklist	468
About the Author	471
Also by Edgardo Fernandez Climent	473

I

Introduction

Chapter 1: The Importance of Cloud Security

A. Overview of Cloud Adoption Trends

As a practitioner with extensive experience in cloud security, I believe it is imperative to understand the landscape of cloud adoption, as it forms the foundation of our discussion on cloud security posture management (CSPM). This chapter delves into the trends driving cloud adoption and the associated security implications, setting the stage for a comprehensive understanding of CSPM.

A.1 The Rise of Cloud Computing

Over the past decade, cloud computing has transformed from a burgeoning technology to a cornerstone of modern IT infrastructure. Organizations across industries are increasingly migrating to the cloud to leverage its numerous benefits, including scalability, cost efficiency, and flexibility.

A.1.1 Historical Context

The concept of cloud computing dates back to the 1960s, with the development of time-sharing systems. However, it wasn't until the mid-2000s that cloud computing gained significant traction. The launch of Amazon Web Services (AWS) in 2006 marked a pivotal moment, introducing the first widely adopted Infrastructure as a Service (IaaS) platform.

A.1.2 Adoption Statistics

According to a 2023 report by Gartner, global spending on public cloud services is expected to reach $591.8 billion by the end of the year, a 20.7% increase from 2022. This rapid growth highlights the pervasive adoption of cloud services across sectors, from small businesses to large enterprises.

A.1.3 Key Drivers of Cloud Adoption

Several factors contribute to the widespread adoption of cloud computing:

- **Cost Efficiency:** Cloud services eliminate the need for significant upfront capital expenditure on hardware and software, shifting to a more manageable operational expenditure model.
- **Scalability:** Cloud providers offer scalable resources that can be adjusted based on demand, ensuring optimal performance and cost management.
- **Flexibility and Agility:** Cloud environments enable rapid deployment and provisioning of resources, facilitating faster innovation and time-to-market.

- **Global Reach:** Cloud services provide global accessibility, allowing organizations to seamlessly operate and collaborate across different geographies.

A.2 Cloud Service Models

Understanding the different cloud service models is crucial for grasping the nuances of cloud security. The primary models include:

- **Infrastructure as a Service (IaaS):** This provides virtualized computing resources over the Internet. Examples include AWS EC2, Microsoft Azure VMs, and Google Cloud Compute Engine.
- **Platform as a Service (PaaS):** This type of service offers a platform allowing customers to develop, run, and manage applications without dealing with the underlying infrastructure. Examples include AWS Elastic Beanstalk, Google App Engine, and Microsoft Azure App Services.
- **Software as a Service (SaaS):** Delivers software applications over the internet on a subscription basis. Examples include Microsoft Office 365, Salesforce, and Google Workspace.

Each service model presents unique security challenges and responsibilities, which will be explored in subsequent chapters.

A.3 Cloud Deployment Models

Cloud deployment models define how cloud services are made available to users. The main models are:

- **Public Cloud:** Services are delivered over the public internet and shared across multiple organizations. Examples include AWS, Microsoft Azure, and Google Cloud Platform.
- **Private Cloud:** Services are maintained on a private network for a single organization, providing greater control and security.
- **Hybrid Cloud:** This model combines public and private cloud environments, allowing data and applications to be shared between them. It offers greater flexibility and optimizes existing infrastructure.
- **Multi-cloud:** Involves using multiple cloud services from different providers, reducing dependency on a single provider, and enhancing resilience.

A.4 Security Implications of Cloud Adoption

While cloud adoption offers numerous benefits, it also introduces new security challenges. As organizations migrate to the cloud, they must address the following security considerations:

- **Data Security:** Ensuring the confidentiality, integrity, and availability of data stored and processed in the cloud.
- **Compliance:** Adhering to industry-specific regulations and standards, such as GDPR, HIPAA, and PCI-DSS.
- **Access Control:** Implementing robust identity and access management (IAM) practices to prevent unauthorized access.
- **Threat Detection and Response:** Monitor potential threats and swiftly respond to incidents.
- **Misconfigurations:** Identifying and rectifying cloud service misconfigurations that could expose sensitive data or resources.

A.5 Conclusion

IT professionals securing cloud environments must understand the trends driving cloud adoption and the associated security implications. As we progress through this guide, we will delve deeper into Cloud Security Posture Management (CSPM) and how it addresses these challenges, providing you with the knowledge and tools needed to safeguard your cloud infrastructure effectively.

B. Common Security Challenges in Cloud Environments

In the rapidly evolving landscape of cloud computing, security remains a paramount concern for organizations leveraging cloud services. While cloud providers implement robust security measures, the shared responsibility model necessitates that users also play a crucial role in securing their cloud environments. This section explores the most prevalent security challenges organizations face in the cloud, offering insights into the complexities and necessary mitigation strategies.

B.1 The Shared Responsibility Model

Before diving into specific challenges, it's important to understand the shared responsibility model that governs cloud security. This model delineates the security responsibilities of the cloud service provider (CSP) and the customer:

Cloud Service Provider (CSP) Responsibilities:

- Physical security of data centers
- Hardware and software infrastructure
- Network controls and virtualization

Customer Responsibilities:

- Data encryption and integrity
- Identity and access management (IAM)
- Configuration and management of cloud resources

Misunderstanding this model can lead to gaps in security, making it essential for organizations to define and understand their roles clearly.

B.2 Data Breaches and Data Loss

Data breaches remain one of the most significant security threats in cloud environments. Sensitive data stored in the cloud can be a prime target for cybercriminals. Common causes of data breaches include:

Misconfigured Cloud Storage:

- Publicly accessible storage buckets and databases can expose sensitive information.
- **Example:** In 2017, a misconfigured AWS S3 bucket exposed the personal information of over 198 million American voters.

Insufficient Access Controls:

- Weak or improperly managed access controls can allow unauthorized users to access sensitive data.

- **Example:** An attacker exploits weak IAM policies to access critical data.

Mitigation Strategies:

- Implement strict access controls and regularly review IAM policies.
- Encrypting data at rest and in transit.
- Conducting regular audits and using tools like AWS Config to detect misconfigurations.

B.3 Identity and Access Management (IAM)

Effective identity and access management is crucial for securing cloud environments. Common IAM challenges include:

Excessive Permissions:

- Users or applications with excessive permissions can perform unauthorized actions.
- **Example:** A developer granted admin-level access for a temporary task but not revoked after completion.

Credential Compromise:

- Compromised credentials can lead to unauthorized access and data breaches.
- **Example:** Phishing attacks targeting cloud credentials.

Mitigation Strategies:

- Implementing the least privilege principle ensures users have only the

permissions they need.
- Using multi-factor authentication (MFA) to enhance login security.
- Regularly rotating and auditing credentials.

B.4 Insecure APIs

APIs are a critical component of cloud services, enabling integration and automation. However, insecure APIs can expose vulnerabilities:

Unsecured Endpoints:

- Publicly accessible APIs without proper authentication and encryption can be exploited.
- **Example:** An attacker accessing a poorly secured API to retrieve sensitive data.

Improper Rate Limiting:

- Lack of rate limiting can lead to denial-of-service attacks.
- **Example:** An API endpoint is overwhelmed with requests, disrupting service.

Mitigation Strategies:

- Securing APIs with strong authentication and encryption.
- Implementing rate limiting and monitoring API usage.
- Regularly testing and validating API security.

B.5 Compliance and Regulatory Challenges

Organizations must comply with various industry regulations and standards, which can be complex in cloud environments:

Data Sovereignty:

- Ensuring data resides within specific geographic boundaries to comply with local laws.
- **Example:** GDPR requires data of EU citizens to be stored and processed within the EU.

Auditing and Reporting:

- Maintaining detailed logs and reports to demonstrate compliance.
- **Example:** Healthcare organizations must comply with HIPAA requirements for data protection.

Mitigation Strategies:

- Selecting cloud providers that offer compliance certifications relevant to your industry.
- Using CSPM tools to monitor compliance status continuously.
- Implementing data residency controls and encryption.

B.6 Threat Detection and Incident Response

Effective threat detection and incident response are critical for mitigating security incidents in the cloud:

Lack of Visibility:

- Limited visibility into cloud environments can hinder threat detection.
- **Example:** An undetected intrusion leading to data exfiltration.

Slow Response Times:

- Delayed responses to security incidents can exacerbate the damage.
- **Example:** Slow identification and containment of a malware attack.

Mitigation Strategies:

- Implementing comprehensive logging and monitoring solutions.
- Using automated tools for real-time threat detection and response.
- Regularly testing and updating incident response plans.

B.7 Conclusion

The security challenges in cloud environments are multifaceted and require a proactive and comprehensive approach. Organizations can significantly enhance their cloud security posture by understanding the shared responsibility model and addressing common security issues such as data breaches, IAM, insecure APIs, compliance, and threat detection. In subsequent chapters, we will delve deeper into cloud security posture management (CSPM) and explore practical solutions and strategies to mitigate these challenges, ensuring a robust and secure cloud infrastructure.

C. Introduction to Cloud Security Posture Management (CSPM)

As organizations increasingly migrate to the cloud, managing and securing their cloud environments has become a critical priority. This section provides an in-depth introduction to Cloud Security Posture Management (CSPM), explaining its significance, core components, and the value it brings to modern IT infrastructures.

C.1 Understanding CSPM

Cloud Security Posture Management (CSPM) refers to continuously monitoring and assessing cloud environments to ensure they adhere to security best practices and regulatory requirements. CSPM tools automate the identification and remediation of misconfigurations and vulnerabilities, thereby maintaining an optimal security posture.

C.1.1 Definition and Scope

CSPM encompasses a range of activities aimed at securing cloud environments:

- **Configuration Management:** Ensuring that cloud resources are configured according to security best practices.
- **Compliance Monitoring:** Continuously checking for adherence to regulatory standards such as GDPR, HIPAA, and PCI-DSS.
- **Risk Assessment:** Identifying and prioritizing security risks based on their potential impact.

- **Automated Remediation:** Automatically fixing or recommending fixes for identified issues.

C.1.2 The Evolution of CSPM

CSPM has evolved in response to cloud environments' growing complexity and scale. Traditional security measures, which were largely manual and reactive, proved insufficient for the dynamic nature of cloud infrastructures. CSPM emerged as a proactive and automated approach to address these challenges.

C.2 Key Components of CSPM

To effectively manage and secure cloud environments, CSPM tools typically include several key components:

C.2.1 Continuous Monitoring

Continuous monitoring is the cornerstone of CSPM. It involves real-time surveillance of cloud resources to detect misconfigurations, vulnerabilities, and compliance issues. This ensures that any deviations from security policies are promptly identified and addressed.

Example: A CSPM tool continuously scans cloud storage buckets to ensure they are not publicly accessible unless explicitly required.

C.2.2 Risk Assessment and Prioritization

CSPM tools assess the security posture of cloud environments by evaluating identified risks. These risks are then prioritized based on their potential impact on the organization. This allows IT teams to focus on the most critical issues first.

Example: A misconfigured firewall rule that exposes a sensitive database to the internet would be prioritized over a less critical configuration issue.

C.2.3 Compliance Management

CSPM tools help organizations adhere to regulatory requirements by continuously monitoring compliance status and generating reports. This is crucial for industries with stringent data protection laws.

Example: A healthcare organization using a CSPM tool to ensure compliance with HIPAA by monitoring the security of patient data stored in the cloud.

C.2.4 Automated Remediation

Many CSPM tools offer automated remediation capabilities, where certain misconfigurations can be automatically corrected without manual intervention. This significantly reduces the time and effort required to maintain a secure cloud environment.

Example: Automatically changing the permissions of an overly permissive storage bucket to restrict public access.

C.2.5 Visibility and Reporting

CSPM tools provide comprehensive visibility into the security posture of cloud environments through detailed dashboards and reports. These insights help organizations understand their security status and track improvements over time.

Example: A security dashboard showing the number of compliance violations, risk levels, and remediation actions taken over the past month.

C.3 Benefits of Implementing CSPM

Implementing CSPM brings numerous benefits to organizations, enhancing their overall security posture and operational efficiency:

C.3.1 Enhanced Security

By continuously monitoring cloud environments and automating the detection and remediation of security issues, CSPM significantly reduces the risk of data breaches and other security incidents.

Example: Detecting and mitigating a misconfigured network security group that could allow unauthorized access to critical applications.

C.3.2 Improved Compliance

CSPM helps organizations maintain compliance with industry regulations by providing real-time visibility into compliance status and generating necessary reports.

Example: Automatically generating compliance reports for an annual audit, showing adherence to PCI-DSS standards.

C.3.3 Operational Efficiency

Automating routine security tasks reduces the burden on IT teams, allowing them to focus on more strategic initiatives. This leads to better resource allocation and improved operational efficiency.

Example: Freeing up IT staff to work on innovative projects rather than spending time manually checking cloud configurations.

C.3.4 Proactive Risk Management

CSPM enables organizations to proactively manage risks by identifying potential issues before attackers can exploit them. This proactive approach is critical in the fast-paced world of cloud computing.

Example: Identifying and addressing vulnerabilities in a development environment before deploying applications to production.

C.4 Real-World Applications of CSPM

CSPM tools are widely used across industries to enhance cloud security and compliance. Here are a few real-world applications:

- **Financial Services:** Ensuring compliance with regulations such as GDPR and PCI-DSS while protecting sensitive financial data.
- **Healthcare:** Maintaining HIPAA compliance and securing patient data stored in cloud environments.
- **Retail:** Protecting customer information and ensuring compliance with data protection laws in a dynamic e-commerce landscape.
- **Technology:** Safeguarding intellectual property and sensitive data in a rapidly evolving technology sector.

C.5 Conclusion

Cloud Security Posture Management (CSPM) is essential to modern cloud security strategies. CSPM helps organizations maintain a robust security posture in an increasingly complex and dynamic cloud landscape by continuously monitoring cloud environments, assessing risks, ensuring compliance, and automating remediation. As we proceed through this guide, we will explore practical steps and best practices for implementing CSPM, equipping you with the knowledge and tools necessary to secure your cloud infrastructure effectively.

D. Benefits of Implementing Cloud Security Posture Management (CSPM)

As cloud environments grow increasingly complex and integral to business operations, the importance of robust security measures cannot be overstated. Cloud Security Posture Management (CSPM) offers a comprehensive solution to the unique challenges posed by cloud security. This section will explore the multifaceted benefits of implementing CSPM in your organization, from enhancing security and compliance to improving operational efficiency and fostering proactive risk management.

D.1 Enhanced Security

One of the most significant benefits of CSPM is the enhancement of overall security in cloud environments. CSPM tools provide continuous monitoring, automated detection, and remediation of security issues, ensuring your cloud infrastructure remains secure and resilient against threats.

D.1.1 Continuous Monitoring and Real-Time Alerts

CSPM tools continuously monitor your cloud environment, identifying real-time misconfigurations, vulnerabilities, and potential threats. This allows immediate action, reducing the window of opportunity for attackers.

Example: A CSPM tool detects an open storage bucket that is inadvertently accessible to the public and sends an alert to the security team, prompting immediate corrective action.

D.1.2 Automated Remediation

Automated remediation capabilities allow CSPM tools to fix certain security issues without manual intervention, significantly reducing the time and effort required to maintain a secure environment.

Example: Automatically applying the correct security settings to a misconfigured cloud resource to prevent unauthorized access.

D.1.3 Threat Detection and Response

CSPM tools integrate with existing security frameworks to enhance threat detection and response capabilities. CSPM tools can identify sophisticated threats and initiate appropriate responses by correlating data from various sources.

Example: Detecting unusual access patterns that indicate a potential insider threat and triggering an automated response to contain the threat.

D.2 Improved Compliance

Compliance with industry regulations and standards is a critical aspect of cloud security. CSPM tools help organizations ensure continuous compliance by automating compliance checks and providing comprehensive reporting capabilities.

D.2.1 Continuous Compliance Monitoring

CSPM tools continuously monitor cloud environments against compliance frameworks such as GDPR, HIPAA, and PCI-DSS. This ensures that any deviations from compliance standards are promptly identified and addressed.

Example: Regularly scanning for compliance with GDPR data protection requirements and alerting the security team to any non-compliant configurations.

D.2.2 Automated Compliance Reporting

Automated reporting features streamline the process of generating compliance reports, saving time and reducing the risk of human error. These reports can be easily shared with auditors and regulatory bodies.

Example: Generating a comprehensive PCI-DSS compliance report for an upcoming audit detailing all security measures in place and any recent compliance incidents.

D.2.3 Policy Enforcement

CSPM tools enforce compliance policies by ensuring that cloud configurations adhere to predefined security policies. This proactive approach prevents non-compliant configurations from being deployed.

Example: Preventing the deployment of cloud resources that do not meet the organization's security policy requirements.

D.3 Operational Efficiency

By automating routine security tasks and providing actionable insights, CSPM tools enhance operational efficiency and free up IT and security teams to focus on more strategic initiatives.

D.3.1 Reduced Manual Effort

Automating the detection and remediation of security issues reduces the manual effort required to maintain a secure cloud environment. This allows security teams to concentrate on high-priority tasks and strategic planning.

Example: Automating checking and updating firewall rules, freeing up the security team to focus on threat hunting and incident response.

D.3.2 Enhanced Visibility and Control

CSPM tools provide comprehensive visibility into cloud environments' security posture through intuitive dashboards and detailed reports. This enables better decision-making and more effective management of cloud resources.

Example: Using a CSPM dashboard to gain an overview of the current security status, including identified risks, compliance status, and remediation actions taken.

D.3.3 Streamlined Incident Management

Integrating CSPM tools with incident management systems streamlines the incident response process, ensuring that security incidents are quickly identified, triaged, and resolved.

Example: Automatically creating incident tickets in a service management tool when a security issue is detected, ensuring prompt attention and resolution.

D.4 Proactive Risk Management

CSPM tools enable organizations to adopt a proactive approach to risk management by identifying and addressing potential security issues before they can be exploited.

D.4.1 Early Detection of Vulnerabilities

By continuously scanning for vulnerabilities, CSPM tools help identify potential security issues early, allowing organizations to take preventive measures before attackers can exploit them.

Example: Identifying a misconfigured identity and access management (IAM) policy that could allow and correct excessive permissions before it can be exploited.

D.4.2 Risk-Based Prioritization

CSPM tools prioritize security issues based on their potential impact, ensuring that the most critical vulnerabilities are addressed first. This risk-based approach optimizes resource allocation and enhances overall security.

Example: Prioritizing the remediation of a high-severity vulnerability in a critical cloud service over lower-severity issues in less critical services.

D.4.3 Continuous Improvement

CSPM tools facilitate continuous improvement of security practices by providing insights into recurring issues and trends. This allows organizations to refine their security policies and practices over time.

Example: Analyzing CSPM reports to identify common misconfigurations and updating security policies to prevent these issues in the future.

D.5 Conclusion

Implementing Cloud Security Posture Management (CSPM) offers many benefits, from enhancing security and ensuring compliance to improving operational efficiency and fostering proactive risk management. As we progress through this guide, we will explore practical steps and best practices for implementing CSPM, equipping you with the knowledge and tools necessary to secure your cloud infrastructure effectively. Understanding these benefits highlights the value of CSPM and underscores the importance of adopting a comprehensive and proactive approach to cloud security in today's dynamic IT landscape.

II

Understanding CSPM

Chapter 2: Fundamentals of CSPM

A. Definition and Core Principles

In today's digital landscape, cloud computing is critical to most organizations' IT infrastructure. As cloud environments expand and evolve, ensuring their security becomes increasingly complex. This is where Cloud Security Posture Management (CSPM) comes into play. CSPM is essential for maintaining cloud environments' security, compliance, and health. In this chapter, we will define CSPM and explore its core principles.

A.1 Definition of CSPM

Cloud Security Posture Management (CSPM) refers to continuously monitoring, assessing, and managing cloud environments' security configurations and compliance. CSPM tools help organizations identify and remediate security risks, enforce best practices, and maintain compliance with regulatory standards.

CSPM involves a proactive approach to cloud security, preventing misconfigurations and vulnerabilities before they can be exploited. It encompasses various activities, from automated scanning and policy enforcement to detailed reporting and remediation guidance.

Key Aspects of CSPM:

- **Continuous Monitoring:** Ongoing assessment of cloud environments to detect security issues in real time.
- **Compliance Management:** Ensuring that cloud configurations adhere to industry regulations and standards.
- **Risk Assessment and Remediation:** Identifying, prioritizing, and addressing security risks.
- **Visibility and Reporting:** Providing insights into the security posture through dashboards and reports.

A.2 Core Principles of CSPM

The effectiveness of CSPM is grounded in several core principles that guide its implementation and operation. Understanding these principles is crucial for leveraging CSPM to enhance cloud security.

A.2.1 Continuous Monitoring and Real-Time Assessment

Continuous monitoring is the foundation of CSPM. It involves the real-time assessment of cloud environments to detect misconfigurations, vulnerabilities, and compliance issues as they arise. This proactive approach ensures that security issues are identified and addressed promptly, minimizing the exposure window.

Example: A CSPM tool continuously scans an organization's cloud infrastructure, identifying an open database instance that could potentially expose sensitive data. The security team receives immediate alerts, prompting quick remediation.

A.2.2 Automation and Scalability

Manual security management is impractical due to the dynamic and scalable nature of the cloud environment. CSPM leverages automation to scale security operations, ensuring consistent and efficient application of security policies across all cloud resources.

Example: Automated enforcement of encryption policies across all storage buckets, ensuring that data at rest is always protected without manual intervention.

A.2.3 Risk-Based Prioritization

Not all security issues are created equal. CSPM tools prioritize risks based on their potential impact, allowing organizations to focus on the most critical vulnerabilities first. This risk-based approach optimizes resource allocation and enhances overall security posture.

Example: Prioritizing the remediation of a misconfigured firewall rule that exposes a critical application to the internet over less severe configuration issues.

A.2.4 Compliance and Policy Enforcement

CSPM ensures cloud environments comply with relevant industry regulations and internal security policies. It continuously checks configurations against predefined compliance frameworks and policies, generating alerts and reports for any deviations.

Example: Ensuring that all cloud resources comply with GDPR by regularly auditing data protection measures and generating compliance reports for regulators.

A.2.5 Visibility and Accountability

Effective CSPM provides comprehensive visibility into cloud environments' security posture. Detailed dashboards and reports offer insights into current security status, compliance levels, and remediation actions taken. This visibility is crucial for accountability and informed decision-making.

Example: Using a CSPM dashboard to track the number of security incidents detected, their severity, and the time to remediate them.

A.2.6 Proactive Threat Management

CSPM tools detect and remediate existing issues and help anticipate and prevent future threats. By analyzing patterns and trends, they can predict potential vulnerabilities and recommend Preventive measures.

Example: Identifying a pattern of failed login attempts that could indicate a brute-force attack and suggesting additional security measures, such as multi-factor authentication.

A.3 The Role of CSPM in Cloud Security

CSPM plays a critical role in maintaining the security of cloud environments. It addresses several key challenges unique to cloud computing, including:

- **Dynamic Environments:** Cloud environments are highly dynamic, with resources being frequently added, modified, or removed. CSPM ensures continuous security oversight in this ever-changing landscape.
- **Complex Configurations:** Cloud infrastructures often involve complex configurations that can be difficult to manage manually. CSPM automates the detection and remediation of configuration issues.
- **Shared Responsibility:** In the cloud, security is a shared responsibility between the cloud provider and the customer. CSPM helps organizations fulfill their part of this responsibility by managing their security configurations effectively.

A.4 Conclusion

Cloud Security Posture Management (CSPM) is an essential practice for any organization utilizing cloud services. By understanding its definition and core principles—continuous monitoring, automation, risk-based prioritization, compliance, visibility, and proactive threat management—IT professionals can effectively implement CSPM to enhance their cloud security posture. As we delve deeper into CSPM in the following chapters, we will explore practical implementation strategies, tools, and best practices to help you secure your cloud environments comprehensively and efficiently.

B. Key Components of CSPM

Cloud Security Posture Management (CSPM) is a comprehensive approach to securing cloud environments. It involves continuous monitoring, assessment, and remediation of security configurations. To effectively implement CSPM, it is essential to understand its key components. Each component plays a critical role in maintaining and enhancing the security posture of cloud infrastructures.

B.1 Continuous Monitoring

Continuous monitoring is the backbone of CSPM, providing real-time visibility into the security state of cloud environments. This component involves the following activities:

B.1.1 Real-Time Surveillance

CSPM tools continuously scan cloud resources to detect misconfigurations, vulnerabilities, and compliance issues. This real-time surveillance ensures that any deviations from security policies are promptly identified and addressed.

Example: A CSPM tool continuously monitors AWS S3 buckets for public accessibility and sends alerts if a bucket is inadvertently made public.

B.1.2 Dynamic Inventory

Maintaining an up-to-date inventory of cloud resources is crucial for effective security management. CSPM tools automatically discover and catalog cloud assets, ensuring comprehensive coverage and visibility.

Example: Automatically discovering new virtual machines, databases, and storage instances as they are provisioned in the cloud environment.

B.2 Risk Assessment and Prioritization

Effective risk management is central to CSPM. This component focuses on identifying, assessing, and prioritizing security risks based on their potential impact.

B.2.1 Vulnerability Detection

CSPM tools scan cloud resources for known vulnerabilities, such as outdated software versions, insecure configurations, and missing security patches.

Example: Detecting a virtual machine running an outdated operating system vulnerable to a recently discovered exploit.

B.2.2 Risk Scoring and Prioritization

Once vulnerabilities are identified, CSPM tools assign risk scores based on severity, potential impact, and exploitability. This helps organizations prioritize remediation efforts.

Example: Assigning a higher risk score to a critical database with a weak password policy than to a non-critical development server with the same issue.

B.3 Compliance Management

Ensuring compliance with industry regulations and internal security policies is a critical aspect of CSPM. This component involves continuous compliance checks and automated reporting.

B.3.1 Continuous Compliance Checks

CSPM tools continuously evaluate cloud configurations against predefined compliance frameworks (e.g., GDPR, HIPAA, PCI-DSS) and internal policies. Any deviations are flagged for remediation.

Example: Regularly checking that all data stored in the cloud is encrypted at rest to comply with GDPR requirements.

B.3.2 Automated Compliance Reporting

Generating compliance reports manually can be time-consuming and prone to errors. CSPM tools automate the generation of detailed compliance reports, simplifying audits and regulatory reviews.

Example: Automatically generating a HIPAA compliance report that details encryption status, access controls, and incident response measures.

B.4 Automated Remediation

Automated remediation capabilities significantly enhance the efficiency of CSPM by addressing security issues without manual intervention.

B.4.1 Predefined Remediation Actions

CSPM tools can be configured with predefined remediation actions for common security issues. When a misconfiguration or vulnerability is detected, the tool automatically applies the appropriate fix.

Example: Automatically applying the correct security group settings to a misconfigured virtual machine to restrict unauthorized access.

B.4.2 Custom Remediation Workflows

In addition to predefined actions, CSPM tools allow organizations to create custom remediation workflows tailored to their specific needs and policies.

Example: Creating a custom workflow that triggers an approval process before applying critical updates to production environments.

B.5 Visibility and Reporting

Comprehensive visibility and detailed reporting are essential for understanding the security posture of cloud environments and making informed decisions.

B.5.1 Interactive Dashboards

CSPM tools provide interactive dashboards that offer real-time insights into the security status of cloud resources. These dashboards display key metrics, trends, and alerts in an easy-to-understand format.

Example: A dashboard showing the current number of high-risk vulnerabilities, compliance violations, and recent remediation actions.

B.5.2 Detailed Reports

In addition to dashboards, CSPM tools generate detailed reports that provide in-depth analysis of security issues, compliance status, and remediation efforts. These reports are essential for audits, regulatory reviews, and internal assessments.

Example: A report detailing the findings of a recent security scan, including identified vulnerabilities, their risk scores, and the actions taken to address them.

B.6 Integration with Existing Tools and Workflows

Effective CSPM involves seamless integration with existing security tools and operational workflows, ensuring a unified approach to cloud security management.

B.6.1 Integration with SIEM and SOAR

CSPM tools often integrate with Security Information and Event Management (SIEM) and Security Orchestration, Automation, and Response (SOAR) platforms to enhance threat detection and incident response capabilities.

Example: Integrating CSPM with a SIEM platform to correlate cloud security events with on-premises incidents, providing a holistic view of the security landscape.

B.6.2 API and Automation Capabilities

CSPM tools provide APIs and automation capabilities that allow organizations to integrate security processes into their DevOps pipelines and other automated workflows.

Example: Using APIs to trigger CSPM scans as part of a continuous integration/continuous deployment (CI/CD) pipeline, ensuring that security checks are performed before deploying new applications.

B.7 Proactive Threat Management

Proactive threat management is a key component of CSPM. It focuses on identifying and mitigating potential security threats before they can be exploited.

B.7.1 Threat Intelligence Integration

CSPM tools often integrate with threat intelligence feeds to stay updated on the latest threats and vulnerabilities. This enables proactive identification and mitigation of emerging risks.

Example: Integrating with a threat intelligence service to receive alerts about newly discovered vulnerabilities that could affect the cloud environment.

B.7.2 Predictive Analytics

Leveraging machine learning and predictive analytics, CSPM tools can identify patterns and trends indicating potential security threats. This allows organizations to take preventive measures.

Example: Using predictive analytics to identify unusual login patterns that may indicate a brute force attack in progress and automatically implementing additional security controls.

B.8 Conclusion

Understanding the key components of Cloud Security Posture Management (CSPM) is essential for effectively securing cloud environments. Continuous monitoring, risk assessment, compliance management, automated remediation, visibility and reporting, integration with existing tools, and proactive threat management form the foundation of CSPM. By leveraging these components, organizations can maintain a robust security posture, ensure compliance with regulatory requirements, and proactively manage security risks in their cloud infrastructures. As we progress through this guide, we will delve deeper into practical implementation strategies and best practices to help you fully harness the power of CSPM.

C. CSPM vs. Traditional Security Measures

As cloud computing becomes more prevalent, traditional security measures often need to be improved to address the unique challenges cloud environments pose. Cloud Security Posture Management (CSPM) offers a more dynamic and comprehensive approach to cloud security. This section will compare CSPM with traditional security measures, highlighting each approach's differences, advantages, and limitations.

C.1 Overview of Traditional Security Measures

Traditional security measures were developed primarily for on-premises infrastructures and have been adapted to varying extents for use in cloud environments. These measures typically include:

- **Firewalls:** Hardware or software solutions that control incoming and outgoing network traffic based on predetermined security rules.
- **Intrusion Detection Systems (IDS) and Intrusion Prevention Systems (IPS):** Tools that monitor network or system activities for malicious activities or policy violations.
- **Antivirus Software:** Programs designed to detect, prevent, and remove malware.
- **Patch Management:** The process of distributing and applying updates to software to fix vulnerabilities.
- **Access Control Systems:** Mechanisms that regulate who or what can view or use resources in a computing environment.

While these measures form the bedrock of traditional security, they have several limitations when applied to cloud environments.

C.2 Limitations of Traditional Security Measures in Cloud Environments

Traditional security measures face several challenges in cloud environments due to their static and reactive nature:

C.2.1 Lack of Visibility

Traditional security tools often need more visibility into cloud resources and configurations. Cloud environments are dynamic, with resources frequently added, modified, or removed, making it difficult for traditional tools to maintain accurate and comprehensive visibility.

Example: An on-premises firewall may not be able to see the configurations and security status of cloud-based virtual machines and storage services.

C.2.2 Scalability Issues

Cloud environments are highly scalable, with resources expanding and contracting based on demand. Traditional security measures designed for static infrastructures must help keep pace with this elasticity.

Example: An intrusion detection system (IDS) designed for a fixed number of servers may not effectively scale to monitor thousands of cloud instances.

C.2.3 Manual Processes

Traditional security measures often rely on manual processes for configuration, monitoring, and remediation. This manual approach is not feasible in the fast-paced, automated cloud environments where changes occur frequently and at scale.

Example: Manually applying security patches to hundreds of cloud instances is time-consuming and error-prone.

C.2.4 Inadequate Response to Misconfigurations

Traditional security measures focus on detecting and preventing external threats but may not adequately address internal misconfigurations, a significant cause of security incidents in cloud environments.

Example: A traditional antivirus program cannot detect a misconfigured storage bucket that is publicly accessible, potentially exposing sensitive data.

C.3 Advantages of CSPM over Traditional Security Measures

Cloud Security Posture Management (CSPM) addresses the limitations of traditional security measures by offering a more adaptive, automated, and comprehensive approach to cloud security. Here are some key advantages of CSPM:

C.3.1 Continuous and Comprehensive Visibility

CSPM tools continuously monitor cloud environments, offering real-time visibility into all cloud resources and configurations. This comprehensive visibility is crucial for identifying and addressing security issues promptly.

Example: A CSPM tool continuously scans all cloud resources, providing a real-time inventory and identifying misconfigurations or vulnerabilities.

C.3.2 Scalability and Automation

CSPM tools are designed to scale with cloud environments, automatically adjusting to adding or removing resources. They automate many security processes, reducing the need for manual intervention and improving efficiency.

Example: Automatically applying security policies to new cloud instances as they are provisioned, ensuring consistent security across all resources.

C.3.3 Proactive Risk Management

CSPM tools proactively identify and mitigate security risks, focusing on external threats and internal misconfigurations. This proactive approach helps prevent security incidents before they occur.

Example: Automatically detecting and remediating an overly permissive IAM policy that could allow unauthorized access to sensitive data.

C.3.4 Compliance Automation

CSPM tools continuously monitor compliance with industry regulations and internal security policies, automating compliance checks and generating detailed reports. This ensures ongoing compliance and simplifies audit processes.

Example: Regularly generating compliance reports for GDPR detailing encryption status, access controls, and data protection measures.

C.3.5 Integration with DevOps and CI/CD Pipelines

CSPM tools integrate seamlessly with DevOps and continuous integration/continuous deployment (CI/CD) pipelines, embedding security into the development process. This ensures that security checks are performed at every development lifecycle stage.

Example: Integrating CSPM scans into a CI/CD pipeline to automatically check for security issues before deploying new applications to production.

C.4 Case Study: CSPM vs. Traditional Security Measures

To illustrate the differences between CSPM and traditional security measures, consider the following case study:

Scenario: A financial services company is migrating its infrastructure to the cloud. The company needs to ensure the security and compliance of its cloud environment while maintaining operational efficiency.

Traditional Security Approach:

Tools Used: Firewalls, IDS/IPS, antivirus software, manual patch management.

Challenges:

- Limited visibility into cloud resources.
- Scalability issues with monitoring tools.
- Manual processes for configuration and remediation.
- Difficulty ensuring compliance with financial regulations.

CSPM Approach:

Tools Used: The CSPM tool is integrated with SIEM and CI/CD pipelines.

Benefits:

- Continuous and comprehensive visibility into all cloud resources.
- Automated scalability and security processes.
- Proactive identification and remediation of security risks.
- Continuous compliance monitoring and automated reporting.

Outcome: By implementing CSPM, the company achieved a more secure and compliant cloud environment, reduced the burden on its IT staff, and improved its overall security posture.

C.5 Conclusion

While traditional security measures provide a foundation for securing IT environments, they often need to be improved for cloud infrastructures' dynamic and scalable nature. Cloud Security Posture Management (CSPM) offers a more comprehensive, automated, and proactive approach to cloud security, addressing the limitations of traditional security measures. By leveraging CSPM, organizations can enhance their security posture, ensure compliance, and efficiently manage the complexities of cloud environments. As we progress through this guide, we will explore practical implementation strategies and best practices for integrating CSPM into your cloud security framework.

Chapter 3: CSPM Tools and Solutions

A. Overview of Leading CSPM Tools

Cloud Security Posture Management (CSPM) tools play a crucial role in maintaining the security and compliance of cloud environments. These tools help organizations identify and remediate misconfigurations, enforce best practices, and ensure continuous compliance with regulatory requirements. This section provides an overview of some of the leading CSPM tools available in the market, highlighting their key features and benefits.

A.1 Palo Alto Networks Prisma Cloud

Prisma Cloud by Palo Alto Networks is a comprehensive CSPM solution that provides visibility, governance, and compliance across multiple platforms, including AWS, Azure, and Google Cloud.

A.1.1 Key Features

- **Unified Visibility:** Offers a single pane of glass for monitoring and managing security across multi-cloud environments.
- **Automated Compliance:** Continuously checks for compliance with industry standards such as CIS, GDPR, HIPAA, and PCI-DSS.
- **Risk Prioritization:** Uses machine learning to prioritize risks based on severity and potential impact.
- **Threat Detection and Response:** Provides real-time threat detection and automated response capabilities.

A.1.2 Benefits

- **Comprehensive Coverage:** Supports many cloud services and resources.
- **Scalability:** Easily scales with growing cloud environments.
- **Integration:** Integrates with other security tools and platforms, enhancing overall security posture.

Example: A financial institution uses Prisma Cloud to monitor its multi-cloud environment, ensuring compliance with PCI-DSS and detecting potential security threats in real time.

A.2 Check Point CloudGuard

Check Point CloudGuard is a robust CSPM solution that provides advanced threat prevention, security management, and compliance assurance for cloud environments.

A.2.1 Key Features

- **Advanced Threat Prevention:** Protects against known and unknown threats using AI and machine learning.
- **Automated Security Policies:** Enforces security policies automatically based on best practices and compliance requirements.
- **Real-Time Monitoring:** Continuously monitors cloud environments for misconfigurations and vulnerabilities.
- **Compliance Management:** Supports compliance frameworks such as NIST, ISO 27001, and SOC 2.

A.2.2 Benefits

- **Proactive Security:** Prevents threats before they can impact the cloud environment.
- **Ease of Use:** Provides an intuitive interface and automated processes, reducing the need for manual intervention.
- **Flexibility:** Supports multiple cloud platforms and integrates with existing security infrastructures.

Example: A healthcare provider uses CloudGuard to ensure HIPAA compliance and protect patient data stored in the cloud from advanced cyber threats.

A.3 AWS Security Hub

AWS Security Hub is a native CSPM solution for AWS environments, offering a comprehensive view of security alerts and compliance status across AWS accounts.

A.3.1 Key Features

- **Centralized Dashboard:** Provides a unified view of security alerts from various AWS services and third-party tools.
- **Automated Compliance Checks:** Continuously monitors AWS resources for compliance with standards such as CIS AWS Foundations Benchmark and AWS best practices.
- **Security Findings Aggregation:** Aggregates security findings from AWS services like Amazon GuardDuty, Amazon Inspector, and AWS Config.
- **Actionable Insights:** Provides actionable recommendations for improving security posture.

A.3.2 Benefits

- **Seamless Integration:** Integrates seamlessly with other AWS services, providing a cohesive security solution.
- **Cost-Effective:** Being a native AWS service, it leverages existing AWS infrastructure, reducing the need for additional tools.
- **Ease of Deployment:** Easy to set up and configure within AWS environments.

Example: An e-commerce company uses AWS Security Hub to monitor its AWS accounts for security threats and ensure compliance with industry standards.

A.4 Microsoft Azure Security Center

Azure Security Center is a CSPM solution that provides advanced threat protection and continuous security assessment for Azure environments.

A.4.1 Key Features

- **Unified Security Management:** Centralized security policies and configurations management across Azure resources.
- **Advanced Threat Protection:** Uses AI and behavioral analytics to detect and respond to threats.
- **Regulatory Compliance:** Continuously assesses compliance with standards such as ISO 27001, PCI-DSS, and Azure Security Benchmark.
- **Security Recommendations:** Provides actionable recommendations to improve security posture.

A.4.2 Benefits

- **Integrated Solution:** Deep integration with Azure services, enhancing overall security management.
- **Proactive Security:** Proactively identifies and mitigates security risks.
- **Cost Efficiency:** Optimizes resource usage and reduces security management costs.

Example: A manufacturing company uses Azure Security Center to protect its intellectual property and ensure compliance with industry regulations.

A.5 Google Cloud Security Command Center (SCC)

Google Cloud Security Command Center (SCC) is a CSPM solution that offers comprehensive security and risk management for Google Cloud Platform (GCP) environments.

A.5.1 Key Features

- **Centralized Security Management:** Provides a unified view of security posture and risks across GCP resources.
- **Threat Detection:** Machine learning detects threats and anomalies in real-time.
- **Compliance Monitoring:** Ensures compliance with regulatory standards such as GDPR, HIPAA, and PCI-DSS.
- **Customizable Dashboards:** Offers customizable dashboards for monitoring security metrics and trends.

A.5.2 Benefits

- **Real-Time Security:** Provides real-time threat detection and response capabilities.
- **Customizability:** Allows customization of security policies and dashboards to meet specific organizational needs.
- **Integration:** Integrates with other Google Cloud services and third-party security tools.

Example: A tech startup uses Google Cloud SCC to secure its cloud infrastructure, detect real-time threats, and maintain compliance with

GDPR.

A.6 Open Source CSPM Tools

In addition to commercial solutions, several open-source CSPM tools are available, providing cost-effective options for managing cloud security posture.

A.6.1 Prowler

Prowler is an open-source security tool designed to perform AWS security best practices assessments, audits, and hardening.

Key Features:

- **AWS CIS Benchmarking:** Performs checks based on the CIS AWS Foundations Benchmark.
- **Custom Checks:** Allows customization of security checks to meet specific requirements.
- **Continuous Monitoring:** Supports continuous monitoring and alerting for AWS environments.

Benefits:

- **Cost-Effective:** Free to use and customize, reducing costs associated with commercial tools.
- **Community Support:** Backed by a strong community, offering regular updates and enhancements.

Example: A small business uses Prowler to perform regular security audits of its AWS environment, ensuring adherence to best practices.

A.6.2 ScoutSuite

ScoutSuite is an open-source multi-cloud security auditing tool that comprehensively assesses cloud environments.

Key Features:

- **Multi-Cloud Support:** Supports AWS, Azure, and GCP.
- **Detailed Reports:** Generates detailed security reports highlighting vulnerabilities and misconfigurations.
- **Customizable:** Allows customization of checks and reports to suit specific needs.

Benefits:

- **Flexibility:** Supports multiple cloud platforms, providing a unified security assessment tool.
- **Community-Driven:** Continuously improved by contributions from the community.

Example: A cybersecurity consultancy uses ScoutSuite to perform security assessments for clients using various cloud platforms.

A.7 Conclusion

The landscape of CSPM tools is diverse, offering various solutions to meet organizational needs. Leading commercial tools like Prisma Cloud, CloudGuard, AWS Security Hub, Azure Security Center, and Google Cloud SCC provide comprehensive features for managing and securing cloud environments. Additionally, open-source tools like Prowler and ScoutSuite offer cost-effective alternatives with robust capabilities. By selecting the right CSPM tool, organizations can enhance their cloud security posture, ensure compliance, and proactively manage risks in their cloud environments. As we move forward, we will explore practical implementation strategies and best practices for integrating these tools into your cloud security framework.

B. Criteria for Selecting a CSPM Tool

Selecting the right Cloud Security Posture Management (CSPM) tool is critical for effectively securing your cloud environments. With numerous options available, each offering a variety of features, it can be challenging to determine which tool best fits your organization's needs. This section outlines the key criteria to consider when selecting a CSPM tool, ensuring you choose a solution that aligns with your security objectives, compliance requirements, and operational workflows.

B.1 Comprehensive Coverage

A CSPM tool must comprehensively cover all cloud services and resources used within your organization. This ensures that no part of your cloud environment is left unmonitored, reducing the risk of security vulnerabilities.

B.1.1 Multi-Cloud Support

Given the increasing adoption of multi-cloud strategies, it is important to select a CSPM tool that supports multiple cloud platforms, such as AWS, Azure, and Google Cloud Platform. This capability ensures unified security management across different environments.

Example: An enterprise using AWS for its primary applications and Azure for its data analytics requires a CSPM tool that can effectively monitor and manage security across both platforms.

B.1.2 Resource and Service Coverage

Ensure the CSPM tool covers many cloud resources and services, including compute, storage, databases, networking, and serverless functions. Comprehensive coverage ensures the security of all aspects of your cloud infrastructure.

Example: A CSPM tool should be able to monitor AWS EC2 instances, S3 buckets, RDS databases, VPC configurations, and Lambda functions.

B.2 Compliance and Regulatory Support

Compliance with industry regulations and standards is a critical aspect of cloud security. A CSPM tool should support the compliance frameworks relevant to your organization and automate compliance checks.

B.2.1 Predefined Compliance Policies

Look for CSPM tools, including predefined policies for common compliance frameworks such as GDPR, HIPAA, PCI-DSS, ISO 27001, and SOC 2. These policies facilitate quick and easy compliance assessments.

Example: A healthcare provider needs a CSPM tool that automatically checks for HIPAA compliance, ensuring patient data is properly protected.

B.2.2 Custom Policy Creation

In addition to predefined policies, the ability to create custom compliance policies tailored to your organization's specific requirements is crucial. This flexibility allows for the enforcement of internal security standards and practices.

Example: A financial institution may need to create custom policies to enforce internal data protection standards beyond PCI-DSS requirements.

B.3 Automation and Remediation

Automation is a key feature of CSPM tools. It reduces the manual effort required to maintain security and compliance in cloud environments. The tool should offer robust automation capabilities for detecting and remediating security issues.

B.3.1 Automated Detection

Choose a CSPM tool that detects misconfigurations, vulnerabilities, and compliance violations. This ensures the timely identification of security issues without needing constant manual monitoring.

Example: Automatically detect when a storage bucket becomes publicly accessible and flag it for immediate action.

B.3.2 Automated Remediation

A valuable feature is the ability to remediate common security issues automatically. This capability minimizes the time and effort required to fix problems and ensures consistent application of security best practices.

Example: Automatically applying the correct security settings to an exposed storage bucket, ensuring it is no longer publicly accessible.

B.4 Integration Capabilities

A CSPM tool should integrate seamlessly with your existing security and operational tools, enhancing overall security operations without creating silos.

B.4.1 SIEM and SOAR Integration

Integration with Security Information and Event Management (SIEM) and Security Orchestration, Automation, and Response (SOAR) platforms is essential for comprehensive threat detection and incident response.

Example: Integrating the CSPM tool with a SIEM system to correlate cloud security events with on-premises security data, providing a unified view of the organization's security posture.

B.4.2 DevOps and CI/CD Integration

Ensure the CSPM tool can integrate with your DevOps and Continuous Integration/Continuous Deployment (CI/CD) pipelines. This integration allows for the continuous monitoring of security throughout the development lifecycle.

Example: Integrating CSPM scans into a CI/CD pipeline to automatically check for security issues before deploying new applications.

B.5 Usability and Reporting

The usability of the CSPM tool and its reporting capabilities are crucial for effective security management. The tool should provide intuitive interfaces and comprehensive reporting features.

B.5.1 User-Friendly Interface

A user-friendly interface simplifies configuring and managing the CSPM tool, making it accessible to security professionals with varying levels of expertise.

Example: An intuitive dashboard that visualizes security posture, compliance status, and remediation actions.

B.5.2 Detailed Reporting

Detailed reporting capabilities are essential for tracking security and compliance status over time. Look for tools that offer customizable reports that can be easily shared with stakeholders.

Example: Generating detailed compliance reports for regulatory audits, highlighting adherence to GDPR and PCI-DSS standards.

B.6 Scalability and Performance

As your cloud environment grows, the CSPM tool should be able to scale accordingly without compromising performance. Assess the tool's scalability and ability to handle large and complex cloud environments.

B.6.1 Performance Metrics

Evaluate the CSPM tool's performance in terms of scanning speed, accuracy, and resource utilization. High-performance tools provide timely and reliable security assessments without significantly impacting cloud operations.

Example: A CSPM tool that can quickly scan thousands of cloud resources without causing noticeable performance degradation.

B.6.2 Scalability Features

Ensure the CSPM tool can scale to accommodate increasing cloud resources and services as your organization grows. This scalability is essential for maintaining consistent security coverage.

Example: A CSPM tool that can rapidly provision new cloud instances during peak business periods.

B.7 Vendor Support and Community

The level of support the CSPM tool vendor provides, as well as the strength of its user community, are important factors to consider. Reliable support ensures that issues can be quickly resolved, while an active community can provide valuable insights and resources.

B.7.1 Vendor Support

Assess the vendor's support offerings, including availability, response times, and the range of support channels (e.g., phone, email, chat). Quality vendor support can significantly enhance the tool's usability and effectiveness.

Example: A CSPM tool vendor that offers 24/7 support with fast response times for critical issues.

B.7.2 User Community

An active user community can provide additional resources like forums, user groups, and knowledge bases. Community engagement can help you leverage best practices and troubleshoot common issues.

Example: Participating in a CSPM tool's user forum to learn from other users' experiences and share solutions to common challenges.

B.8 Cost and Licensing

Finally, the cost and licensing options of the CSPM tool should be considered. The total cost of ownership should align with your organization's budget while providing the necessary features and capabilities.

B.8.1 Pricing Models

Evaluate pricing models, such as subscription-based, pay-as-you-go, or perpetual licensing. Choose a model that aligns with your financial strategy and provides flexibility as your cloud environment evolves.

Example: A subscription-based CSPM tool that offers scalable pricing based on the number of cloud resources monitored.

B.8.2 Value for Money

Assess the value provided by the CSPM tool relative to its cost. Consider factors such as the range of features, the quality of support, and the tool's overall impact on your security posture.

Example: A CSPM tool that provides comprehensive coverage, automation, and integration capabilities at a competitive price, offering high value for money.

B.9 Conclusion

Selecting the right CSPM tool is a critical decision that can significantly impact your organization's cloud security posture. By considering factors such as comprehensive coverage, compliance support, automation capabilities, integration with existing tools, usability, scalability, vendor support, and cost, you can choose a CSPM solution that best meets your needs. As we continue through this guide, we will explore practical implementation strategies and best practices for effectively deploying and leveraging CSPM tools in your cloud environment.

C. Comparison of CSPM Tools

With the increasing adoption of cloud computing, organizations must choose the right Cloud Security Posture Management (CSPM) tools to ensure their cloud environments are secure and compliant. This section compares several leading CSPM tools, highlighting their strengths, weaknesses, and ideal use cases to help you make an informed decision.

C.1 Palo Alto Networks Prisma Cloud

Overview: Prisma Cloud by Palo Alto Networks is a comprehensive CSPM solution that provides visibility, governance, and compliance across multiple cloud platforms.

Strengths:

- **Multi-Cloud Support:** Supports AWS, Azure, Google Cloud, and other cloud platforms.
- **Comprehensive Security:** Offers extensive features, including threat detection, compliance checks, and risk management.
- **Scalability:** Easily scales with growing cloud environments.
- **User-Friendly Interface:** Provides an intuitive dashboard and detailed reports.

Weaknesses:

- **Cost:** Higher cost than other CSPM tools, which may be a consideration

for smaller organizations.
- **Complexity:** The extensive feature set can overwhelm smaller teams or those new to CSPM.

Ideal Use Cases:

- Large enterprises with complex, multi-cloud environments.
- Organizations requiring comprehensive security and compliance features.

Example: A multinational corporation uses Prisma Cloud to manage and secure its multi-cloud infrastructure, ensuring compliance with global regulations and detecting potential threats in real time.

C.2 Check Point CloudGuard

Overview: CloudGuard by Check Point is a robust CSPM tool that provides advanced threat prevention, security management, and compliance assurance for cloud environments.

Strengths:

- **Advanced Threat Prevention:** Uses AI and machine learning to detect and prevent threats.
- **Automated Security Policies:** Enforces security policies automatically based on best practices and compliance requirements.
- **Real-Time Monitoring:** Continuously monitors cloud environments for misconfigurations and vulnerabilities.
- **Ease of Use:** Offers an intuitive interface and automated processes, reducing the need for manual intervention.

Weaknesses:

- **Integration:** Limited integration with non-Check Point products compared to other CSPM tools.
- **Learning Curve:** Some users may need help with the initial setup and configuration.

Ideal Use Cases:

- Organizations looking for advanced threat prevention and automated security policy enforcement.
- Companies with existing Check Point security products are seeking integrated solutions.

Example: A healthcare provider uses CloudGuard to ensure HIPAA compliance and protect patient data stored in the cloud from advanced cyber threats.

C.3 AWS Security Hub

Overview: AWS Security Hub is a native CSPM solution for AWS environments. It provides a comprehensive view of security alerts and compliance status across AWS accounts.

Strengths:

- **Seamless Integration:** Integrates smoothly with other AWS services, providing a cohesive security solution.
- **Cost-Effective:** Utilizes existing AWS infrastructure, reducing the need for additional tools.
- **Ease of Deployment:** Simple to set up and configure within AWS

CHAPTER 3: CSPM TOOLS AND SOLUTIONS

environments.
- **Centralized Dashboard:** Provides a unified view of security alerts from various AWS services and third-party tools.

Weaknesses:

- **AWS-Centric:** Limited to AWS environments, making it unsuitable for multi-cloud strategies.
- **Feature Set:** It may lack advanced features in more comprehensive CSPM tools.

Ideal Use Cases:

- Organizations primarily use AWS for their cloud infrastructure.
- Companies looking for a cost-effective, integrated solution for AWS security management.

Example: An e-commerce company uses AWS Security Hub to monitor its AWS accounts for security threats and ensure compliance with industry standards.

C.4 Microsoft Azure Security Center

Overview: Azure Security Center is a CSPM solution that provides advanced threat protection and continuous security assessment for Azure environments.

Strengths:

- **Integrated Solution:** Deep integration with Azure services, enhancing overall security management.

- **Advanced Threat Protection:** Uses AI and behavioral analytics to detect and respond to threats.
- **Regulatory Compliance:** Continuously assesses compliance with standards such as ISO 27001, PCI-DSS, and Azure Security Benchmark.
- **Security Recommendations:** Provides actionable recommendations to improve security posture.

Weaknesses:

- **Azure-Centric:** Primarily designed for Azure environments, with limited support for other cloud platforms.
- **Complexity:** Some users may find navigating the extensive features and settings complex.

Ideal Use Cases:

- Organizations heavily invested in Microsoft Azure.
- Companies seeking advanced threat protection and compliance management within Azure environments.

Example: A manufacturing company uses Azure Security Center to protect its intellectual property and ensure compliance with industry regulations.

C.5 Google Cloud Security Command Center (SCC)

Overview: Google Cloud Security Command Center (SCC) offers comprehensive security and risk management for Google Cloud Platform (GCP) environments.

Strengths:

- **Real-Time Security:** Provides real-time threat detection and response capabilities.
- **Customizability:** Allows customization of security policies and dashboards to meet specific organizational needs.
- **Integration:** Integrates with other Google Cloud services and third-party security tools.
- **Centralized Security Management:** Provides a unified view of security posture and risks across GCP resources.

Weaknesses:

- **GCP-Centric:** Limited to GCP environments, making it less suitable for multi-cloud strategies.
- **Learning Curve:** Some users may need help with the initial setup and configuration.

Ideal Use Cases:

- Organizations primarily use the Google Cloud Platform.
- Companies looking for customizable security management and real-time threat detection in GCP.

Example: A tech startup uses Google Cloud SCC to secure its cloud infrastructure, detect real-time threats, and maintain compliance with GDPR.

C.6 Open Source CSPM Tools

C.6.1 Prowler

Overview: Prowler is an open-source security tool designed to perform AWS security best practices assessments, audits, and hardening.

Strengths:

- **Cost-Effective:** Free to use and customize, reducing costs associated with commercial tools.
- **Community Support:** Backed by a strong community, offering regular updates and enhancements.
- **AWS CIS Benchmarking:** Performs checks based on the CIS AWS Foundations Benchmark.
- **Custom Checks:** Allows customization of security checks to meet specific requirements.

Weaknesses:

- **AWS-Only:** Limited to AWS environments, lacking support for other cloud platforms.
- **Manual Effort:** This requires manual effort for setup and customization, which may be challenging for some users.

Ideal Use Cases:

- Small to medium-sized businesses using AWS.
- Organizations looking for a cost-effective CSPM solution with community support.

Example: A small business uses Prowler to perform regular security audits of its AWS environment, ensuring adherence to best practices.

C.6.2 ScoutSuite

Overview: ScoutSuite is an open-source multi-cloud security auditing tool that comprehensively assesses cloud environments.

Strengths:

- **Multi-Cloud Support:** Supports AWS, Azure, and GCP.
- **Detailed Reports:** Generates detailed security reports highlighting vulnerabilities and misconfigurations.
- **Customizable:** Allows customization of checks and reports to suit specific needs.
- **Community-Driven:** Continuously improved by contributions from the community.

Weaknesses:

- **Manual Setup:** This requires manual setup and configuration, which can be time-consuming.
- **Limited Support:** May lack the advanced features and vendor support of commercial tools.

Ideal Use Cases:

- Organizations with multi-cloud strategies.
- Companies seeking a flexible, cost-effective CSPM tool with multi-cloud support.

Example: A cybersecurity consultancy uses ScoutSuite to perform security assessments for clients using various cloud platforms.

C.7 Comparison Summary

When comparing CSPM tools, it's essential to consider factors such as platform support, feature set, ease of use, cost, and your organization's specific needs. Here's a summary table for quick reference:

CSPM Tool	Platforms Supported	Key Strengths	Key Weaknesses	Ideal Use Cases
Palo Alto Networks Prisma Cloud	Multi-Cloud (AWS, Azure, GCP)	Comprehensive security, scalability, user-friendly interface	Higher cost, complexity	Large enterprises with complex, multi-cloud environments
Check Point CloudGuard	Multi-Cloud (AWS, Azure, GCP)	Advanced threat prevention, automated security policies	Limited integration, learning curve	Organizations looking for advanced threat prevention
AWS Security Hub	AWS	Seamless integration, cost-effective, easy deployment	AWS-centric, limited advanced features	AWS-centric organizations
Azure Security Center	Azure	Integrated solution, advanced threat protection	Azure-centric, complexity	Organizations heavily invested in Microsoft Azure
Google Cloud SCC	GCP	Real-time security, customizability, integration	GCP-centric, learning curve	Organizations primarily using Google Cloud Platform

Prowler	AWS	Cost-effective, community support, AWS CIS benchmarking	AWS-only, manual effort	Small to medium-sized businesses using AWS
ScoutSuite	AWS, Azure, GCP	Multi-cloud support, detailed reports, customizability	Manual setup, limited support	Organizations with multi-cloud strategies

C.8 Conclusion

Choosing the right CSPM tool is critical in securing your cloud environment. By understanding the strengths and weaknesses of each tool and considering factors such as platform support, feature set, ease of use, and cost, you can select a CSPM solution that best fits your organization's needs. As we continue through this guide, we will explore practical implementation strategies and best practices for integrating CSPM tools into your cloud security framework.

III

Planning and Preparation

Chapter 4: Assessing Your Cloud Environment

A. Inventorying Cloud Resources

A thorough inventory of cloud resources is the foundation of any effective Cloud Security Posture Management (CSPM) strategy. Accurate and comprehensive knowledge of all assets within your cloud environment is crucial for maintaining security, managing risks, and ensuring compliance. This chapter will explore the importance of inventorying cloud resources, the steps involved in creating a comprehensive inventory, and best practices for maintaining and updating your inventory.

A.1 Importance of Inventorying Cloud Resources

Inventorying cloud resources is essential for several reasons:

A.1.1 Visibility and Control

An accurate inventory provides visibility into all assets deployed across your cloud environment. This visibility is crucial for controlling your infrastructure and ensuring all resources are accounted for and properly managed.

Example: A comprehensive inventory helps identify orphaned resources, such as unused virtual machines or storage buckets, which can be decommissioned to reduce costs and minimize security risks.

A.1.2 Security and Compliance

Understanding the full scope of your cloud environment is necessary for effective security management and compliance monitoring. An inventory allows you to apply security policies consistently and ensure all resources comply with regulatory requirements.

Example: By inventorying all databases in your environment, you can ensure each is configured with the appropriate encryption and access controls to meet compliance standards such as GDPR or HIPAA.

A.1.3 Risk Management

Identifying all resources within your cloud environment helps you assess and manage risks. Knowing what assets, configurations, and security postures exist enables you to prioritize remediation efforts and allocate resources effectively.

Example: An inventory can reveal critical assets, such as customer databases, requiring more stringent security measures than less sensitive resources like development servers.

A.2 Steps for Creating a Comprehensive Inventory

Creating a comprehensive inventory involves several steps, from initial discovery to ongoing maintenance. Here's a detailed look at each step:

A.2.1 Initial Discovery

The initial discovery phase involves identifying all existing resources in your cloud environment. This can be achieved through automated tools cloud service providers provide or third-party solutions.

Tools and Techniques:

- **Cloud Provider Tools:** AWS Config, Azure Resource Graph, Google Cloud Asset Inventory.
- **Third-Party Tools:** CloudHealth by VMware, CloudCheckr, or open-source tools like Prowler and ScoutSuite.

Example: Using AWS Config to automatically discover and record all AWS resources, including EC2 instances, S3 buckets, RDS databases, and IAM roles.

A.2.2 Classification and Tagging

Once discovered, resources should be classified and tagged based on various criteria, such as type, environment (production, development, testing), owner, and criticality. Effective tagging helps organize and manage resources efficiently.

Best Practices for Tagging:

- **Consistency:** Use a consistent tagging schema across all resources to ensure uniformity and ease of management.
- **Relevance:** Include tags that provide meaningful information, such as 'Environment', 'Owner', 'Department', 'Cost Center', and 'Compliance'.

Example: To facilitate management and compliance tracking, all production databases should be tagged with 'Environment: Production', 'Owner: DBA_Team', and 'Compliance: PCI-DSS'.

A.2.3 Documentation and Reporting

Documenting the inventory involves creating detailed records of all resources, including their configurations, dependencies, and security postures. This documentation references security assessments, audits, and compliance checks.

Documentation Elements:

- **Resource Details:** Type, name, identifier, location.
- **Configuration:** Security settings, access controls, network configura-

tions.
- **Dependencies:** Relationships with other resources (e.g., a web server linked to a database).
- **Security Posture:** Compliance status, known vulnerabilities, remediation actions.

Example: Maintaining a centralized inventory database that records all EC2 instances, configurations (e.g., security groups, IAM roles), and compliance statuses.

A.2.4 Ongoing Maintenance and Updates

Cloud environments are dynamic, with resources frequently added, modified, or removed. Ongoing maintenance of the inventory is essential to ensure its accuracy and relevance.

Best Practices for Maintenance:

- **Regular Audits:** Conduct periodic audits to verify the accuracy of the inventory and update it with any changes.
- **Automation:** Automation tools monitor the environment continuously and update the inventory in real time.
- **Change Management:** Integrate inventory updates with your change management processes to ensure that any modifications to the cloud environment are reflected in the inventory.

Example: Using AWS Config Rules to automatically track changes to resource configurations and update the inventory accordingly.

A.3 Best Practices for Inventorying Cloud Resources

To ensure a comprehensive and effective inventory, follow these best practices:

A.3.1 Leverage Automation

Automation is key to maintaining an accurate and up-to-date inventory. Use cloud-native tools and third-party solutions to automate resource discovery, tagging, and documentation.

Example: Implementing automated scripts that leverage AWS Lambda functions to tag new resources based on predefined policies.

A.3.2 Standardize Naming Conventions

Standardized naming conventions make it easier to identify and manage resources. Consistent naming also helps organize resources and facilitates automation.

Example: Adopting a naming convention like 'Project-Environment-ResourceType-UniqueID' (e.g., 'SalesApp-Prod-EC2-01') for all resources.

A.3.3 Implement Role-Based Access Control (RBAC)

Ensure that only authorized personnel can modify the inventory or the resources it tracks. Implement RBAC to restrict access based on roles and responsibilities.

Example: Grant inventory modification permissions only to cloud administrators and security teams while providing read-only access to other stakeholders.

A.3.4 Regular Training and Awareness

Regularly train your teams on the importance of maintaining an accurate inventory and the procedures for tagging and documenting resources. Awareness programs help in ensuring compliance with inventory management policies.

Example: Conducting quarterly training sessions for DevOps and security teams on best practices for inventory management and compliance requirements.

A.4 Tools for Inventorying Cloud Resources

Several tools can assist in creating and maintaining an accurate inventory of cloud resources. Here are some recommended tools:

A.4.1 AWS Config

Overview: AWS Config is a service that enables you to assess, audit, and evaluate the configurations of your AWS resources.

Features:

- Continuous monitoring of resource configurations.
- Automatic recording of configuration changes.
- Integration with AWS CloudTrail for detailed audit logs.

Example: Using AWS Config to automatically record changes to security group configurations and generate compliance reports.

A.4.2 Azure Resource Graph

Overview: Azure Resource Graph is a service designed to explore and query Azure resources at scale.

Features:

- Powerful query capabilities for resource management.
- Real-time resource inventory and visibility.
- Integration with Azure Policy for compliance monitoring.

Example: Querying Azure Resource Graph to generate a report of all virtual machines and their compliance statuses.

A.4.3 Google Cloud Asset Inventory

Overview: Google Cloud Asset Inventory provides a real-time view of all assets in Google Cloud.

A.5 Conclusion

Inventorying cloud resources is a fundamental step in establishing a robust CSPM strategy. Organizations can achieve better visibility, control, and security over their cloud environments by creating a comprehensive inventory and maintaining a c. Leveraging automation, standardizing practices, and using effective tools are critical to the success of this process. As we progress, we'll explore further steps in assessing your cloud environment, setting goals and objectives, and using tools to ensure you configure CSP to secure your cloud infrastructure effectively.

B. Identifying Security Requirements and Compliance Needs

Identifying security and compliance requirements is critical in assessing your cloud environment. This process ensures that all security measures align with organizational goals, industry standards, and regulatory requirements. This section will explore identifying security requirements, understanding compliance needs, and developing a framework for maintaining security and compliance in your cloud environment.

B.1 Understanding Security Requirements

Security requirements are the specific conditions or capabilities a system must meet to protect data, applications, and services within a cloud environment. Various factors influence these, including organizational goals, threat landscapes, and best practice requirements.

B.1.1 Organizational Goals and Objectives

Your organization's goals and objectives play a significant role in shaping your security requirements. These goals may include protecting sensitive data, ensuring service availability, maintaining customer trust, and complying with legal obligations.

Example: A financial institution prioritizes protecting customer financial data and ensuring the availability of online banking services, influencing its security requirements for encryption, access controls, and disaster recovery.

B.1.2 Threat Landscape and Risk Assessment

A thorough risk assessment helps identify potential threats and vulnerabilities specific to your cloud environment. Understanding the threat landscape allows you to prioritize security measures based on the likelihood and impact of different risks.

Steps for Risk Assessment:

- **Identify Assets:** List all critical assets, such as data, applications, and infrastructure components.
- **Identify Threats:** Determine potential threats, including cyberattacks, data breaches, insider threats, and natural disasters.
- **Assess Vulnerabilities:** Evaluate vulnerabilities in your cloud environment that threats could exploit.
- **Evaluate Impact:** Assess each threat's potential impact on your assets, considering data loss, financial loss, and reputational damage.

Example: A healthcare provider identifies patient data as a critical asset and evaluates threats such as ransomware attacks and data breaches. This leads to security requirements for robust encryption and regular security audits.

B.1.3 Best Practices and Industry Standards

Adhering to industry best practices and standards helps ensure your security measures are comprehensive and effective. These standards provide guidelines and frameworks for implementing security controls in cloud environments.

Key Standards and Frameworks:

- **NIST Cybersecurity Framework:** Provides comprehensive guidelines for managing and reducing cybersecurity risks.
- **CIS Controls:** Offers a prioritized set of actions to protect against cyber threats.
- **ISO/IEC 27001:** Specifies requirements for establishing, implementing, maintaining, and continually improving an information security management system (ISMS).

Example: An e-commerce company adopts CIS Controls to establish a baseline for its security practices, including network security, access controls, and incident response.

B.2 Understanding Compliance Needs

Compliance requirements are dictated by industry regulations, legal obligations, and an organization's internal policies. These requirements ensure that your cloud environment meets necessary legal and regulatory standards.

B.2.1 Identifying Relevant Regulations

The first step in understanding compliance needs is identifying the regulations and standards relevant to your industry and geographic location. These regulations dictate the security measures required to protect sensitive data and ensure privacy.

Common Regulations:

- **GDPR (General Data Protection Regulation):** Applies to organizations handling the personal data of EU citizens, requiring stringent data protection measures.
- **HIPAA (Health Insurance Portability and Accountability Act):** This act regulates the protection of health information in the United States.
- **PCI-DSS (Payment Card Industry Data Security Standard):** Sets security standards for organizations that handle payment card information.

Example: A multinational company operating in Europe and the US must comply with GDPR and HIPAA, influencing its requirements for data encryption, access controls, and data breach response.

B.2.2 Conducting a Compliance Gap Analysis

A compliance gap analysis helps identify areas where your security measures fall short of regulatory requirements. This analysis guides the development of a compliance plan to address these gaps.

Steps for Compliance Gap Analysis:

- **Review Requirements:** Understand the specific requirements of each relevant regulation.
- **Assess Current Measures:** Evaluate your security measures and controls against these requirements.
- **Identify Gaps:** Document gaps where current measures do not meet compliance standards.
- **Develop a Remediation Plan:** Create a plan to address identified gaps and achieve compliance.

Example: An organization evaluates its data protection measures against GDPR requirements and identifies gaps in data encryption and access controls, leading to a remediation plan to implement stronger encryption and multi-factor authentication.

B.2.3 Implementing Compliance Controls

Once compliance gaps are identified, the necessary controls to meet regulatory requirements will be implemented. These controls should be integrated into your security strategy and continuously monitored for effectiveness.

Compliance Controls:

- **Data Protection:** Implement encryption, data masking, and secure data disposal measures.
- **Access Controls:** Use role-based access control (RBAC), multi-factor authentication (MFA), and regular access reviews.
- **Monitoring and Auditing:** Continuously monitor cloud environments for compliance and conduct regular audits to ensure ongoing adherence to regulations.

Example: To comply with PCI-DSS, a retail company implements encryption for payment data, restricts access to cardholder data, and conducts regular security audits.

B.3 Developing a Security and Compliance Framework

A comprehensive security and compliance framework helps integrate security requirements and compliance needs into a cohesive strategy. This framework guides the implementation, monitoring, and continuous improvement of security measures.

B.3.1 Security Policies and Procedures

Develop and document security policies and procedures that outline the specific measures and controls to be implemented. These policies should align with organizational goals, regulatory requirements, and industry best practices.

Example: A financial institution develops a data protection policy with encryption standards, access control measures, and incident response procedures.

B.3.2 Training and Awareness Programs

Regular training and awareness programs ensure that employees understand their roles and responsibilities in maintaining security and compliance. These programs should cover policies, procedures, and best practices.

Example: Conducting quarterly training sessions for employees on data protection best practices and compliance requirements for handling sensitive customer information.

B.3.3 Continuous Monitoring and Improvement

Implement continuous monitoring to detect security and compliance issues in real-time. Automated tools monitor cloud environments and generate alerts for deviations from established policies and standards. Regularly review and update security measures to address emerging threats and changing regulations.

Example: Using a CSPM tool to continuously monitor cloud configurations for compliance with GDPR and generate alerts for any non-compliant resources.

B.4 Tools for Identifying Security and Compliance Needs

Several tools can assist in identifying and managing security requirements and compliance needs:

B.4.1 AWS Security Hub

Overview: AWS Security Hub provides a comprehensive view of your security posture and compliance status across AWS accounts.

Features:

- Aggregates security findings from AWS services and third-party tools.
- Provides automated compliance checks for standards such as CIS AWS Foundations Benchmark and PCI-DSS.
- Generates detailed reports and dashboards for monitoring security and compliance.

Example: Using AWS Security Hub to assess compliance with CIS benchmarks and monitor security findings from Amazon GuardDuty and AWS Config.

B.4.2 Azure Security Center

Overview: Azure Security Center offers advanced threat protection and continuous security assessment for Azure environments.

Features:

- Provides unified security management and advanced threat protection.
- Continuously assesses compliance with standards such as ISO 27001, PCI-DSS, and Azure Security Benchmark.
- Offers actionable security recommendations and automated remediation.

Example: Azure Security Center will be used to monitor compliance with PCI-DSS and implement security recommendations to protect sensitive payment data.

B.4.3 Google Cloud Security Command Center (SCC)

Overview: Google Cloud Security Command Center (SCC) provides comprehensive security and risk management for Google Cloud Platform (GCP) environments.

Features:

- Offers real-time visibility into security posture and compliance status.
- Integrates with GCP services for threat detection and response.
- Provides customizable dashboards and automated compliance checks.

Example: Using Google Cloud SCC to monitor compliance with GDPR and detect potential security threats in real-time.

B.5 Conclusion

Identifying security and compliance requirements is critical in assessing your cloud environment. You can develop a comprehensive security and compliance framework by understanding organizational goals, conducting risk assessments, adhering to best practices, and ensuring compliance with relevant regulations. Leveraging automated tools and continuous monitoring further enhances your ability to maintain a secure and compliant cloud environment. As we move forward, we will explore practical steps for setting goals and objectives and configuring CSPM tools to secure your cloud infrastructure effectively.

- Real-time inventory management.
- Detailed asset metadata.
- Integration with Cloud Security Command Center (SCC) for security assessments.

Example: Using Cloud Asset Inventory to track the lifecycle of cloud resources and ensure compliance with organizational policies.

C. Conducting a Risk Assessment

Conducting a risk assessment is a fundamental step in securing your cloud environment. It involves identifying potential threats, evaluating vulnerabilities, and assessing the impact of security incidents on your organization. A thorough risk assessment enables you to prioritize security measures and allocate resources effectively. This section will explore the steps in conducting a risk assessment and the best practices and tools to aid this process.

C.1 Importance of Risk Assessment

A risk assessment helps you understand the security posture of your cloud environment, identify potential weaknesses, and implement measures to mitigate risks. This proactive approach is essential for:

- **Protecting Sensitive Data:** Protecting sensitive information against unauthorized access and breaches.
- **Maintaining Compliance:** Meeting regulatory requirements and industry standards to avoid legal penalties and reputational damage.
- **Preventing Downtime:** Mitigating risks that could lead to service disruptions, ensuring business continuity.
- **Optimizing Resource Allocation:** Prioritizing security investments based on the severity and likelihood of risks.

C.2 Steps in Conducting a Risk Assessment

Risk assessment involves several key steps, from identifying assets to implementing mitigation strategies. Here's a detailed look at each step:

C.2.1 Identify Assets

The first step in a risk assessment is to identify all assets within your cloud environment. Assets include data, applications, services, and infrastructure components critical to your organization's operations.

Example: An e-commerce company identifies its customer database, payment processing system, and web application as critical assets.

C.2.2 Identify Threats

Next, identify potential threats that could compromise the security of your assets. Threats can be internal or external, including cyberattacks, natural disasters, human error, and system failures.

Common Threats:

- **Cyberattacks:** Phishing, malware, ransomware, denial-of-service (DoS) attacks.
- **Insider Threats:** Malicious actions by employees or contractors.
- **Natural Disasters:** Floods, earthquakes, fires.
- **Human Error:** Accidental data deletion and misconfigurations.
- **System Failures:** Hardware or software malfunctions.

Example: The e-commerce company identifies threats such as DDoS attacks on its web application, ransomware targeting its customer database, and insider threats from employees accessing sensitive data.

C.2.3 Identify Vulnerabilities

Assess the vulnerabilities in your cloud environment that identified threats that could be exploited. Vulnerabilities are weaknesses or gaps in your security controls that could be exploited to gain unauthorized access or cause harm.

Common Vulnerabilities:

- **Unpatched Software:** Systems or applications must be updated with the latest security patches.
- **Weak Passwords:** Use of easily guessable or reused passwords.
- **Misconfigurations:** Incorrect settings that expose resources to unauthorized access.
- **Lack of Encryption:** Data is not encrypted at rest or in transit.

Example: The e-commerce company identifies vulnerabilities such as unpatched software on its web servers, weak passwords used by employees, and misconfigured security groups in its cloud environment.

C.2.4 Evaluate Impact

Assess the potential impact of each threat exploiting a vulnerability. The impact can be measured regarding financial loss, reputational damage, legal consequences, and operational disruption.

Impact Categories:

- **Financial Impact:** Direct financial losses, costs of remediation, and potential fines.
- **Reputational Impact:** Damage to brand reputation and customer trust.
- **Legal Impact:** Legal consequences of non-compliance with regulations.
- **Operational Impact:** Disruption to business operations and service delivery.

Example: The e-commerce company evaluates the impact of a DDoS attack on its web application, considering potential revenue loss, customer dissatisfaction, and reputational damage.

C.2.5 Determine Likelihood

Estimate the likelihood of each threat exploiting a vulnerability. Likelihood can be assessed based on historical data, threat intelligence, and expert judgment.

Likelihood Levels:

- **High:** Threats likely to occur based on past incidents or known vulnerabilities.
- **Medium:** Threats that are possible but not highly probable.
- **Low:** Threats that are unlikely to occur but still possible.

Example: The e-commerce company assesses the likelihood of a ransomware attack on its customer database as high due to recent industry trends and known vulnerabilities in its software.

C.2.6 Assess Risk

Combine the impact and likelihood to assess the overall risk for each threat-vulnerability pair. This helps prioritize risks based on their potential severity and probability of occurrence.

Risk Matrix:

- **High Risk:** High impact and high likelihood; requires immediate

attention and mitigation.
- **Medium Risk:** Moderate impact or likelihood; requires monitoring and mitigation planning.
- **Low Risk:** Low impact and low likelihood; may require minimal monitoring or acceptance.

Example: The e-commerce company uses a risk matrix to categorize the risk of a DDoS attack on its web application as high, given the high impact on revenue and customer trust and a moderate likelihood based on recent attack trends.

C.2.7 Develop Mitigation Strategies

Develop strategies to mitigate identified risks. Mitigation strategies may include implementing security controls, enhancing monitoring and detection capabilities, and developing incident response plans.

Mitigation Strategies:

- **Preventive Controls:** Measures to prevent security incidents, such as firewalls, intrusion detection systems, and regular software updates.
- **Detective Controls:** Measures to detect security incidents, such as continuous monitoring, logging, and alerting.
- **Corrective Controls:** Measures to respond to and recover from security incidents, such as incident response plans and disaster recovery procedures.

Example: The e-commerce company develops a mitigation strategy for DDoS attacks by implementing a web application firewall (WAF), enhancing network monitoring, and creating an incident response plan for DDoS scenarios.

C.2.8 Document and Review

Document and review the risk assessment findings regularly. This documentation should include identified assets, threats, vulnerabilities, impacts, likelihoods, and mitigation strategies.

Documentation Components:

- **Risk Assessment Report:** Detailed report of the risk assessment process and findings.
- **Risk Register:** A dynamic document that tracks identified risks, their status, and mitigation efforts.
- **Action Plans:** Specific action plans for implementing mitigation strategies and improving security posture.

Example: The e-commerce company maintains a risk register that is reviewed and updated quarterly. The register tracks the status of identified risks and the implementation of mitigation measures.

C.3 Best Practices for Risk Assessment

To ensure a thorough and effective risk assessment, follow these best practices:

C.3.1 Involve Stakeholders

Involve relevant stakeholders from different departments, including IT, security, compliance, and business units. Stakeholder involvement ensures a comprehensive understanding of risks and aligns security measures with business objectives.

Example: Including IT, security, and legal department representatives in the risk assessment process to provide diverse perspectives on potential risks and impacts.

C.3.2 Use a Structured Methodology

Adopt a structured methodology for risk assessment, such as the NIST Risk Management Framework (RMF) or ISO 31000. A structured approach ensures consistency and thoroughness in identifying and evaluating risks.

Example: Using the NIST RMF to guide the risk assessment process, from categorizing assets to selecting and implementing security controls.

C.3.3 Leverage Automated Tools

Utilize automated tools to enhance the efficiency and accuracy of the risk assessment process. Automated tools can help identify assets, detect vulnerabilities, and generate risk reports.

Example: Using tools like AWS Config, Azure Security Center, or third-party solutions like Qualys or Tenable to automate asset discovery, vulnerability scanning, and risk assessment reporting.

C.3.4 Regularly Update Risk Assessments

Regularly update risk assessments to account for changes in the threat landscape, new vulnerabilities, and changes in the cloud environment. Continuous assessment ensures that security measures remain effective and relevant.

Example: Conduct quarterly risk assessments to review new threats, vulnerabilities, and changes in the cloud infrastructure and update mitigation strategies accordingly.

C.4 Tools for Conducting Risk Assessments

Several tools can assist in conducting comprehensive risk assessments in cloud environments:

C.4.1 AWS Config

Overview: AWS Config provides continuous monitoring and assessment of AWS resource configurations, helping identify risks and compliance issues.

Features:

- Automatic detection of configuration changes.
- Integration with AWS Security Hub for consolidated risk reporting.
- Predefined and custom rules for compliance and security assessments.

Example: AWS Config can monitor the configuration of EC2 instances and detect non-compliant settings that could pose security risks.

C.4.2 Azure Security Center

Overview: Azure Security Center offers advanced threat protection and continuous security assessment for Azure environments.

Features:

- Continuous assessment of security posture and compliance.
- Integration with Azure Sentinel for threat detection and response.
- Recommendations for mitigating identified risks.

Example: Using Azure Security Center to assess the security posture of virtual machines and implement recommended security controls to mitigate identified risks.

C.4.3 Qualys Cloud Platform

Overview: Qualys Cloud Platform provides comprehensive vulnerability management, continuous monitoring, and risk assessment for cloud environments.

Features:

- Automated vulnerability scanning and risk assessment.
- Detailed reporting and risk prioritization.
- Integration with SIEM and ITSM tools for enhanced threat detection and response.

Example: Using Qualys to perform regular vulnerability scans of cloud resources, prioritize risks based on impact and likelihood, and generate detailed risk assessment reports.

C.5 Conclusion

Conducting a thorough risk assessment is essential for securing your cloud environment and protecting critical assets. You can prioritize risks and develop effective mitigation strategies by identifying assets, threats, vulnerabilities, impacts, and likelihoods. Leveraging best practices and automated tools further enhances the efficiency and accuracy of the risk assessment process. As we move forward, we'll explore practical steps for setting goals and objectives and configuring CSPM tools to secure your cloud infrastructure effectively.

Chapter 5: Setting Goals and Objectives

A. Defining Clear Security Goals

Establishing clear security goals is crucial in developing a robust Cloud Security Posture Management (CSPM) strategy. Well-defined security goals provide direction, ensure alignment with business objectives, and serve as a foundation for measuring progress and success. In this section, we will explore the importance of defining clear security goals, the process of setting these goals, and examples of effective security goals in a cloud environment.

A.1 Importance of Clear Security Goals

Clear security goals are essential for several reasons:

A.1.1 Strategic Alignment

Security goals must align with the overall business objectives and strategies. This alignment ensures that security efforts support the organization's mission and contribute to achieving broader business outcomes.

Example: A financial services company aims to enhance customer trust and satisfaction. Aligning security goals such as protecting customer data and ensuring service availability directly supports this objective.

A.1.2 Resource Allocation

Defined security goals help efficiently allocate resources, including time, budget, and personnel. By prioritizing security initiatives based on these goals, organizations can ensure that resources are used effectively to address the most critical areas.

Example: Prioritizing investment in advanced threat detection tools to reduce the time to detect and respond to security incidents.

A.1.3 Performance Measurement

Clear security goals provide a basis for measuring performance and progress. By setting specific, measurable targets, organizations can track their success over time and identify areas for improvement.

Example: Setting a goal to reduce the number of security incidents by 25% within the next year and using this metric to measure the effectiveness of security initiatives.

A.2 Process of Setting Security Goals

Setting security goals involves several key steps:

A.2.1 Assessing the Current Security Posture

Before defining security goals, it is essential to assess the current security posture of the cloud environment. This assessment provides a baseline understanding of strengths, weaknesses, and areas that require improvement.

Steps for Assessing Security Posture:

- **Inventory Assets:** Identify all assets in the cloud environment.
- **Evaluate Controls:** Assess the effectiveness of existing security controls.
- **Identify Risks:** Determine current and potential risks to the cloud environment.
- **Review Compliance:** Check compliance with relevant regulations and standards.

Example: Conducting a security assessment using tools like AWS Security Hub or Azure Security Center to evaluate the current security state and identify gaps.

A.2.2 Engaging Stakeholders

Engage key stakeholders from various departments, including IT, security, compliance, and business units. Stakeholder input ensures that security goals are comprehensive, realistic, and aligned with organizational priorities.

Example: Holding workshops with IT, legal, and finance representatives to gather input on security priorities and objectives.

A.2.3 Defining SMART Goals

Security goals should be SMART: Specific, Measurable, Achievable, Relevant, and Time-bound. This framework ensures that goals are clear, actionable, and trackable.

Components of SMART Goals:

- **Specific:** Clearly define what is to be achieved.
- **Measurable:** Establish criteria for measuring progress.
- **Achievable:** Ensure the goal is realistic, given available resources.
- **Relevant:** Align the goal with broader business objectives.
- **Time-bound:** Set a deadline for achieving the goal.

Example: Setting a goal to "implement multi-factor authentication (MFA) for all critical cloud services within six months" is a SMART goal.

CHAPTER 5: SETTING GOALS AND OBJECTIVES

A.2.4 Prioritizing Goals

Not all security goals can be achieved simultaneously. Prioritize goals based on risk severity, regulatory requirements, and business impact. High-priority goals should address the most critical security needs and have the greatest potential impact.

Example: Prioritizing the goal of encrypting sensitive data at rest and in transit to meet regulatory requirements and protect critical information.

A.2.5 Developing an Action Plan

Once security goals are defined and prioritized, develop an action plan that outlines the steps required to achieve each goal. The action plan should include specific tasks, responsible parties, timelines, and required resources.

Example: Creating an action plan to implement MFA, including tasks such as selecting an MFA solution, configuring MFA for cloud services, training employees, and monitoring implementation progress.

A.3 Examples of Effective Security Goals

Here are some examples of effective security goals for a cloud environment:

A.3.1 Enhancing Data Protection

Goal: Implement encryption for all sensitive data stored in the cloud within the next six months.

Action Plan:

- Identify all sensitive data.
- Select encryption tools and technologies.
- Implement encryption for data at rest and in transit.
- Verify encryption effectiveness through regular audits.

Example: A healthcare organization implements encryption to protect patient records, ensuring compliance with HIPAA requirements.

A.3.2 Reducing Incident Response Time

Goal: Reduce the average time to detect and respond to security incidents by 50% within the next year.

Action Plan:

- Implement advanced threat detection tools.
- Develop and test incident response plans.
- Train security personnel on incident response procedures.
- Monitor and review incident response performance.

Example: An e-commerce company enhances its threat detection capabilities and trains its security team to respond more quickly to potential breaches, minimizing the impact of security incidents.

A.3.3 Achieving Regulatory Compliance

Goal: Achieve full compliance with GDPR within the next nine months.

Action Plan:

- Conduct a compliance gap analysis.
- Implement necessary controls and measures.
- Train employees on GDPR requirements.
- Regularly audit compliance status and address any issues.

Example: A multinational corporation implements data protection measures and trains its staff to ensure compliance with GDPR, avoid legal penalties, and protect customer privacy.

A.3.4 Improving Access Controls

Goal: Implement role-based access control (RBAC) for all cloud resources within the next six months.

Action Plan:

- Define roles and access levels.
- Configure RBAC policies in cloud services.
- Train employees on RBAC policies and procedures.
- Monitor access controls and adjust as needed.

Example: A financial institution implements RBAC to ensure that employees only have access to the data and systems necessary for their roles, reducing the risk of insider threats.

A.4 Monitoring and Revisiting Security Goals

Security goals should not be static. Monitor progress toward achieving these goals regularly and revisit them periodically to ensure they remain relevant and effective. Adjust goals as needed to address new threats, changes in the cloud environment, and evolving business objectives.

Best Practices for Monitoring and Revisiting Goals:

- Regular Reviews: Schedule regular reviews of security goals and progress involving key stakeholders.
- Performance Metrics: Use specific metrics to track progress and measure success.
- Continuous Improvement: Adjust and refine goals based on lessons learned and changes in the security landscape.

Example: A company reviews its security goals quarterly, using metrics such as the number of security incidents, time to resolution, and compliance audit results to assess progress and make necessary adjustments.

A.5 Conclusion

Defining clear security goals is vital in developing an effective CSPM strategy. Organizations can set actionable and measurable targets by aligning security goals with business objectives, engaging stakeholders, and using the SMART framework. Regular monitoring and revisiting of these goals ensure continuous improvement and adaptation to the evolving threat landscape. As we continue, we will explore practical steps for configuring CSPM tools to achieve these goals and secure your cloud environment effectively.

B. Establishing Key Performance Indicators (KPIs)

Key Performance Indicators (KPIs) are essential metrics used to measure the effectiveness of your cloud security initiatives. By establishing KPIs, you can track progress towards your security goals, identify areas for improvement, and demonstrate the value of your security investments. This section will explore the importance of KPIs, selecting and defining relevant KPIs, and examples of effective KPIs for cloud security.

B.1 Importance of KPIs

KPIs play a critical role in cloud security management for several reasons:

B.1.1 Performance Measurement

KPIs provide a quantifiable means of assessing the performance of your security measures. You can track these metrics to determine whether your security initiatives achieve their intended outcomes.

Example: Monitoring the average time to resolve security incidents helps assess the efficiency of your incident response process.

B.1.2 Continuous Improvement

KPIs help identify areas where security measures may be lacking or require enhancement. You can implement targeted improvements to strengthen your security posture by analyzing KPI data.

Example: Analyzing the number of recurring vulnerabilities can highlight the need for better patch management practices.

B.1.3 Accountability and Reporting

KPIs provide a basis for reporting security performance to stakeholders, including executives, board members, and regulatory bodies. Clear metrics show the effectiveness of your security program and ensure further investment.

Example: Report the percentage of systems compliant with security standards to the board of directors.

B.2 Selecting and Defining Relevant KPIs

Selecting and defining KPIs involves several key steps to ensure they are meaningful and aligned with your security goals:

B.2.1 Align with Security Goals

KPIs should directly relate to your security goals. Ensure that each KPI provides insight into the progress towards achieving specific objectives.

Example: If your goal is to enhance data protection, a relevant KPI could be the percentage of encrypted sensitive data.

B.2.2 Make KPIs SMART

KPIs should be Specific, Measurable, Achievable, Relevant, and Time-bound (SMART). This ensures that they are clear, actionable, and trackable over time.

Example: A KPI to "reduce the average time to detect security incidents by 30% within six months" is SMART.

B.2.3 Use a Balanced Approach

Use a balanced set of KPIs to cover different aspects of cloud security, including prevention, detection, response, and compliance. This comprehensive approach provides a holistic view of your security posture.

Example: Combining KPIs for incident detection time, compliance status, and user access reviews to cover various security dimensions.

B.2.4 Define Clear Metrics

Define clear and precise metrics for each KPI. Ensure the data required to measure these metrics is readily available and reliable.

Example: Defining a metric for "average time to resolve security incidents" based on incident response logs.

B.3 Examples of Effective KPIs for Cloud Security

Here are some examples of effective KPIs for monitoring cloud security:

B.3.1 Incident Detection and Response

KPI: Average Time to Detect Security Incidents (MTTD)

Definition: The average time to detect security incidents from the initial occurrence.

Metric: (Sum of time taken to detect each incident) / (Total number of incidents detected)

Example: Tracking MTTD helps assess the effectiveness of your threat detection tools and processes.

KPI: Average Time to Resolve Security Incidents (MTTR)

Definition: The average time to resolve security incidents from detection to resolution.

Metric: (Sum of time taken to resolve each incident) / (Total number of incidents resolved)

Example: Monitoring MTTR helps evaluate the efficiency of your incident response process and identify areas for improvement.

B.3.2 Vulnerability Management

KPI: Percentage of Critical Vulnerabilities Remediated

Definition: The percentage of critical vulnerabilities identified and remediated within a specified time frame.

Metric: (Number of critical vulnerabilities remediated) / (Total number of critical vulnerabilities identified) * 100

Example: This KPI helps assess the effectiveness of your vulnerability management program and prioritize critical issues.

KPI: Average Time to Patch Vulnerabilities

Definition: The average time taken to apply patches to identified vulnerabilities.

Metric: (Sum of time taken to patch each vulnerability) / (Total number of vulnerabilities patched)

Example: Tracking this KPI helps ensure timely patching and reduce the risk of exploitation.

B.3.3 Compliance and Governance

KPI: Percentage of Systems in Compliance with Security Policies

Definition: The percentage of cloud systems that comply with defined security policies and standards.

Metric: (Number of compliant systems) / (Total number of systems assessed) * 100

Example: This KPI helps monitor adherence to security policies and identify non-compliant systems that require attention.

KPI: Number of Compliance Violations Detected

Definition: The number of compliance violations detected during audits or continuous monitoring.

Metric: Total number of compliance violations detected within a specified period.

Example: Tracking this KPI helps identify areas where compliance efforts must be strengthened.

B.3.4 Access Management

KPI: Number of Unauthorized Access Attempts

Definition: The total number of unauthorized access attempts detected within a specified period.

Metric: Total number of unauthorized access attempts detected.

Example: Monitoring this KPI helps assess the effectiveness of access control measures and identify potential insider threats.

KPI: Percentage of Users with Expired Credentials

Definition: The percentage of users whose credentials have expired but have yet to be updated or revoked.

Metric: (Number of users with expired credentials) / (Total number of users) * 100

Example: This KPI helps ensure that user credentials are regularly updated and unauthorized access is minimized.

B.4 Best Practices for Monitoring KPIs

To effectively monitor and utilize KPIs, follow these best practices:

B.4.1 Automate Data Collection

Automate the collection and analysis of KPI data using security tools and dashboards. This reduces manual effort and ensures timely and accurate data.

Example: Using a SIEM (Security Information and Event Management) system automatically collects and analyzes security incident data for KPI reporting.

B.4.2 Regularly Review and Update KPIs

Regularly review and update KPIs to remain relevant and aligned with evolving security goals and threat landscapes.

Example: Conducting quarterly reviews of KPIs to assess their effectiveness and make adjustments based on new security challenges.

B.4.3 Communicate KPI Results

Communicate KPI results to stakeholders through regular reports and dashboards. Clear communication ensures stakeholders are informed about security performance and can support necessary improvements.

Example: Providing monthly security performance reports to executives and IT management, highlighting key KPIs and trends.

B.4.4 Use KPIs for Continuous Improvement

Use KPI data to drive continuous improvement in your security program. Analyze trends, identify root causes of issues, and implement corrective actions.

Example: Analyzing an increase in unauthorized access attempts to identify and address weaknesses in access control measures.

B.5 Tools for Monitoring KPIs

Several tools can assist in monitoring and reporting KPIs for cloud security:

B.5.1 AWS Security Hub

Overview: AWS Security Hub provides a comprehensive view of your security posture and compliance status across AWS accounts.

Features:

- Aggregates security findings from AWS services and third-party tools.
- Provides automated compliance checks and security alerts.
- Generates detailed dashboards and reports for KPI monitoring.

Example: AWS Security Hub can be used to track KPIs such as the number of security incidents detected and resolved within AWS environments.

B.5.2 Azure Security Center

Overview: Azure Security Center offers advanced threat protection and continuous security assessment for Azure environments.

Features:

- Provides real-time security monitoring and threat detection.
- Continuously assesses compliance with security standards and policies.
- Offers customizable dashboards and reports for KPI tracking.

Example: Using Azure Security Center to monitor KPIs such as compliance status and the average time to patch vulnerabilities.

B.5.3 Google Cloud Security Command Center (SCC)

Overview: Google Cloud Security Command Center (SCC) provides comprehensive security and risk management for Google Cloud Platform (GCP) environments.

Features:

- Offers real-time visibility into security posture and compliance status.
- Integrates with GCP services for threat detection and response.
- Provides customizable dashboards and automated reporting for KPI monitoring.

Example: Using Google Cloud SCC to track KPIs such as the number of compliance violations and the percentage of systems with up-to-date security patches.

B.6 Conclusion

Establishing KPIs is a critical component of effective cloud security management. By selecting relevant SMART KPIs and using them to measure performance, organizations can track progress towards security goals, identify areas for improvement, and ensure accountability. Leveraging automated tools and following best practices for KPI monitoring further enhances the ability to maintain a robust security posture. As we move forward, we will explore practical steps for configuring CSPM tools to achieve these goals and secure your cloud environment effectively.

C. Aligning CSPM Goals with Business Objectives

Aligning Cloud Security Posture Management (CSPM) goals with business objectives is essential for ensuring that security efforts support the organization's broader mission and strategic goals. This alignment helps secure executive buy-in, optimize resource allocation, and demonstrate the value of security initiatives in driving business success. This section will explore the importance of alignment, strategies for achieving it, and examples of aligned CSPM goals.

C.1 Importance of Aligning CSPM Goals with Business Objectives

C.1.1 Strategic Integration

Aligning CSPM goals with business objectives ensures that security initiatives are integrated into the organization's strategic plan. This integration facilitates a cohesive approach in which security measures directly contribute to achieving business goals.

Example: A retail company prioritizes customer trust as a business objective. Aligning CSPM goals to enhance data protection and ensure compliance with data privacy regulations directly supports this objective.

C.1.2 Resource Optimization

When CSPM goals are aligned with business objectives, resources can be allocated more effectively. Organizations can prioritize investments in security measures that significantly impact business success, ensuring optimal use of time, budget, and personnel.

Example: A financial services firm focuses on transaction security to maintain customer confidence. Prioritizing CSPM resources towards advanced fraud detection and prevention technologies aligns with this business objective.

C.1.3 Executive Buy-In

Executive support is crucial for the success of security initiatives. Aligning CSPM goals with business objectives makes it easier to secure executive buy-in, as it demonstrates how security measures contribute to the organization's overall success.

Example: Presenting a CSPM goal to reduce the risk of data breaches, which aligns with the business objective of protecting intellectual property, can help gain executive approval for necessary security investments.

C.1.4 Performance Measurement

Aligned goals facilitate the measurement of both security and business performance. Organizations can track progress towards CSPM goals and their impact on achieving business objectives, ensuring accountability and continuous improvement.

Example: Measuring the reduction in security incidents and correlating it with increased customer satisfaction and reduced churn rates.

C.2 Strategies for Aligning CSPM Goals with Business Objectives

C.2.1 Understand Business Objectives

The first step in aligning CSPM goals with business objectives is thoroughly understanding the organization's strategic goals and priorities. This understanding forms the basis for defining relevant and supportive CSPM goals.

Steps to Understand Business Objectives:

- **Engage with Leadership:** Conduct meetings and discussions with executive leadership to understand strategic goals and priorities.
- **Review Strategic Documents:** Study the organization's mission statement, strategic plan, and annual reports to gain insights into business objectives.
- **Identify Key Metrics:** Identify the key performance indicators (KPIs) that the organization uses to measure business success.

Example: A healthcare organization's strategic goal is to enhance patient trust and satisfaction. Key metrics include patient data protection and compliance with healthcare regulations.

C.2.2 Map CSPM Goals to Business Objectives

Once you understand the business objectives, map specific CSPM goals to them. This mapping ensures that each security goal directly contributes to achieving a broader business goal.

Mapping Process:

- Identify Security Needs: Determine the security needs that align with business objectives.
- Define Specific Goals: Define specific CSPM goals that address these security needs.
- Establish Metrics: Establish metrics to measure the success of CSPM goals and their impact on business objectives.

Example: For a business objective to enhance customer trust, a CSPM goal could be to implement comprehensive data encryption measures. Metrics could include the percentage of data encrypted and the number of data breaches prevented.

C.2.3 Involve Stakeholders

Involving stakeholders from various departments ensures that CSPM goals are comprehensive and aligned with the needs of different business units. Stakeholder involvement fosters collaboration and buy-in across the organization.

Stakeholder Engagement:

- **Cross-Functional Teams:** Form cross-functional teams with repre-

sentatives from IT, security, compliance, finance, and business units.
- **Workshops and Brainstorming:** Conduct workshops and brainstorming sessions to gather input and perspectives on aligning CSPM goals with business objectives.
- **Regular Updates:** Provide stakeholders with regular updates on the progress of CSPM initiatives and their impact on business goals.

Example: Involving the marketing department in discussions about data protection can highlight the importance of securing customer data for marketing campaigns and customer engagement.

C.2.4 Communicate the Value of CSPM

Effectively communicating the value of CSPM initiatives in terms of business impact is crucial for gaining support and demonstrating success. You can use business language and metrics to explain how CSPM contributes to achieving strategic goals.

Communication Strategies:

- **Business Impact Reports:** Create reports that translate technical security metrics into business impact, such as cost savings from prevented breaches or increased customer retention due to enhanced security.
- **Executive Summaries:** Provide executive summaries highlighting the alignment of CSPM goals with business objectives and their impact on business performance.
- **Success Stories:** Share success stories and case studies that illustrate the positive impact of CSPM initiatives on business outcomes.

Example: Presenting a report that shows how implementing advanced threat detection reduced security incidents by 40%, resulting in cost savings and improved customer trust.

C.3 Examples of Aligned CSPM Goals

C.3.1 Enhancing Customer Trust

Business Objective: Enhance customer trust and satisfaction.

Aligned CSPM Goal: Implement comprehensive data protection measures to safeguard customer information.

Metrics:

- Percentage of customer data encrypted.
- Number of data breaches reported.
- Customer satisfaction scores related to data privacy.

Example: A retail company implements encryption for all customer data stored in the cloud, monitors access to this data, and regularly audits its security practices to ensure compliance with data protection regulations.

C.3.2 Ensuring Regulatory Compliance

Business Objective: Ensure compliance with industry regulations to avoid legal penalties and maintain operational integrity.

Aligned CSPM Goal: Ensure compliance with relevant regulations such as

GDPR, HIPAA, or PCI-DSS.

Metrics:

- The number of compliance violations detected and resolved.
- Audit findings and compliance scores.
- Time is taken to achieve compliance with new regulations.

Example: A healthcare provider focuses on achieving HIPAA compliance by implementing security controls, conducting regular compliance audits, and training staff on data protection requirements.

C.3.3 Protecting Intellectual Property

Business Objective: Protect intellectual property to maintain competitive advantage and support innovation.

Aligned CSPM Goal: Implement advanced security measures to prevent unauthorized access to sensitive intellectual property.

Metrics:

- Number of unauthorized access attempts detected and blocked.
- Incidents of intellectual property theft or loss.
- Employee training completion rates on data protection.

Example: A technology company deploys advanced threat detection tools, enforces strict access controls, and educates employees on protecting intellectual property.

C.3.4 Reducing Operational Disruption

Business Objective: Minimize operational disruptions to ensure continuous service delivery and business continuity.

Aligned CSPM Goal: Enhance incident detection and response capabilities to reduce the impact of security incidents on operations.

Metrics:

- Average time to detect and resolve security incidents.
- Number of incidents causing operational downtime.
- Recovery time objectives (RTO) and recovery point objectives (RPO) were achieved.

Example: A financial institution invests in a Security Operations Center (SOC) to monitor and respond to security incidents 24/7, ensuring that any disruptions are quickly identified and mitigated.

C.4 Best Practices for Aligning CSPM Goals

C.4.1 Continuous Alignment

Ensure that CSPM goals are continuously aligned with evolving business objectives. Regularly review and update goals to reflect changes in business strategy, threat landscape, and regulatory requirements.

Example: Conducting annual reviews of CSPM goals and adjusting them based on new business initiatives or emerging security threats.

C.4.2 Performance Metrics

Use performance metrics to track the alignment and impact of CSPM goals. Regularly monitor and report on these metrics to demonstrate the effectiveness of security initiatives in supporting business objectives.

Example: Using a dashboard to track key metrics such as reducing security incidents, compliance status, and customer satisfaction scores.

C.4.3 Stakeholder Collaboration

Foster ongoing collaboration with stakeholders to ensure that CSPM goals remain relevant and support business objectives. Engage stakeholders in goal-setting, implementation, and evaluation processes.

Example: Holding quarterly meetings with cross-functional teams to discuss progress, challenges, and opportunities for improving CSPM initiatives.

C.5 Conclusion

Aligning CSPM goals with business objectives is critical for ensuring that security efforts contribute to the organization's success. Organizations can create a cohesive and impactful security strategy by understanding business objectives, mapping CSPM goals, involving stakeholders, and effectively communicating the value of CSPM. Regular monitoring and adjustment of CSPM goals ensure continuous alignment and support for business growth and resilience. As we continue, we will explore practical steps for configuring CSPM tools to achieve these aligned goals and secure your cloud environment effectively.

IV

Implementation Steps

Chapter 6: Configuring CSPM Tools

A. Setting Up the CSPM Environment

Configuring your Cloud Security Posture Management (CSPM) tools is critical in securing your cloud environment. Proper setup ensures your CSPM tools can effectively monitor, assess, and remediate security risks. This section will guide you through setting up the CSPM environment, including initial configurations, integration with cloud services, and best practices for optimizing the tool's performance.

A.1 Initial Configuration

A.1.1 Selecting the Right CSPM Tool

The first step in setting up your CSPM environment is selecting the right tool for your organization's needs. Consider factors such as the cloud platforms you use, the specific security requirements of your industry, and your budget.

Example Tools:

- **Palo Alto Networks Prisma Cloud:** Ideal for multi-cloud environments and advanced security features.
- **AWS Security Hub:** Best for organizations heavily invested in AWS.
- **Azure Security Center:** Suitable for enterprises using Microsoft Azure.
- **Google Cloud Security Command Center (SCC):** Designed for Google Cloud Platform users.
- **Open Source Tools:** Prowler for AWS and ScoutSuite for multi-cloud support.

A.1.2 Creating a Deployment Plan

Develop a deployment plan that outlines the steps for installing and configuring the CSPM tool. The plan should include tasks, timelines, resources needed, and roles and responsibilities.

Key Components of the Deployment Plan:

- **Objectives:** Define what you aim to achieve with the CSPM tool.
- **Scope:** Specify the cloud environments and resources to be monitored.
- **Timeline:** Establish a realistic timeline for the deployment.
- **Resources:** Identify the necessary resources, including personnel, budget, and tools.
- **Responsibilities:** Assign roles and responsibilities to team members.

A.1.3 Setting Up the CSPM Tool

To set up the CSPM tool, follow the vendor's installation and configuration guidelines. This typically involves deploying the tool within your cloud environment, configuring access permissions, and setting up initial security policies.

Steps for Setting Up:

- **Install the CSPM Tool:** To install the CSPM tool in your cloud environment, use the vendor-provided installation package or deployment script.
- **Configure Access:** Grant the CSPM tool appropriate permissions to access your cloud resources. This may involve creating an IAM role in AWS, a service principal in Azure, or a service account in GCP.
- **Initial Configuration:** Configure basic settings such as monitoring regions, resource types, and notification preferences.

Example: Setting up AWS Security Hub involves enabling the service in the AWS Management Console, configuring IAM roles for access, and setting up initial security standards such as the CIS AWS Foundations Benchmark.

A.2 Integration with Cloud Services

A.2.1 Connecting to Cloud Accounts

Integrate the CSPM tool with your cloud accounts to enable monitoring and assessment. This step involves providing the CSPM tool with the credentials and permissions to access your cloud resources.

Example: In AWS, you would create an IAM role with the necessary policies and link it to AWS Security Hub. In Azure, you can register for Azure Security Center with your subscription and configure the necessary role-based access control (RBAC).

A.2.2 Configuring API Access

Most CSPM tools use APIs to interact with cloud services. Ensure API access is configured correctly, allowing the CSPM tool to query resource configurations, monitor activity, and execute remediation actions.

Example: For Google Cloud SCC, you would enable the required APIs in the Google Cloud Console, such as the Security Command Center API, and configure service accounts with appropriate roles.

A.2.3 Setting Up Data Collection

Configure data collection settings to specify what data the CSPM tool should collect and how often. This includes log data, configuration snapshots, and real-time monitoring data.

Example: In AWS Security Hub, configure CloudTrail to log API activity, enable AWS Config for configuration snapshots, and set up GuardDuty for threat detection.

A.2.4 Integrating with SIEM and SOAR Tools

Integrate your CSPM tool with Security Information and Event Management (SIEM) and Security Orchestration, Automation, and Response (SOAR) platforms for comprehensive security management. This integration enables centralized logging, correlation of security events, and automated incident response.

Example: Integrating AWS Security Hub with Splunk (a SIEM tool) allows you to centralize security findings from multiple AWS accounts and correlate them with other security events for holistic analysis.

A.3 Best Practices for Optimizing CSPM Performance

A.3.1 Regularly Update Security Policies

Keep your security policies up to date to address new threats and vulnerabilities. Regularly review and update your CSPM tool's policies to align with the latest security best practices and regulatory requirements.

Example: Regularly update CIS benchmarks and other compliance frameworks in AWS Security. Our environment meets Hub to ensure the latest security standards are met.

A.3.2 Customize Alerts and Notifications

Customize alerts and notifications to ensure that relevant security events are promptly addressed. Configure thresholds and alert preferences based on the criticality of resources and the nature of security findings.

Example: Setting up high-priority alerts for unauthorized access attempts to critical databases and configuring notifications to be sent to the security operations team.

A.3.3 Automate Remediation

Leverage the CSPM tool's automated remediation capabilities to address security issues promptly. Define automation rules for common misconfigurations and vulnerabilities to reduce the manual effort required for remediation.

Example: Azure Security Center's automated remediation feature automatically applies security patches to vulnerable virtual machines.

A.3.4 Conduct Regular Audits

Conduct regular audits of your cloud environment to validate the effectiveness of your CSPM tool and ensure compliance with security policies. Use audit findings to refine your CSPM configurations and improve your overall security posture.

Example: Performing quarterly audits of AWS Security Hub findings to verify that all critical security issues have been addressed and compliance requirements are met.

A.3.5 Monitor and Review Performance

Continuously monitor the performance of your CSPM tool and review its effectiveness in meeting security goals. Use performance metrics and KPIs to track progress and identify areas for improvement.

Example: Monitoring metrics such as the number of security incidents detected, the average time to resolve incidents, and the compliance status of cloud resources.

A.4 Tools for Setting Up the CSPM Environment

A.4.1 AWS Security Hub

Overview: AWS Security Hub provides a comprehensive view of your security posture across AWS accounts, aggregating security findings from various AWS services and third-party tools.

Key Features:

- Integration with AWS Config, Amazon GuardDuty, and AWS CloudTrail.
- Automated compliance checks using CIS AWS Foundations Benchmark.
- Centralized dashboard for monitoring security findings.

Example: Using AWS Security Hub to monitor and manage security across multiple AWS accounts, ensuring compliance with industry standards.

A.4.2 Azure Security Center

Overview: Azure Security Center offers advanced threat protection and continuous security assessment for Azure environments.

Key Features:

- Integration with Azure Defender, Azure Policy, and Azure Monitor.
- Real-time threat detection and automated remediation.
- Continuous compliance assessment and reporting.

Example: Using Azure Security Center to protect Azure resources from threats, ensure compliance with regulatory requirements, and automate security management.

A.4.3 Google Cloud Security Command Center (SCC)

Overview: Google Cloud Security Command Center (SCC) provides comprehensive security and risk management for Google Cloud Platform environments.

Key Features:

- Integration with Google Cloud services such as Cloud IAM, Cloud Logging, and Cloud Storage.
- Real-time visibility into security posture and compliance status.
- Customizable dashboards and automated alerts.

Example: Using Google Cloud SCC to monitor security across GCP projects, detect and respond to threats, and maintain compliance with industry standards.

A.4.4 Open Source Tools (Prowler and ScoutSuite)

Overview: Open-source tools like Prowler and ScoutSuite offer cost-effective CSPM solutions for AWS and multi-cloud environments.

Key Features:

- Comprehensive security assessments based on industry best practices.
- Customizable checks and detailed reporting.
- Community support and regular updates.

Example: Prowler performs regular security audits of an AWS environment, ensuring compliance with CIS benchmarks and best practices.

A.5 Conclusion

Setting up the CSPM environment is crucial in securing your cloud infrastructure. By following best practices for initial configuration, integrating with cloud services, and optimizing performance, you can ensure that your CSPM tool effectively monitors, assesses, and remediates security risks. Leveraging the right tools and maintaining continuous improvement will help you achieve a robust and resilient security posture. As we move forward, we will explore further steps in configuring CSPM tools, including continuous monitoring and assessment, remediation and response, and integrating CSPM with DevOps practices.

B. Integrating CSPM Tools with Existing Systems

Integrating Cloud Security Posture Management (CSPM) tools with your existing systems is crucial for maximizing the effectiveness of your security strategy. Proper integration ensures seamless data flow, enhances visibility, and enables automated responses to security incidents. This section will explore the importance of integration, the steps involved in integrating CSPM tools with existing systems, and best practices to ensure successful integration.

B.1 Importance of Integrating CSPM Tools

B.1.1 Enhanced Visibility

Integrating existing systems provides a unified view of your security posture across different platforms and services. This holistic visibility is essential for effectively identifying and mitigating security risks.

Example: Integrating AWS Security Hub with your SIEM system allows you to correlate cloud security findings with on-premises security events, providing a comprehensive view of your organization's security landscape.

B.1.2 Streamlined Operations

Integration automates the flow of security data between systems, reducing the need for manual intervention and streamlining security operations. This leads to faster detection and response times for security incidents.

Example: Automated alerting and incident creation in a SOAR platform when a critical vulnerability is detected by your CSPM tool.

B.1.3 Improved Incident Response

Integrating CSPM tools with incident response systems allows you to automate and enhance your response to security incidents. This ensures that incidents are promptly detected, investigated, and resolved.

Example: Integrating Azure Security Center with an incident response platform to automatically generate and track incident response workflows for detected threats.

B.2 Steps for Integrating CSPM Tools with Existing Systems

B.2.1 Assess Integration Requirements

Begin by assessing the integration requirements for your CSPM tools and existing systems. Identify the key systems that need to be integrated, the data that needs to be exchanged, and the objectives of the integration.

Key Systems to Consider:

- **SIEM (Security Information and Event Management):** For centralized logging and correlation of security events.
- **SOAR (Security Orchestration, Automation, and Response):** Automating incident response workflows.
- **ITSM (IT Service Management):** For managing security incidents and

changes.
- **DevOps Tools:** These are used to integrate security into the development pipeline.
- **Compliance Management Systems:** This is used to ensure regulatory compliance.

Example: Assessing the need to integrate AWS Security Hub with Splunk (SIEM), ServiceNow (ITSM), and Jenkins (DevOps pipeline) to achieve comprehensive security management.

B.2.2 Configure API Access and Permissions

Most CSPM tools and existing systems provide APIs for integration. Configure API access and permissions to enable secure communication between the systems. Ensure that only authorized systems and users have access to the APIs.

Steps for Configuring API Access:

- **Create API Keys or Tokens:** Generate API keys or tokens for authentication.
- **Assign Permissions:** Grant the necessary permissions to the API keys or tokens.
- **Secure API Endpoints:** Use encryption and secure communication protocols to protect API endpoints.

Example: Generating an API key in AWS Security Hub and configuring it with appropriate read and write permissions for integration with Splunk.

B.2.3 Set Up Data Collection and Exchange

Configure the data collection and exchange settings to ensure relevant security data is sent from the CSPM tool to the integrated systems. Define what data needs to be collected, how often it should be sent, and the data format.

Key Data to Collect and Exchange:

- **Security Findings and Alerts:** Information about detected vulnerabilities, threats, and misconfigurations.
- **Configuration Data:** Details of cloud resource configurations and changes.
- **Compliance Reports:** Information on compliance status and violations.

Example: Configuring AWS Security Hub to send security findings to Splunk in real-time using AWS CloudWatch Events and Kinesis Data Firehose.

B.2.4 Configure Automated Workflows

Set up automated workflows to streamline security operations and incident response. Define the actions to take when the CSPM tool detects specific security events.

Examples of Automated Workflows:

- **Incident Creation:** An incident in the ITSM system is automatically created when a critical security finding is detected.
- **Alerting:** Send alerts to the security operations team via email, SMS, or chat.

- **Remediation:** Trigger automated remediation actions, such as applying patches or changing configurations.

Example: Azure Logic Apps can create automated workflows that generate ServiceNow incidents for high-severity alerts detected by Azure Security Center.

B.2.5 Test and Validate Integration

After configuring the integration, thoroughly test and validate the setup to ensure data is exchanged correctly and automated workflows function as intended. Perform end-to-end testing to identify and resolve any issues.

Testing Steps:

- **Simulate Security Events:** Generate test security findings and alerts to verify data collection and workflows.
- **Check Data Accuracy:** Ensure the data sent to integrated systems is accurate and complete.
- **Validate Workflows:** Test automated workflows to ensure they trigger the correct actions.

Example: Simulating a security incident in AWS Security Hub and verifying that it is correctly logged in Splunk and generates an incident in ServiceNow.

B.2.6 Monitor and Maintain Integration

Continuously monitor the integration to ensure it remains effective and address any issues. Regularly review and update integration settings to accommodate changes in your cloud environment and security requirements.

Monitoring and Maintenance Activities:

- **Monitor Data Flows:** Use monitoring tools to track data flows between systems and detect anomalies.
- **Review Logs:** Regularly review logs to identify and troubleshoot integration issues.
- **Update Configurations:** Adjust API permissions, data collection settings, and workflows as needed.

Example: Setting up monitoring dashboards in Splunk to track data ingestion from AWS Security Hub and alerting on any data transfer failures.

B.3 Best Practices for Successful Integration

B.3.1 Ensure Data Consistency

Maintain data consistency between the CSPM tool and integrated systems. Ensure the data format, naming conventions, and timestamps are consistent to avoid discrepancies.

Example: Standardizing the format of security findings sent from AWS Security Hub to Splunk to ensure consistent and accurate logging.

B.3.2 Implement Security Controls

Implement robust security controls to secure the integration. Protect API keys and tokens, use encryption for data transmission, and restrict access based on the principle of least privilege.

Example: Using AWS IAM policies to restrict API access to only the necessary resources and actions for the integration with Splunk.

B.3.3 Regularly Update Integrations

Update integration settings regularly to reflect changes in your cloud environment, security policies, and business requirements. Ensure that the integration remains aligned with your security goals and objectives.

Example: Updating automated workflows in Azure Logic Apps to address new compliance requirements or changes in security policies.

B.3.4 Document Integration Processes

Document the integration processes, including configuration settings, workflows, and troubleshooting steps. This documentation is a reference for maintaining the integration and training of new team members.

Example: Creating detailed documentation for integrating AWS Security Hub with ServiceNow, including API configurations, workflow definitions, and common issues.

B.3.5 Foster Collaboration

To ensure successful integration, Foster collaboration between security, IT, and development teams. Engage stakeholders in planning, implementing, and maintaining the integration to address concerns and ensure alignment with business objectives.

Example: Holding regular meetings with security operations, IT, and DevOps team representatives to discuss integration progress and address any challenges.

B.4 Tools for Integrating CSPM with Existing Systems

B.4.1 AWS Security Hub

Integration Features:

- Supports integration with SIEM tools like Splunk, QRadar, and Sumo Logic.
- Uses AWS CloudWatch Events and AWS Lambda for custom integrations.
- Provides APIs for data access and automation.

Example: Integrating AWS Security Hub with Splunk to centralize security findings and correlate them with on-premises security events.

B.4.2 Azure Security Center

Integration Features:

- Integrates with Azure Sentinel for advanced threat detection and response.
- Supports integration with ITSM tools like ServiceNow and JIRA.
- Provides APIs and Azure Logic Apps for custom workflows.

Example: Azure Logic Apps can create automated workflows that generate incidents in ServiceNow based on alerts from the Azure Security Center.

B.4.3 Google Cloud Security Command Center (SCC)

Integration Features:

- Integrates with Google Cloud services such as Cloud Logging and Cloud Monitoring.
- Supports third-party SIEM and SOAR integrations via APIs.
- Provides customizable dashboards and alerts.

Example: Integrating Google Cloud SCC with Splunk to aggregate and analyze security findings across GCP projects.

B.4.4 Open Source Tools (Prowler and ScoutSuite)

Integration Features:

- Provides CLI-based outputs that can be integrated with SIEM and logging tools.
- Supports custom scripts and automation for data collection and reporting.
- Community-driven support for various integrations.

Example: Using Prowler to generate security assessment reports for AWS and integrating the reports with a central logging system for analysis.

B.5 Conclusion

Integrating CSPM tools with existing systems is essential for creating a cohesive and efficient security management framework. Following the steps outlined in this section and adhering to best practices can ensure seamless data flow, enhance visibility, and improve incident response capabilities. Leveraging the right tools and maintaining continuous stakeholder collaboration will help you achieve a robust and integrated security posture. As we proceed,

we will explore further steps in configuring CSPM tools, including continuous monitoring and assessment, remediation and response, and integrating CSPM with DevOps practices.

C. Initial Configuration and Setup

Properly configuring and setting up your Cloud Security Posture Management (CSPM) tools is crucial to effectively managing and securing your cloud environments. This section will guide you through the initial configuration and setup process, ensuring your CSPM tools are correctly deployed, integrated, and optimized for your specific security needs.

C.1 Choosing the Right CSPM Tool

Before starting the configuration, selecting the CSPM tool that best fits your organization's requirements is essential. Consider factors such as compatibility with your cloud platform(s), feature set, scalability, and cost.

Popular CSPM Tools:

- **Palo Alto Networks Prisma Cloud**
- **AWS Security Hub**
- **Azure Security Center**
- **Google Cloud Security Command Center (SCC)**
- **Open Source Tools: Prowler (for AWS), ScoutSuite (for multi-cloud environments)**

Example: If your organization primarily uses AWS, AWS Security Hub would be suitable due to its seamless integration with other AWS services.

C.2 Pre-Configuration Planning

C.2.1 Define Objectives and Scope

Clearly define what you aim to achieve with the CSPM tool and the scope of its deployment. Identify which cloud accounts, regions, and services will be monitored.

Steps:

- **Objectives:** Enhance security, ensure compliance, and improve visibility.
- **Scope:** Specify cloud accounts, regions, and resource types to be included.

Example: A financial institution might define objectives such as achieving PCI-DSS compliance and enhancing threat detection across all its AWS accounts in the US and Europe.

C.2.2 Assign Roles and Responsibilities

Determine who will be responsible for setting up, configuring, and managing the CSPM tool. Define clear roles and responsibilities within the team.

Roles:

- **CSPM Administrator:** Oversees the configuration and management of the CSPM tool.
- **Security Analysts:** Monitor alerts and manage incidents.
- **IT Operations:** Handle integrations with existing systems and workflows.

Example: Assigning the CSPM Administrator role to a senior security engineer and Security Analysts roles to team members specialized in incident response.

C.3 Setting Up the CSPM Tool

C.3.1 Installation and Deployment

Follow the vendor's guidelines to install and deploy the CSPM tool in your cloud environment.

Steps for Installation:

- **Obtain the CSPM Tool:** Download or access the tool through your cloud provider's marketplace or vendor website.
- **Deploy the Tool:** Use the provided deployment scripts or follow the installation steps to deploy the tool.

Example: Deploying AWS Security Hub involves enabling the service in the AWS Management Console and configuring it to monitor selected AWS accounts.

C.3.2 Configuring Access Permissions

Ensure the CSPM tool has the necessary permissions to access and monitor your cloud resources. This typically involves setting up roles and permissions.

Steps:

- **Create IAM Roles (AWS):** Create IAM roles using the necessary policies.
- **Service Principals (Azure):** Register the CSPM tool as a service principal with the required permissions.

- **Service Accounts (GCP):** Create service accounts with appropriate roles.

Example: In AWS, create an IAM role with policies that grant read-only access to AWS Config, CloudTrail, and other necessary services, then link this role to AWS Security Hub.

C.3.3 Initial Configuration

Perform the CSPM tool's initial configuration to set up basic settings, such as monitoring regions, types of resources, and compliance frameworks.

Steps:

- **Select Regions:** Choose the geographic regions where the tool will monitor resources.
- **Define Resource Types:** Specify which types of resources (e.g., EC2 instances, S3 buckets) the tool will monitor.
- **Configure Compliance Frameworks:** Select and configure compliance standards such as CIS, GDPR, HIPAA, etc.

Example: In AWS Security Hub, enable the CIS AWS Foundations Benchmark standard to check compliance against CIS guidelines automatically.

C.4 Integration with Cloud Services

C.4.1 Connecting Cloud Accounts

Integrate the CSPM tool with your cloud accounts to enable it to collect and analyze data.

Steps:

- Link Accounts: Use the CSPM tool's interface to link your cloud accounts.
- Verify Access: Ensure the tool can access and collect data from the linked accounts.

Example: In AWS Security Hub, link multiple AWS accounts by configuring AWS Organizations and setting up a master account to manage security findings centrally.

C.4.2 Configuring Data Sources

Set up data sources to ensure the CSPM tool collects relevant security data from your cloud environment.

Data Sources:

- **Configuration Data:** AWS Config, Azure Resource Graph.
- **Log Data:** CloudTrail (AWS), Activity Log (Azure), Cloud Logging (GCP).
- **Threat Intelligence:** Amazon GuardDuty, Azure Sentinel, Google Cloud Security Scanner.

Example: In AWS, configure AWS Config to monitor continuously, record configuration changes, and integrate it with AWS Security Hub.

C.4.3 Setting Up Automated Workflows

Automate common tasks and responses to streamline security operations and ensure timely action on security findings.

Steps:

- **Define Automation Rules:** Set up rules for automated actions based on security findings.
- **Integrate with SOAR Tools:** For advanced automation, integrate with Security Orchestration, Automation, and Response (SOAR) tools.

Example: Configure AWS Lambda functions to remediate common misconfigurations detected by the AWS Security Hub automatically.

C.5 Initial Security Policies and Baselines

C.5.1 Establishing Security Policies

Define and implement initial security policies within the CSPM tool to guide its monitoring and assessment activities.

Steps:

- **Select Policies:** Choose from predefined policies or create custom policies based on your security requirements.
- **Configure Policies:** Adjust policy settings to match your organizational standards.

Example: In Azure Security Center, select and configure policies for network security, data protection, and identity management.

C.5.2 Setting Baselines

Establish baselines for normal behavior and configurations to help the CSPM tool identify deviations and potential security issues.

Steps:

- Baseline Configuration: Define baseline configurations for critical resources.
- Baseline Behavior: Establish normal activity patterns for monitoring purposes.

Example: In Google Cloud SCC, configure baseline settings for VM instances, firewall rules, and IAM policies to detect anomalies.

C.6 Monitoring and Fine-Tuning

C.6.1 Initial Monitoring

After configuration, monitor the CSPM tool's findings to ensure it functions correctly and captures and alerts on relevant security data.

Steps:

- **Monitor Alerts:** Review initial alerts and findings to validate accuracy.

- **Adjust Sensitivity:** Fine-tune alert thresholds to balance sensitivity and relevance.

Example: In AWS Security Hub, review initial security findings, adjust configurations to reduce false positives, and focus on critical issues.

C.6.2 Fine-Tuning Configurations

Continuously refine the CSPM tool's settings and policies based on initial monitoring results and feedback from the security team.

Steps:

- **Review Findings:** Regularly review security findings and adjust policies as needed.
- **Update Configurations:** Modify configurations to improve detection accuracy and coverage.

Example: Update security policies in Azure Security Center based on security analysts' feedback and threat landscape changes.

C.7 Documentation and Training

C.7.1 Documenting Configuration

Maintain comprehensive documentation of the CSPM tool's configuration, including settings, policies, and integration details. This documentation serves as a reference for future adjustments and troubleshooting.

Example: Create a detailed configuration guide for AWS Security Hub, documenting IAM roles, linked accounts, data sources, and policy settings.

C.7.2 Training the Team

Ensure your security team is well-trained in using and managing the CSPM tool. Provide training sessions and resources to help them understand the tool's capabilities and how to respond to findings.

Training Components:

- **Tool Overview:** Introduction to the CSPM tool's features and interface.
- **Policy Management:** How to configure and manage security policies.
- **Incident Response:** Procedures for handling security alerts and incidents.

Example: Conducting a training session for security analysts to use AWS Security Hub's dashboard, interpret findings, and execute remediation actions.

C.8 Conclusion

The initial configuration and setup of CSPM tools are critical to establishing a robust cloud security posture. Following the outlined steps and best practices ensures your CSPM tool is correctly deployed, integrated, and optimized for your specific security needs. Continuous monitoring, fine-tuning, and training will help maintain and enhance the effectiveness of your CSPM tool, enabling you to protect your cloud environment proactively. As we move forward, we will explore further steps in configuring CSPM tools, including continuous monitoring and assessment, remediation and response, and integrating CSPM with DevOps practices.

D. Hands-On Exercise: Installing and Configuring an Open Source CSPM Tool (Prowler)

This hands-on exercise will teach you how to install and configure Prowler, an open-source Cloud Security Posture Management (CSPM) tool designed for AWS environments. Prowler helps you assess the security posture of your AWS accounts by performing security best practices assessments, audits, and compliance checks. This section provides a step-by-step installation guide, instructions for configuring Prowler for AWS, and guidance on running your first scan.

D.1 Step-by-Step Installation Guide

D.1.1 Prerequisites

Before installing Prowler, ensure that you have the following prerequisites:

- **AWS CLI:** Installed and configured with appropriate IAM permissions.
- **Python:** Installed on your system (Python 3.7 or later is recommended).
- **Git:** Installed for cloning the Prowler repository.

Example: Ensure you have administrator or read-only access permissions on the AWS account you intend to scan.

D.1.2 Cloning the Prowler Repository

To install Prowler, start by cloning the Prowler repository from GitHub.

1. Open a terminal window.

2. Run the following command to clone the repository:

sh

git clone https://github.com/prowler-cloud/prowler.git

3. Change to the Prowler directory:

sh

cd prowler

D.1.3 Installing Dependencies

Prowler requires certain dependencies to run. Install these dependencies using the following commands:

1. Create a virtual environment (optional but recommended):

sh

python3 -m venv prowler-venv
   source prowler-venv/bin/activate

2. Install the required Python packages:

sh

pip install -r requirements.txt

D.2 Configuring Prowler for AWS

D.2.1 Setting Up AWS CLI

Ensure that the AWS CLI is configured with the necessary credentials and permissions.

1. If you haven't already configured the AWS CLI, run the following:

sh

aws configure

2. When prompted, enter your AWS Access Key ID, Secret Access Key, region, and output format.

Example: You might enter 'us-west-2' for the region and 'json' for the output format.

D.2.2 Configuring Prowler

Prowler uses AWS CLI configuration to access your AWS account. Ensure the IAM user or role has the necessary permissions to perform security assessments.

Example IAM Policy:

json

{

"Version": "2012-10-17",

"Statement": [

{

"Effect": "Allow",

"Action": [

"iam:ListUsers",

"iam:ListRoles",

"iam:ListGroups",

"iam:ListPolicies",

"iam:ListAttachedUserPolicies",

"iam:ListAttachedGroupPolicies",

"iam:ListAttachedRolePolicies",

"iam:GetAccountSummary",

"ec2:DescribeInstances",

"ec2:DescribeSecurityGroups",

"s3:ListAllMyBuckets",

"cloudtrail:DescribeTrails",

"cloudtrail:GetTrailStatus",

"cloudtrail:LookupEvents",

"config:DescribeConfigRules",

"config:GetComplianceDetailsByConfigRule",

"config:GetComplianceSummaryByConfigRule",

"config:DescribeConfigurationRecorders",

"config:DescribeConfigurationRecorderStatus",

"config:DescribeDeliveryChannels",

"config:DescribeDeliveryChannelStatus",

"logs:DescribeLogGroups",

"logs:DescribeLogStreams",

"logs:GetLogEvents",

"logs:FilterLogEvents",

"logs:DescribeMetricFilters",

"logs:PutMetricFilter",

"logs:DeleteMetricFilter",

"kms:ListKeys",

"kms:DescribeKey"

],

"Resource": "*"

}

]

}

Attach this policy to the IAM user or role the AWS CLI uses.

D.3 Running Your First Scan

D.3.1 Running Prowler

Now that Prowler is installed and configured, you can run your first scan. Prowler provides various command-line options to customize the scan.

1. To run a basic scan, execute the following command:

sh

./prowler

This command runs a full scan using default settings and outputs the results to the terminal.

D.3.2 Customizing the Scan

Prowler allows you to customize the scan based on your needs. Here are some common options:

Specifying Checks: Run specific checks using the '-c' option.

sh

./prowler -c check12,check22

Output Format: Change the output format using the '-M' option.

sh

./prowler -M json

Saving Results: Save the results to a file using output redirection.

sh

./prowler -M json > prowler-results.json

D.3.3 Reviewing Scan Results

After the scan is completed, review the results to identify security issues and areas for improvement.

Example Output:

json

{

"AccountId": "123456789012",

"Region": "us-west-2",

"Service": "EC2",

"Severity": "High",

"Check": "check12",

"Message": "EC2 instance without IAM role detected",

"ResourceId": "i-0abcd1234efgh5678"

}

Use the scan results to prioritize remediation efforts based on the severity and impact of the findings.

D.4 Best Practices for Using Prowler

D.4.1 Regular Scans

Run Prowler scans regularly to continuously monitor your AWS environment and maintain a strong security posture.

Example: Schedule weekly scans using a cron job or a scheduled task in your CI/CD pipeline.

D.4.2 Automating Remediation

Integrate Prowler with automation tools to remediate common security issues and scan automatically identified duri.

Example: Use AWS Lambda functions to automatically apply security group rules based on Prowler's findings.

D.4.3 Reporting and Alerts

Set up reporting and alerting mechanisms to notify your security team of critical findings.

Example: Configure Prowler to send scan results to an SNS topic or a Slack channel for immediate alerts.

D.5 Conclusion

Installing and configuring Prowler provides a robust foundation for monitoring and improving the security posture of your AWS environment. Following the step-by-step guide and best practices outlined in this section, you can effectively utilize Prowler to identify and remediate security issues, ensuring compliance with industry standards and best practices. As you become more familiar with Prowler, consider integrating it with other security tools and workflows to enhance your overall cloud security strategy.

Chapter 7: Continuous Monitoring and Assessment

A. Setting Up Continuous Monitoring

Continuous monitoring is a critical component of maintaining a secure cloud environment. It involves the ongoing assessment of your cloud infrastructure to detect and respond to real-time security threats, misconfigurations, and compliance issues. This chapter will guide you through setting up continuous monitoring, including selecting the right tools, configuring monitoring services, and implementing best practices for effective monitoring.

A.1 Importance of Continuous Monitoring

A.1.1 Real-Time Threat Detection

Continuous monitoring enables real-time detection of security threats, allowing immediate response and mitigation. This proactive approach minimizes the potential damage caused by security incidents.

Example: Detecting a brute force attack on an AWS EC2 instance in real-time and automatically blocking the offending IP addresses.

A.1.2 Compliance Assurance

Maintaining compliance with industry standards and regulations is an ongoing process. Continuous monitoring ensures that your cloud environment consistently meets compliance requirements, reducing the risk of non-compliance penalties.

Example: Regularly checking the configuration of AWS S3 buckets to ensure they comply with GDPR data protection requirements.

A.1.3 Operational Efficiency

Automating the monitoring process reduces the need for manual oversight, freeing up resources and improving operational efficiency. It also ensures that security issues are promptly identified and addressed.

Example: Automatically generating alerts for configuration changes that deviate from established security policies.

A.2 Selecting the Right Monitoring Tools

Choosing the appropriate tools for continuous monitoring is essential for effective cloud security management. Consider tools that integrate seamlessly with your cloud platforms and provide comprehensive monitoring capabilities.

A.2.1 AWS Tools

- **Amazon CloudWatch:** Provides monitoring and observability of AWS resources and applications, including metrics collection, log monitoring, and alarms.
- **AWS Config:** Continuously monitors and records AWS resource configurations and evaluates them against desired configurations.
- **Amazon GuardDuty:** Offers threat detection and continuous security monitoring to protect AWS accounts and workloads.

A.2.2 Azure Tools

- **Azure Monitor:** Collects and analyzes telemetry data from Azure resources and applications, providing insights and alerts.
- **Azure Security Center:** Offers continuous assessment of security posture and advanced threat protection for Azure environments.
- **Azure Policy:** Enforces organization-specific policies and compliance standards across Azure resources.

A.2.3 Google Cloud Tools

- **Google Cloud Monitoring:** Provides visibility into the performance, uptime, and overall health of cloud resources.
- **Google Cloud Security Command Center (SCC):** Centralizes security management and threat detection for GCP environments.
- **Google Cloud Audit Logs:** Tracks administrative and data access

actions within Google Cloud.

A.2.4 Multi-Cloud and Open-Source Tools

- **Datadog:** Offers comprehensive monitoring and security capabilities for multi-cloud environments.
- **Prometheus:** An open-source monitoring system that collects metrics from configured targets at specified intervals.
- **Prowler:** An open-source tool for AWS that provides continuous security assessments and compliance checks.

A.3 Configuring Monitoring Services

Once you have selected the appropriate monitoring tools, configure them to ensure comprehensive and continuous monitoring of your cloud environment.

A.3.1 Setting Up Metrics Collection

Configure your monitoring tools to collect metrics from all relevant cloud resources. Metrics provide quantitative data on resource performance, utilization, and health.

Example (AWS CloudWatch):

- **Create a CloudWatch Dashboard:** Set up a dashboard to visualize

metrics.
- **Configure Metrics:** Select metrics to monitor, such as CPU utilization, network traffic, and disk I/O.
- **Set Alarms:** Create alarms to notify you when metrics exceed predefined thresholds.

sh

```
aws cloudwatch put-metric-alarm
    --alarm-name HighCPUUtilization
    --metric-name CPUUtilization
    --namespace AWS/EC2
    --statistic Average
    --period 300
    --threshold 80
    --comparison-operator GreaterThanOrEqualToThreshold
    --evaluation-periods 2
    --alarm-actions arn:aws:sns:us-west-2:123456789012:my-sns-topic
```

A.3.2 Enabling Log Monitoring

Logs provide detailed information about resource activities and are crucial for troubleshooting and security investigations. Enable log collection and monitoring to gain insights into system behavior and detect anomalies.

Example (AWS CloudTrail and CloudWatch Logs):

1. **Enable CloudTrail:** Enable AWS CloudTrail to log API calls and resource activity.
2. **Create Log Groups:** Create log groups in CloudWatch Logs to organize log data.
3. **Set Up Log Streams:** Configure log streams to collect logs from various resources.

sh

```
aws cloudtrail create-trail
   --name my-trail
   --s3-bucket-name my-cloudtrail-logs

aws logs create-log-group
   --log-group-name my
   -log-group

aws logs create-log-stream
   --log-group-name my-log-group
   --log-stream-name my-log-stream
```

A.3.3 Configuring Alerts and Notifications

Set up alerts and notifications to ensure that relevant stakeholders are informed of critical security events and can respond promptly.

Example (AWS SNS and CloudWatch):

1. **Create an SNS Topic:** Set up an SNS topic to send notifications.

```sh
aws sns create-topic —name my-sns-topic
```

2. **Subscribe to the Topic:** Add subscribers to the SNS topic (e.g., email, SMS).

```sh
aws sns subscribe
  —topic-arn arn:aws:sns:us-west-2:123456789012:my-sns-topic
  —protocol email
  —notification-endpoint my-email@example.com
```

3. **Create CloudWatch Alarms:** Configure CloudWatch alarms to notify the SNS topic.

```sh
aws cloudwatch put-metric-alarm
  —alarm-name HighCPUUtilization
  —metric-name CPUUtilization
  —namespace AWS/EC2
  —statistic Average
  —period 300
  —threshold 80
  —comparison-operator GreaterThanOrEqualToThreshold
  —evaluation-periods 2
  —alarm-actions arn:aws:sns:us-west-2:123456789012:my-sns-topic
```

A.3.4 Implementing Compliance Checks

Use compliance monitoring tools to continuously assess your cloud environment against regulatory standards and internal policies.

Example (AWS Config):

1. Set Up AWS Config: Enable AWS Config to record resource configurations.

sh

```
aws configservice put-configuration-recorder
  —configuration-recorder name=
  myrecorder,roleARN=arn:aws:iam
  ::123456789012:role/my-config-role

aws configservice start-configuration-recorder
  —configuration-recorder-name my-recorder
```

2. Create Config Rules: Define rules to evaluate resource configurations.

sh

```
aws configservice put-config-rule
  —config-rule file://config-rule.json
```

Sample Config Rule (config-rule.json):

json

{

```
"ConfigRuleName": "s3-bucket-encryption",

"Description": "Checks whether S3 buckets

have default encryption enabled.",

"Scope": {

"ComplianceResourceTypes": [

"AWS::S3::Bucket"

]

},

"Source": {

"Owner": "AWS",

"SourceIdentifier": "S3_BUCKET_SERVER
   _SIDE_ENCRYPTION_ENABLED"

},

"InputParameters": "{}",

"MaximumExecutionFrequency": "Six_Hours",

"ConfigRuleState": "ACTIVE"

}
```

A.4 Best Practices for Effective Continuous Monitoring

A.4.1 Establish Baselines

Define and document baseline configurations and behavior patterns for your cloud resources. Baselines serve as a reference for detecting deviations and potential security issues.

Example: Establishing a baseline for network traffic patterns to detect anomalies such as unexpected spikes or drops.

A.4.2 Automate Responses

Automate responses to common security events to reduce the time required for remediation and minimize human error.

Example: Using AWS Lambda functions to remediate non-compliant security group rules detected by AWS Config automatically.

A.4.3 Regularly Review and Update Configurations

Continuously review and update monitoring configurations to adapt to changes in your cloud environment and evolving security threats.

Example: Periodically reviewing CloudWatch alarm thresholds and Config rules to ensure they remain effective and relevant.

A.4.4 Integrate with Incident Response

Ensure that continuous monitoring is integrated with your incident response process. This integration enables quick identification, investigation, and remediation of security incidents.

Example: Configuring Azure Security Center to automatically create incidents in an ITSM tool like ServiceNow for high-severity alerts.

A.4.5 Train Your Team

Provide ongoing training for your security and IT teams to ensure they are proficient in using monitoring tools and responding to alerts.

Example: Conducting regular training sessions on interpreting CloudWatch metrics and logs and responding to GuardDuty findings.

A.5 Conclusion

Continuous monitoring is essential for maintaining a secure and compliant cloud environment. By carefully selecting and configuring monitoring tools, establishing baselines, automating responses, and integrating with incident response processes, you can ensure your cloud environment is continuously monitored and protected against emerging threats. Regular reviews and team training further enhance the effectiveness of your monitoring efforts, helping you maintain a robust security posture. As we move forward, we will explore further steps in implementing CSPM tools, including remediation and response strategies and integrating CSPM with DevOps practices.

B. Automated Scanning and Risk Detection

Automated scanning and risk detection are fundamental to a robust cloud security strategy. These processes enable continuous assessment of your cloud environment, ensuring that potential vulnerabilities and risks are identified and addressed promptly. This section will explore the importance of automated scanning and risk detection, the tools and technologies available, and best practices for implementing these processes effectively.

B.1 Importance of Automated Scanning and Risk Detection

B.1.1 Proactive Risk Management

Automated scanning allows for continuously and proactively identifying security vulnerabilities and misconfigurations. This proactive approach helps mitigate risks before malicious actors can exploit them.

Example: Regularly scanning AWS EC2 instances for known vulnerabilities and applying patches to prevent exploitation.

B.1.2 Compliance and Audit Readiness

Automated scanning helps ensure ongoing compliance with industry standards and regulatory requirements by continuously monitoring your cloud environment against predefined policies and benchmarks.

Example: Using automated scans to ensure compliance with PCI-DSS by checking that all databases storing credit card information are encrypted.

B.1.3 Operational Efficiency

Automation reduces the manual effort required for security assessments, allowing security teams to focus on more strategic tasks. It also ensures consistent and repeatable assessments across the entire cloud environment.

Example: Automating scanning new cloud resources upon deployment to ensure they meet security standards from the outset.

B.2 Tools and Technologies for Automated Scanning and Risk Detection

The right tools for automated scanning and risk detection are critical for effective cloud security management. Here are some popular tools and technologies across different cloud platforms:

B.2.1 AWS Tools

- **Amazon Inspector:** An automated security assessment service that helps improve the security and compliance of applications deployed on AWS.
- **AWS Config:** Continuously monitors and records your AWS resource configurations and allows automated compliance checking.
- **Amazon GuardDuty:** Provides continuous monitoring for malicious activity and unauthorized behavior.

B.2.2 Azure Tools

- **Azure Security Center:** Offers continuous security assessment and advanced threat protection for Azure resources.
- **Azure Policy:** Ensures that resources comply with organizational standards and regulatory requirements by applying policies automatically.
- **Azure Defender:** Provides threat protection for Azure workloads.

B.2.3 Google Cloud Tools

- **Google Cloud Security Command Center (SCC):** Centralizes security management and provides risk detection for GCP resources.
- **Google Cloud Armor:** Provides DDoS protection and access control for applications running on GCP.
- **Google Cloud Security Scanner:** Identifies vulnerabilities in web applications running on Google Cloud.

B.2.4 Multi-Cloud and Open-Source Tools

- **Prowler:** An open-source tool for AWS security best practices assessments and compliance checks.
- **ScoutSuite:** An open-source multi-cloud security-auditing tool that comprehensively assesses cloud environments.
- **Cloud Custodian:** A rules engine for managing and enforcing security policies across AWS, Azure, and GCP.

B.3 Implementing Automated Scanning and Risk Detection

B.3.1 Setting Up Automated Scans

To implement automated scanning, start by configuring your chosen tools to perform regular and comprehensive scans of your cloud environment.

Steps for Setting Up Scans:

- **Select Scanning Tools:** Choose the appropriate tools based on your cloud platform and security needs.
- **Define Scan Scope:** Specify which resources and configurations should be included in the scans.
- **Schedule Scans:** Set up regular scan intervals (e.g., daily, weekly) to ensure continuous coverage.

Example (Setting Up AWS Inspector):

1. **Create Assessment Targets:** Define the EC2 instances to be scanned.

```sh
aws inspector create-assessment-target
   —assessment-target-name
   "MyAssessmentTarget"
   —resource-group-arn "arn:aws:resource-
   groups:region:123456789012:group/MyResourceGroup"
```

2. **Create Assessment Templates:** Define the rules packages and duration for the assessment.

```sh
aws inspector create-assessment-template
   —assessment-template-name
   "MyAssessmentTemplate"
   —duration-in-seconds 3600
   —rules-package-arns
   "arn:aws:inspector:us-west-2:758058086616
   :rulespackage/0-3ewz1hRL" —target-arn
   "arn:aws:inspector:us-west
   -2:123456789012:target/0-abc123"
```

3. **Run Assessment:** Start the assessment run.

```sh
aws inspector start-assessment-run
   —assessment-template-arn
   "arn:aws:inspector:us-west
   -2:123456789012:template/0-abc123"
```

B.3.2 Configuring Risk Detection Rules

Define and configure rules for detecting risks and vulnerabilities. These rules should be based on best practices, regulatory requirements, and your organization's specific security policies.

Example (AWS Config Rules):

1. Create Config Rule: Define a rule to check for unencrypted S3 buckets.

sh

```
aws configservice put-config-rule
   —config-rule-name
   "s3-bucket-encryption"
   —config-rule
   file://s3-bucket-encryption-rule.json
```

Sample Config Rule (s3-bucket-encryption-rule.json):

json

{

"ConfigRuleName": "s3-bucket-encryption",

"Description": "Checks whether S3 buckets have default encryption enabled.",

"Scope": {

"ComplianceResourceTypes": [

"AWS::S3::Bucket"

]

},

"Source": {

"Owner": "AWS",

"SourceIdentifier": "S3_BUCKET_SERVER_SIDE_ENCRYPTION_ENABLED"

},

"InputParameters": "{}",

"MaximumExecutionFrequency": "Six_Hours",

"ConfigRuleState": "ACTIVE"

}

B.3.3 Integrating with CI/CD Pipelines

Integrate automated scanning tools with your CI/CD pipelines to ensure security assessments are part of your development and deployment processes. This practice helps identify and remediate security issues early in the lifecycle.

Steps for Integration:

- **Add Scanning Steps:** Include security scanning steps in your build and deployment scripts.
- **Set Fail Criteria:** Define criteria for failing a build or deployment based on scan results.
- **Automate Remediation:** Use automated workflows to address identified issues before proceeding.

Example (Integrating Prowler with Jenkins):

1. **Install Prowler:** Ensure Prowler is installed on your Jenkins server.
2. **Add Build Step:** Add a build step in Jenkins to run Prowler.

```sh
./prowler -M json > prowler-results.json
```

3. **Set Fail Criteria:** Configure Jenkins to fail the build if critical vulnerabilities are found.

```sh
if grep -q '"Severity": "Critical"' prowler-results.json; then
exit 1
fi
```

B.3.4 Automating Notifications and Remediation

Set up automated notifications and remediation actions to ensure timely response to identified risks. Use alerting tools and automation scripts to handle common issues.

Steps for Automation:

- **Configure Alerts:** Set up alerts to notify relevant stakeholders of critical findings.
- **Define Remediation Actions:** Create automation scripts or use built-in tools to remediate common issues.
- **Implement Workflow Automation:** Use workflow automation tools to coordinate notifications and remediation efforts.

Example (AWS Lambda for Automated Remediation):

1. Create Lambda Function: Define a function to remediate unencrypted S3 buckets.

python

import boto3

def lambda_handler(event, context):

s3 = boto3.client('s3')

buckets = s3.list_buckets()

for bucket in buckets['Buckets']:

CHAPTER 7: CONTINUOUS MONITORING AND ASSESSMENT

```
encryption = s3.get_bucket_encryption(Bucket=bucket['Name'])

if 'ServerSideEncryptionConfiguration' not in encryption:

s3.put_bucket_encryption(

Bucket=bucket['Name'],

ServerSideEncryptionConfiguration={

'Rules': [

{

'ApplyServerSideEncryptionByDefault': {

'SSEAlgorithm': 'AES256'

}

}

]

}

)
```

2. **Set Up Trigger:** Configure AWS Config to trigger the Lambda function when an unencrypted S3 bucket is detected.

sh

```
aws lambda create-event-source-mapping
  —function-name
  MyRemediationFunction
  —event-source-arn
  arn:aws:sqs:us-west
  -2:123456789012:MyConfigQueue
  —batch-size 1
```

B.4 Best Practices for Effective Automated Scanning and Risk Detection

B.4.1 Regularly Update Scanning Tools and Rules

Keep your scanning tools and detection rules up to date to ensure they can identify the latest vulnerabilities and threats. Regular updates help maintain the effectiveness of your automated scanning processes.

Example: Regularly updating Prowler to the latest version to include new checks and improvements.

B.4.2 Prioritize Findings

Implement a risk-based approach to prioritize scan findings based on their severity and potential impact on your organization. Focus on remediating high-severity issues first.

Example: Prioritizing the remediation of critical vulnerabilities identified in internet-facing resources.

B.4.3 Conduct Regular Audits

Audit the results of automated scans regularly to ensure accuracy and completeness. Use audit findings to improve your scanning and risk detection processes.

Example: Conducting quarterly audits of AWS Config compliance results to verify that all rules are correctly applied and no critical resources are missed.

B.4.4 Integrate with Security Information and Event Management (SIEM) Systems

Integrate automated scanning and risk detection tools with your SIEM system to centralize security event management and correlation.

Example: Sending Amazon Inspector findings to Splunk for centralized logging and analysis.

B.4.5 Continuously Improve Processes

Use automated scanning and risk detection feedback to improve your security processes continuously. Review and refine your scanning configurations, rules, and workflows regularly.

Example: Updating AWS Config rules based on new compliance requirements or changes in the threat landscape.

B.5 Conclusion

Automated scanning and risk detection are essential for maintaining a secure and compliant cloud environment. You can ensure continuous assessment and management of security risks by implementing the right tools and technologies, integrating with CI/CD pipelines, automating notifications and remediation, and following best practices. This proactive approach helps you avoid threats, maintain compliance, and improve operational efficiency. As we proceed, we will explore further steps in implementing CSPM tools, including remediation and response strategies and integrating CSPM with DevOps practices.

C. Interpreting CSPM Reports and Dashboards

Interpreting Cloud Security Posture Management (CSPM) reports and dashboards is crucial for understanding your cloud environment's security status, identifying potential risks, and making informed decisions to enhance your security posture. This section will guide you through the key aspects of interpreting CSPM reports and dashboards, including understanding common metrics, recognizing trends, and making data-driven decisions.

C.1 Importance of CSPM Reports and Dashboards

C.1.1 Real-Time Visibility

CSPM dashboards provide real-time visibility into your cloud security posture, enabling you to monitor your resources' status continuously. This immediate insight is essential for detecting and responding to security incidents promptly.

Example: A dashboard showing real-time compliance status across multiple AWS accounts helps security teams quickly identify and address non-compliant resources.

C.1.2 Comprehensive Assessments

CSPM reports compile data from various scans and assessments, offering a comprehensive view of your security posture. They help you understand the overall security health and compliance status of your cloud environment.

Example: A weekly report summarizing the findings of automated scans across all cloud resources, including vulnerabilities, misconfigurations, and compliance violations.

C.1.3 Informed Decision-Making

Interpreting CSPM reports and dashboards allows you to make data-driven decisions to improve your security posture. By understanding the metrics and trends presented, you can prioritize remediation efforts and allocate resources effectively.

Example: Using trend analysis from CSPM reports to identify recurring security issues and allocate resources to address root causes.

C.2 Key Metrics in CSPM Reports and Dashboards

Understanding the key metrics in CSPM reports and dashboards is essential for accurate interpretation and decision-making.

C.2.1 Compliance Metrics

Compliance metrics indicate how well your cloud environment adheres to industry standards and regulatory requirements. Common compliance metrics include:

- **Compliance Score:** A percentage indicating the overall compliance level of your cloud resources.
- **Compliance Violations:** The number and severity of compliance violations detected.
- **Compliance Trends:** Changes in compliance status over time.

Example: An AWS Security Hub dashboard showing a compliance score of 85%, with a detailed list of critical and high-severity compliance violations.

C.2.2 Security Findings

Security findings highlight vulnerabilities, misconfigurations, and other security issues identified in your cloud environment. Key metrics include:

- **Number of Findings:** Total number of security findings.
- **Severity of Findings:** Categorization of findings by severity (e.g., critical, high, medium, low).
- **Open vs. Resolved Findings:** The number of still open findings versus those that have been resolved.

Example: A Google Cloud Security Command Center (SCC) report listing 10 critical findings, 25 high-severity findings, and 40 medium-severity findings, with a trend showing a decrease in open findings over the past month.

C.2.3 Resource Inventory

Resource inventory metrics provide an overview of the resources in your cloud environment, including their configurations and statuses. Key metrics include:

- **Resource Count:** Total number of resources monitored.
- **Resource Types:** Breakdown of resources by type (e.g., EC2 instances, S3 buckets, VMs).
- **Configuration Status:** Compliance status of resource configurations.

Example: An Azure Security Center dashboard showing 200 VMs, 180 compliant and 20 non-compliant based on security configurations.

C.2.4 Activity Logs

Activity logs capture events and actions within your cloud environment, providing insight into user activity and system changes. Key metrics include:

- **Event Count:** Total number of events logged.
- **User Activity:** Summary of user actions, including login attempts, resource modifications, and data access.
- **Anomalous Activity:** Identification of unusual or suspicious activities.

Example: An AWS CloudTrail report showing a spike in failed login attempts over the weekend, indicating potential brute force attacks.

C.3 Recognizing Trends and Patterns

Recognizing trends and patterns in CSPM reports and dashboards helps identify recurring issues and potential security gaps.

C.3.1 Trend Analysis

Trend analysis involves examining changes in security metrics over time to identify patterns and assess the effectiveness of security measures.

Example: Analyzing a trend graph showing a steady decrease in open high-severity findings after implementing automated remediation workflows.

C.3.2 Anomaly Detection

Anomaly detection identifies deviations from normal behavior, which may indicate security incidents or misconfigurations.

Example: Detecting an unexpected increase in outbound network traffic from a normally low-traffic resource could indicate a compromised instance.

C.3.3 Benchmarking

Benchmarking compares your security posture against industry standards and best practices to identify areas for improvement.

Example: Comparing your compliance score with industry benchmarks to identify gaps and prioritize compliance initiatives.

C.4 Making Data-Driven Decisions

Interpreting CSPM reports and dashboards enables you to make informed decisions to enhance your security posture.

C.4.1 Prioritizing Remediation Efforts

Use severity and impact metrics to prioritize remediation efforts. Focus on addressing critical and high-severity findings first to reduce risk exposure.

Example: Prioritizing the remediation of critical vulnerabilities in internet-facing resources to prevent potential breaches.

C.4.2 Allocating Resources

Allocate resources based on the trends and patterns identified in the reports. Ensure your security team has the necessary tools and support to address recurring issues.

Example: Allocating additional resources to improve patch management processes after identifying a trend of recurring unpatched vulnerabilities.

C.4.3 Enhancing Security Policies

Use insights from CSPM reports to refine and enhance your security policies and procedures. Ensure that policies are aligned with current threat landscapes and compliance requirements.

Example: Updating access control policies to enforce multi-factor authentication for all administrative users after detecting suspicious login activities.

C.5 Best Practices for Interpreting CSPM Reports and Dashboards

C.5.1 Regular Reviews

Conduct regular reviews of CSPM reports and dashboards to stay informed about your security posture and address issues promptly.

Example: Scheduling weekly reviews of AWS Security Hub reports to monitor compliance status and security findings.

C.5.2 Collaborative Analysis

Engage stakeholders from different departments in analyzing CSPM reports to gain diverse perspectives and ensure comprehensive risk management.

Example: Involving representatives from the IT, compliance, and business teams in monthly security review meetings.

C.5.3 Actionable Insights

Focus on extracting actionable insights from CSPM reports and dashboards. Identify specific actions that can be taken to address identified risks and improve security.

Example: Developing a remediation plan based on the top three recurring security findings highlighted in the monthly CSPM report.

C.5.4 Continuous Improvement

Use the insights gained from CSPM reports to improve your security posture continuously. Regularly update and refine your security strategies based on evolving threats and compliance requirements.

Example: Implementing a continuous improvement process incorporating CSPM reports' feedback to enhance security policies and practices.

C.6 Conclusion

Interpreting CSPM reports and dashboards is essential for maintaining a secure and compliant cloud environment. You can effectively manage your cloud security posture by understanding key metrics, recognizing trends, and making data-driven decisions. Regular reviews, collaborative analysis, and a focus on actionable insights ensure that your security strategies are aligned with current threats and compliance requirements. We will explore further steps in implementing CSPM tools, including remediation and response strategies and integrating CSPM with DevOps practices.

D. Hands-On Exercise: Continuous Monitoring with Prowler

In this hands-on exercise, you will learn how to set up continuous monitoring with Prowler, an open-source Cloud Security Posture Management (CSPM) tool for AWS. This includes scheduling regular scans and automating the visualization of scan results using dashboards. By the end of this exercise, you will have a fully automated process for monitoring your AWS environment and visualizing security data in an accessible format.

D.1 Scheduling Regular Scans

Regularly scheduled scans are crucial for maintaining continuous visibility into the security posture of your AWS environment. Prowler can be scheduled to run automatically using tools like AWS Lambda and CloudWatch Events.

D.1.1 Setting Up AWS Lambda for Prowler Scans

First, you must set up an AWS Lambda function to run Prowler scans.

Step-by-Step Guide:

1. Create an S3 Bucket for Prowler Outputs:

sh

aws s3 mb s3://my-prowler-output-bucket

2. Create an IAM Role for Lambda:

Create a role with permissions to execute Lambda functions and access necessary AWS services.

json

{

```
"Version": "2012-10-17",

"Statement": [

{

"Effect": "Allow",

"Action": "logs:*",

"Resource": "arn:aws:logs:*:*:*"

},

{

"Effect": "Allow",

"Action": "s3:PutObject",

"Resource": "arn:aws:s3:::my-prowler-output-bucket/*"

},

{

"Effect": "Allow",

"Action": "ec2:DescribeInstances",

"Resource": "*"

},
```

```
{

    "Effect": "Allow",

    "Action": "config:DescribeConfigRules",

    "Resource": "*"

}

]

}
```

Attach this policy to the Lambda execution role.

3. Create the Lambda Function:

Create a Lambda function that runs Prowler and uploads the results to S3. Below is a basic example using Python:

python

import boto3

import subprocess

import datetime

def lambda_handler(event, context):

s3 = boto3.client('s3')

```python
timestamp = datetime.datetime.now().strftime
    ("%Y-%m-%d-%H-%M-%S")

output_file = f'/tmp/prowler-output-{timestamp}.json'

# Run Prowler command

subprocess.run(['/var/task/prowler', '-M', 'json',
    '-S', '-r', 'us-west-2'], stdout=open(output_file, 'w'))

# Upload output to S3

s3.upload_file(output_file, 'my-prowler-output-bucket',
    f'prowler-output-{timestamp}.json')
```

4. Deploy Prowler with Lambda:

Package Prowler and your Lambda function together. You may use a deployment package or AWS Lambda Layers.

sh

```sh
zip -r9 my-deployment-package.zip prowler

lambda_function.py

aws lambda create-function —function-name

ProwlerScanFunction —zip-file
    fileb://my-deployment-package.zip —handler

lambda_function.lambda_handler —runtime python3.8
    —role arn:aws:iam::123456789012:role/my-lambda-role
```

D.1.2 Scheduling the Lambda Function with CloudWatch Events

To automate the execution of your Lambda function, use CloudWatch Events to trigger the function at regular intervals.

Step-by-Step Guide:

1. Create a CloudWatch Events Rule:

sh

```
aws events put-rule
    --schedule-expression "rate(1 day)"
    --name ProwlerScanSchedule
```

2. Add Lambda Function as Target:

sh

```
aws lambda add-permission
    --function-name ProwlerScanFunction
    --statement-id ProwlerEventPermission
    --action 'lambda:InvokeFunction'
    --principal events.amazonaws.com
    --source-arn arn:aws:events:us-west-2:123456789012:rule/ProwlerScanSchedule

aws events put-targets
    --rule ProwlerScanSchedule
    --targets "Id"="1","Arn"="arn:aws:lambda:us-west-2:123456789012:function:ProwlerScanFunction"
```

This setup schedules the Lambda function to run daily, executing Prowler scans and storing the results in the specified S3 bucket.

D.2 Automating Scan Results to Dashboards

Visualizing the results of Prowler scans on dashboards helps quickly identify and address security issues. You can use Amazon QuickSight to create dashboards from the Prowler output stored in S3.

D.2.1 Setting Up Amazon QuickSight

Step-by-Step Guide:

1. Sign Up for Amazon QuickSight:

If you haven't already, sign up for Amazon QuickSight from the AWS Management Console.

2. Create a Data Source in QuickSight:

- Go to the QuickSight console.
- Choose "Manage data" and then "New data set".
- Choose "S3" as the data source.
- Provide the S3 bucket details where Prowler outputs are stored.

3. Prepare the Data:

Configure the data preparation steps to format the Prowler output correctly.

Use the JSON format settings to parse the data.

4. Create Visuals:

- Use the data set created to build visuals such as bar charts, pie charts, and tables.
- For example, create a bar chart showing the number of findings by severity.

5. Build a Dashboard:

Combine multiple visuals to create a comprehensive security dashboard. Save and share the dashboard with your team.

D.2.2 Automating Data Refresh

Ensure that your QuickSight dashboard stays up-to-date with the latest Prowler scan results by automating data refresh.

Step-by-Step Guide:

1. Schedule Data Refresh in QuickSight:

- Go to the data set in QuickSight.
- Set up a refresh schedule to align with the frequency of Prowler scans (e.g., daily).

2. Automate Data Upload:

Ensure that new scan results are automatically uploaded to S3 after each

Prowler scan by the Lambda function.

Example:

The Prowler Lambda function should already handle uploading scan results to S3. Ensure the data format and path remain consistent so that QuickSight can pick up the new files.

python

```
def lambda_handler(event, context):

    s3 = boto3.client('s3')

    timestamp = datetime.datetime.now().strftime
        ("%Y-%m-%d-%H-%M-%S")

    output_file = f'/tmp/prowler-output-{timestamp}.json'

    # Run Prowler command

    subprocess.run(['/var/task/prowler', '-M',
        'json', '-S', '-r', 'us-west-2'], stdout=open(output_file, 'w'))

    # Upload output to S3

    s3.upload_file(output_file, 'my-prowler-output-bucket'
        , f'prowler-output-{timestamp}.json')
```

D.3 Conclusion

By setting up continuous monitoring with Prowler, scheduling regular scans, and automating the visualization of scan results in dashboards like Amazon QuickSight, you can maintain a robust security posture for your AWS environment. This hands-on exercise demonstrates the importance of automation in cloud security, enabling you to promptly detect and respond to security issues. As you become proficient with these tools and processes, consider expanding your monitoring capabilities and integrating additional security measures to enhance your cloud security strategy further.

Chapter 8: Remediation and Response

A. Prioritizing Security Issues

Prioritizing security issues is a critical step in the remediation and response process. It ensures that the most significant threats are addressed promptly, minimizing potential damage and maintaining the security posture of your cloud environment. This section will guide you through the principles and practices of prioritizing security issues, including risk assessment, categorization, and the use of automated tools.

A.1 Importance of Prioritizing Security Issues

A.1.1 Effective Resource Allocation

By prioritizing security issues, organizations can allocate resources more effectively, focusing on high-risk vulnerabilities that could have the most significant impact.

Example: Allocating more resources to patch critical vulnerabilities in internet-facing applications rather than low-risk internal systems.

A.1.2 Reducing Risk Exposure

Addressing the most severe security issues first reduces the overall risk exposure of your cloud environment, protecting sensitive data and maintaining compliance.

Example: Prioritizing the remediation of misconfigured security groups that expose critical databases to the internet.

A.1.3 Enhancing Incident Response

Prioritization helps streamline incident response processes, ensuring the security team can respond quickly to the most pressing threats.

Example: Developing an incident response playbook prioritizes ransomware attacks over less critical issues like low-severity configuration warnings.

A.2 Risk Assessment and Categorization

To effectively prioritize security issues, you must assess the risks associated with each issue and categorize them based on their potential impact and likelihood.

A.2.1 Assessing Impact

Impact assessment evaluates the potential consequences of a security issue if it were to be exploited. Consider factors such as data sensitivity, system criticality, and business operations.

Impact Categories:

- **High Impact:** Issues that could lead to significant data breaches, substantial financial loss, or major operational disruptions.
- **Medium Impact:** Issues that could cause moderate damage, such as partial data exposure or limited operational impact.
- **Low Impact:** Issues with minimal consequences, such as minor configuration errors or non-critical system vulnerabilities.

Example: Classifying a vulnerability in a customer database as having a high impact due to the sensitivity of the data and potential compliance violations.

A.2.2 Assessing Likelihood

Likelihood assessment evaluates the probability that a security issue will be exploited. Consider factors such as exploit availability, attack complexity, and exposure.

Likelihood Categories:

- **High Likelihood:** Issues that are easily exploited, widely known, and exposed to potential attackers.
- **Medium Likelihood:** Issues that require some effort to exploit and

have moderate exposure.
- **Low Likelihood:** Issues that are difficult to exploit, not well-known, or have limited exposure.

Example: Classifying a publicly known SQL injection vulnerability in a web application as high likelihood due to its ease of exploitation and public exposure.

A.2.3 Combining Impact and Likelihood

Combine the impact and likelihood assessments to determine the overall risk level of each security issue. This combined assessment helps prioritize remediation efforts.

Risk Matrix:

Impact / Likelihood	High	Medium	Low
High Impact	Critical Priority	High Priority	Medium Priority
Medium Impact	High Priority	Medium Priority	Low Priority
Low Impact	Medium Priority	Low Priority	Low Priority

Example: A high-impact, high-likelihood issue would be classified as a critical priority, warranting immediate attention and remediation.

A.3 Using Automated Tools for Prioritization

Automated tools can assist in prioritization by continuously assessing and categorizing security issues based on predefined criteria.

A.3.1 AWS Trusted Advisor

AWS Trusted Advisor provides real-time guidance to help you provision your resources following AWS best practices. It includes checks for security vulnerabilities and recommends prioritization.

Example: Using Trusted Advisor to identify and prioritize high-risk security groups with open access to critical resources.

A.3.2 Azure Security Center

Azure Security Center continuously assesses your cloud environment and provides a security score based on identified issues. It prioritizes recommendations based on severity and impact.

Example: Leveraging Azure Security Center's recommendations to prioritize the remediation of high-severity vulnerabilities in virtual machines.

A.3.3 Google Cloud Security Command Center (SCC)

Google Cloud SCC provides a centralized view of your security posture and helps prioritize vulnerabilities and threats based on their risk level.

Example: Using SCC to prioritize high-risk findings such as misconfigured IAM policies that could lead to privilege escalation.

A.3.4 Third-Party and Open Source Tools

Third-party and open-source tools like Tenable.io, Qualys, and Prowler can help prioritize security issues by providing detailed assessments and risk scores.

Example: Using Prowler to perform continuous security assessments and prioritize issues based on the CIS AWS Foundations Benchmark.

A.4 Best Practices for Prioritizing Security Issues

A.4.1 Develop a Risk-Based Approach

Adopt a risk-based approach to prioritize security issues, focusing on the most critical risks that could impact your organization.

Example: Implementing a risk-based vulnerability management program prioritizes patching high-risk vulnerabilities in critical systems.

A.4.2 Regularly Review and Update Prioritization Criteria

Review and update your prioritization criteria regularly to reflect changes in your cloud environment, threat landscape, and business priorities.

Example: Adjusting prioritization criteria to focus on emerging threats like ransomware and supply chain attacks.

A.4.3 Involve Key Stakeholders

Key stakeholders from different departments, including IT, security, compliance, and business units, should be involved in the prioritization process to ensure a comprehensive approach.

Example: Conducting regular risk assessment meetings with security, IT, and compliance team representatives to review and prioritize security issues.

A.4.4 Automate Where Possible

Automate the prioritization process using tools and scripts to ensure consistency and efficiency. Automation helps reduce the manual effort required for continuous risk assessment.

Example: Using AWS Lambda functions to automate the collection and prioritization of security findings from AWS Security Hub.

A.4.5 Document and Communicate Prioritization Decisions

Document and communicate prioritization decisions to relevant stakeholders to ensure transparency and alignment. This helps build consensus and support for remediation efforts.

Example: Creating a detailed report outlining the prioritization process, criteria used, and prioritized security issues and sharing it with the security and executive teams.

A.5 Conclusion

Prioritizing security issues is essential for effective risk management and incident response in a cloud environment. Organizations can ensure they address the most critical risks by assessing the impact and likelihood of security issues, leveraging automated tools, and following best practices. Regular reviews, stakeholder involvement, and automation further enhance the prioritization process, helping maintain a strong security posture. We will explore additional remediation and response strategies to address prioritized security issues and integrate CSPM with DevOps practices as we continue.

B. Automated and Manual Remediation Strategies

Effective remediation strategies are crucial for addressing identified security issues and maintaining a robust security posture in your cloud environment. This section explores automated and manual remediation strategies, providing detailed guidance on their implementation, advantages, and best practices.

B.1 Importance of Remediation

B.1.1 Maintaining Security Posture

Timely remediation of security issues is essential to maintaining the overall security posture of your cloud environment. Addressing vulnerabilities and misconfigurations promptly minimizes the window of opportunity for potential attackers.

Example: Applying patches to known vulnerabilities on time to prevent exploitation.

B.1.2 Compliance and Regulatory Requirements

Many compliance frameworks and regulatory standards require organizations to implement effective remediation processes. Ensuring timely remediation helps maintain compliance and avoid legal penalties.

Example: Ensuring critical vulnerabilities identified during a PCI-DSS audit are remediated within the required timeframe.

B.1.3 Operational Continuity

Remediation strategies help ensure the continuity of business operations by preventing security incidents that could disrupt services or damage critical systems.

Example: Remediating misconfigurations that could lead to denial-of-service (DoS) attacks, ensuring that essential services remain available.

B.2 Automated Remediation Strategies

Automated remediation involves using scripts, tools, and services to resolve security issues automatically without manual intervention. This approach is efficient, consistent, and scalable.

B.2.1 Benefits of Automated Remediation

- **Speed and Efficiency:** Automated remediation can address security issues quickly, reducing the time they remain vulnerable.
- **Consistency:** Automated processes ensure that remediation steps are performed consistently across all affected resources.
- **Scalability:** Automation can handle large-scale environments, managing numerous security issues simultaneously.

B.2.2 Implementing Automated Remediation

Example: AWS Lambda for Automated Remediation

1. Identify Security Issues for Automation:

- Determine which security issues can be safely and effectively remediated automatically. Examples include applying patches, adjusting security group rules, and enabling encryption.

2. Develop Remediation Scripts:

- Write scripts that define the remediation steps for identified security issues. To execute these scripts, use AWS Lambda, Azure Functions, or Google Cloud Functions.

AWS Lambda Example (Enabling S3 Bucket Encryption):

```python
import boto3

def lambda_handler(event, context):

    s3 = boto3.client('s3')

    for bucket in event['buckets']:

        try:

            s3.put_bucket_encryption(
```

```
        Bucket=bucket,
        ServerSideEncryptionConfiguration={
            'Rules': [
                {
                    'ApplyServerSideEncryptionByDefault': {
                        'SSEAlgorithm': 'AES256'
                    }
                }
            ]
        }
    )
    print(f"Enabled encryption on bucket: {bucket}")
except Exception as e:
    print(f"Error enabling encryption on bucket {bucket}: {str(e)}")
```

3. **Set Up Event Triggers:**

- Configure event triggers to execute remediation scripts when specific security issues are detected automatically.

AWS Config Rule Example (Triggering Lambda for Non-Compliant Buckets):

json

```
{
"ConfigRuleName": "s3-bucket-encryption-check",
"Source": {
"Owner": "AWS",
"SourceIdentifier": "S3_BUCKET_SERVER_SIDE_ENCRYPTION_ENABLED"
},
"Scope": {
"ComplianceResourceTypes": [
"AWS::S3::Bucket"
]
},
"InputParameters": "{}",
"MaximumExecutionFrequency": "Six_Hours",
"ConfigRuleState": "ACTIVE"
```

}

4. Monitor and Validate Remediation:

- Continuously monitor the effectiveness of automated remediation. Validate that the issues are resolved and no unintended consequences occur.

AWS CloudWatch Example (Monitoring Lambda Executions):

sh

```sh
aws cloudwatch put-metric-alarm
  --alarm-name LambdaErrors
  --metric-name Errors
  --namespace AWS/Lambda
  --statistic Sum
  --period 300
  --threshold 1
  --comparison-operator GreaterThanOrEqualToThreshold
  --dimensions "Name=FunctionName, Value=MyLambdaFunction"
  --evaluation-periods 1
  --alarm-actions arn:aws:sns:us-west-2:123456789012:MySNSTopic
```

B.2.3 Best Practices for Automated Remediation

- **Test Thoroughly:** Test automation scripts in a staging environment before deploying to production to ensure they work as expected.
- **Use Idempotent Scripts:** Scripts should be able to be run multiple times without causing adverse effects or creating duplicate changes.

- **Implement Fail-Safes:** Include checks and balances to prevent automated remediation from causing disruptions. For example, a script can be limited in the number of resources it can modify simultaneously.

B.3 Manual Remediation Strategies

Manual remediation involves human intervention to resolve security issues. This approach is necessary for complex issues that require analysis, decision-making, and careful execution.

B.3.1 Benefits of Manual Remediation

- **Flexibility:** Allows tailored responses to unique or complex security issues that automated scripts cannot handle.
- **Expert Analysis:** Leverages the expertise and judgment of security professionals to assess and resolve issues effectively.
- **Control:** Provides greater control over the remediation process, ensuring that changes are made thoughtfully and deliberately.

B.3.2 Implementing Manual Remediation

Example: Remediating IAM Policy Misconfigurations

1. **Identify the Issue:**

- Use security tools and dashboards to identify IAM policy misconfigurations that grant excessive permissions.

AWS IAM Example (Finding Overly Permissive Policies):

sh

**aws iam list-policies —query 'Policies[?
   PolicyName==‛AdminAccess‛]' —output json**

2. Analyze the Impact:

- Assess the potential impact of the misconfiguration. Identify which users or roles are affected and what resources they can access.

IAM Policy Analysis:

sh

**aws iam get-policy-version —policy-arn
   arn:aws:iam::aws:policy/AdminAccess —version-id v1**

3. Develop a Remediation Plan:

- Create a plan to modify or replace the misconfigured policy. Ensure that the new policy grants only the necessary permissions.

IAM Policy Modification:

json

{

"Version": "2012-10-17",

```
"Statement": [

{

"Effect": "Allow",

"Action": [

"ec2:Describe*",

"s3:List*"

],

"Resource": "*"

}

]

}
```

4. Implement the Remediation:

- Apply the changes to the affected IAM policies. Monitor for any issues or unintended consequences.

Updating IAM Policy:

```sh
aws iam create-policy
    --policy-name LeastPrivilegePolicy
```

```
--policy-document file://least-privilege-policy.json

aws iam attach-user-policy
  --policy-arn arn:aws:iam
  ::123456789012:policy/LeastPrivilegePolicy
  --user-name UserName
```

5. **Review and Validate:**

- Review the changes to ensure that the misconfiguration is resolved. Validate that the new policy functions as intended without granting excessive permissions.

B.3.3 Best Practices for Manual Remediation

- **Document the Process:** Keep detailed records of the remediation process, including the issue identified, analysis performed, actions taken, and validation results.
- **Involve Stakeholders:** Collaborate with relevant stakeholders, such as application owners and compliance teams, to ensure that remediation efforts align with business requirements.
- **Perform Post-Remediation Reviews:** Conduct reviews after remediation to assess the actions' effectiveness and identify any lessons learned for future improvements.

B.4 Combining Automated and Manual Remediation

A hybrid approach that combines automated and manual remediation strategies often provides the best results. Automate routine, well-defined tasks while reserving manual intervention for complex or high-impact issues.

B.4.1 Example of a Hybrid Approach

Scenario: Managing Vulnerabilities in a Cloud Environment

1. Automated Scanning:

- Automated tools like AWS Inspector or Azure Security Center can scan for vulnerabilities continuously.

2. Automated Remediation:

- Automatically remediate low-complexity issues, such as applying patches or enforcing security group rules, using AWS Lambda or Azure Functions.

3. Manual Analysis and Remediation:

- For high-complexity issues, such as application-level vulnerabilities or critical misconfigurations, perform manual analysis and remediation by security professionals.

4. Continuous Monitoring:

- Implement continuous monitoring to ensure that remediation efforts are effective and that new issues are promptly identified and addressed.

B.4.2 Benefits of a Hybrid Approach

- **Efficiency:** Automates routine tasks to improve efficiency and reduce the workload on security teams.
- **Effectiveness:** Ensures that complex issues receive the attention and expertise they require.
- **Scalability:** Scales to manage large environments by automating common tasks while maintaining the flexibility to handle unique challenges.

B.5 Conclusion

Implementing effective remediation strategies is crucial for maintaining a secure cloud environment. Organizations can efficiently address various security issues by leveraging automated and manual approaches, ensuring that critical vulnerabilities and misconfigurations are resolved promptly. Adopting a hybrid approach that combines the strengths of both methods allows for scalable, flexible, and effective remediation processes. As we move forward, we will explore additional aspects of remediation and response, including integrating CSPM with DevOps practices to enhance security throughout the development lifecycle.

C. Incident Response Planning

Incident response planning is a critical component of a comprehensive cloud security strategy. An effective incident response plan ensures that your organization can quickly and effectively respond to security incidents, minimizing damage and reducing recovery time. This section covers the key elements of incident response planning, including preparation, detection and analysis, containment, eradication, recovery, and post-incident activities.

C.1 Importance of Incident Response Planning

C.1.1 Minimizing Damage

A well-defined incident response plan helps minimize the damage caused by security incidents, protect sensitive data, and maintain business continuity.

Example: Quickly isolating compromised systems to prevent the spread of malware.

C.1.2 Reducing Recovery Time

Efficient incident response reduces the time required to recover from security incidents, restoring normal operations faster.

Example: Implementing automated recovery procedures to restore affected services quickly.

C.1.3 Ensuring Compliance

Many regulatory frameworks require organizations to have an incident response plan in place. Ensuring compliance helps avoid legal penalties and maintain customer trust.

Example: Demonstrating compliance with GDPR by having a documented incident response plan and conducting regular incident response drills.

C.1.4 Improving Security Posture

Continuous improvement of incident response capabilities enhances the overall security posture of your organization.

Example: Analyzing incidents to identify root causes and implementing measures to prevent future occurrences.

C.2 Key Elements of Incident Response Planning

C.2.1 Preparation

Preparation involves establishing and maintaining the tools, policies, and procedures necessary to respond to security incidents effectively.

Key Activities:

- **Developing an Incident Response Plan:** Documenting the processes and procedures to be followed during an incident.
- **Establishing an Incident Response Team:** Assembling a team of qualified individuals responsible for managing incidents.
- **Training and Awareness:** Providing regular training and awareness programs for employees to ensure they understand their roles and responsibilities during an incident.

Example: Creating an incident response plan that outlines roles, responsibilities, communication channels, and escalation procedures.

C.2.2 Detection and Analysis

Detection and analysis involve identifying and understanding security incidents to determine their scope and impact.

Key Activities:

- **Monitoring and Detection:** Implementing monitoring tools and techniques to detect potential security incidents.
- **Incident Analysis:** Analyzing detected incidents to determine their nature, scope, and impact.
- **Incident Classification:** Classifying incidents based on severity and potential impact to prioritize response efforts.

Example: AWS CloudTrail and Amazon GuardDuty are used to detect suspicious activity and analyze logs to understand the incident's scope.

C.2.3 Containment

Containment involves isolating affected systems to prevent further damage and limit the spread of the incident.

Key Activities:

- **Short-Term Containment:** Taking immediate actions to contain the incident and prevent further impact.
- **Long-Term Containment:** Implementing measures to maintain containment until the incident can be fully resolved.

Example: Disconnecting compromised systems from the network prevents malware from spreading to other systems.

C.2.4 Eradication

Eradication involves removing the incident's root cause and ensuring that affected systems are free from malicious activity.

Key Activities:

- **Identifying Root Causes:** Determining the underlying causes of the incident to prevent recurrence.
- **Removing Malware:** Eliminating malware or malicious code from affected systems.
- **Applying Patches and Updates:** Applying necessary patches and updates to address vulnerabilities exploited during the incident.

Example: Using antivirus software to remove malware and applying security patches to vulnerable systems.

C.2.5 Recovery

Recovery involves restoring affected systems and services to normal operations while ensuring the incident does not recur.

Key Activities:

- **Restoring Systems:** Recovering data and restoring systems to their pre-incident state.
- **Validating Recovery:** Ensuring that restored systems are functioning correctly and securely.
- **Monitoring for Recurrence:** Monitoring restored systems to detect any signs of recurrence.

Example: Restoring data from backups and monitoring system logs to ensure no further malicious activity is detected.

C.2.6 Post-Incident Activities

Post-incident activities involve analyzing the incident response process, identifying lessons learned, and implementing improvements.

Key Activities:

- **Incident Analysis:** Conducting a thorough analysis of the incident to understand what happened and why.
- **Lessons Learned:** Identifying lessons learned to improve future

incident response efforts.
- **Updating Incident Response Plan:** Revising the incident response plan based on lessons learned and changes in the environment.

Example: Conducting a post-incident review meeting to discuss what went well and what could be improved, and updating the incident response plan accordingly.

C.3 Developing an Incident Response Plan

An effective incident response plan should be comprehensive, flexible, and regularly updated to address evolving threats and organizational changes.

C.3.1 Establishing an Incident Response Team

Define roles and responsibilities for the incident response team, ensuring team members have the necessary skills and authority to act during an incident.

Example Roles:

- **Incident Response Coordinator:** Oversees the incident response process and coordinates activities.
- **Security Analysts:** Analyze incidents, determine their scope and impact, and recommend remediation actions.
- **System Administrators:** Implement containment, eradication, and recovery measures on affected systems.
- **Communication Lead:** Manages internal and external communications during an incident.

C.3.2 Defining Incident Categories and Severity Levels

Categorize incidents based on their nature and define severity levels to prioritize response efforts.

Example Categories:

- **Malware Infections:** Incidents involving malicious software.
- **Data Breaches:** Incidents involving unauthorized access to sensitive data.
- **Denial of Service:** Incidents involving service disruptions.

Example Severity Levels:

- **Critical:** Incidents causing significant impact to operations or data security.
- **High:** Incidents with the potential to cause major impact.
- **Medium:** Incidents causing limited impact.
- **Low:** Incidents with minimal impact.

C.3.3 Developing Response Procedures

Document detailed response procedures for each incident category and severity level, including specific steps to be taken during detection, containment, eradication, and recovery.

Example Procedure for Malware Infection:

1. **Detection:** Monitor for malware alerts from antivirus software and

endpoint detection tools.
2. **Containment:** Isolate infected systems from the network.
3. **Eradication:** Use antivirus tools to remove malware and conduct a full system scan.
4. **Recovery:** Restore data from backups and apply necessary patches.
5. **Post-Incident:** Conduct a root cause analysis and update security measures.

C.3.4 Communication Plan

Develop a communication plan to ensure clear and effective communication during an incident. This plan should include internal communication channels and external communication guidelines.

Example:

- **Internal Communication:** Use secure communication tools (e.g., encrypted messaging, secure email) to share information with the incident response team and relevant stakeholders.
- **External Communication:** Develop templates for notifying customers, partners, and regulatory bodies about the incident, ensuring compliance with legal requirements.

C.3.5 Testing and Drills

Regularly test and conduct drills to ensure that the incident response plan is effective, and that team members are familiar with their roles and responsibilities.

Example: Conducting tabletop exercises to simulate different incidents and assess the incident response team's readiness.

C.4 Best Practices for Incident Response Planning

C.4.1 Continuous Improvement

Continuously improve your incident response capabilities by incorporating lessons learned from actual incidents and drills.

Example: After a successful incident response, update the plan with any new insights or improvements identified during the post-incident review.

C.4.2 Stakeholder Involvement

Involve key stakeholders from different departments, including IT, security, legal, and communications, in developing and reviewing the incident response plan.

Example: Holding regular meetings with stakeholders to review and update the incident response plan, ensuring it aligns with organizational goals and requirements.

C.4.3 Documentation and Accessibility

Ensure the incident response plan is well-documented, easily accessible, and understood by all relevant personnel.

Example: Storing the incident response plan in a secure, centralized location and providing access to team members through secure channels.

C.4.4 Regular Training

Provide regular training for the incident response team and other relevant personnel to ensure they are prepared to respond effectively to incidents.

Example: Conducting quarterly training sessions to review the incident response plan, update team members on new threats, and practice response procedures.

C.4.5 Integration with Overall Security Strategy

Integrate the incident response plan with your security strategy, ensuring it complements other security measures and processes.

Example: Aligning the incident response plan with the organization's risk management framework and compliance requirements.

C.5 Conclusion

An effective incident response plan is essential for minimizing the impact of security incidents, ensuring compliance, and maintaining business continuity. Organizations can enhance their incident response capabilities by preparing thoroughly, detecting and analyzing incidents, and implementing robust containment, eradication, and recovery procedures. Continuous improvement, stakeholder involvement, and regular training strengthen the incident response plan, ensuring it remains effective despite evolving threats. As we move forward, we will explore additional remediation and response strategies, including integrating CSPM with DevOps practices to enhance security throughout the development lifecycle.

D. Hands-On Exercise: Remediation Strategies with Prowler

In this hands-on exercise, you will learn how to use Prowler, an open-source tool for AWS security best practices and compliance checks, to identify, remediate, and verify critical vulnerabilities in your AWS environment. This exercise will help you identify critical vulnerabilities, apply remediation steps, and verify the effectiveness of your remediation efforts.

D.1 Identifying Critical Vulnerabilities

The first step in the remediation process is identifying critical vulnerabilities within your AWS environment using Prowler.

D.1.1 Running Prowler

To identify critical vulnerabilities, run a Prowler scan on your AWS environment.

Step-by-Step Guide:

1. Install Prowler:

- Clone the Prowler repository and navigate to the directory:

sh

git clone https://github.com/prowler-cloud/prowler.git

cd prowler

2. Run Prowler Scan:

- Execute Prowler to perform a full scan and generate a report:

sh

./prowler -M csv

This command runs all available checks and outputs the results in CSV format.

D.1.2 Reviewing Scan Results

After running the scan, review the results to identify critical vulnerabilities.

Step-by-Step Guide:

1. Locate the Report:

- Find the generated CSV report in the Prowler directory. The file is typically named 'prowler-output.csv'.

2. Open the Report:

- Open the CSV file using a spreadsheet application or a text editor.

3. Identify Critical Findings:

- Filter the report to show only critical findings. Look for columns indicating the severity of each finding, such as "Severity" or "Risk".

Example: Identify rows with "Critical" severity.

D.2 Applying Remediation Steps

Once critical vulnerabilities have been identified, the next step is to apply appropriate remediation steps to address these issues.

D.2.1 Common Critical Vulnerabilities and Remediation

Here are some common critical vulnerabilities and their corresponding remediation steps:

1. Open Security Groups:

- **Vulnerability:** Security groups with overly permissive rules (e.g., 0.0.0.0/0 for all ports).
- **Remediation:** Restrict security group rules to allow only necessary traffic from trusted IP ranges.

Step-by-Step Guide:

1. Identify Open Security Groups:

- According to the Prowler report, security groups should be identified with overly permissive rules.

2. Modify Security Group Rules:

- Use the AWS Management Console or AWS CLI to modify security group rules.

```sh
aws ec2 revoke-security-group-ingress
   —group-id sg-12345678 —protocol tcp —port 22
   —cidr 0.0.0.0/0

aws ec2 authorize-security-group-ingress
```

    —group-id sg-12345678 —protocol tcp
    —port 22 —cidr 192.168.1.0/24

2. Unencrypted S3 Buckets:

- **Vulnerability:** S3 buckets without server-side encryption enabled.
- **Remediation:** Enable server-side encryption for all S3 buckets.

Step-by-Step Guide:

1. Identify Unencrypted S3 Buckets:

- From the Prowler report, identify S3 buckets without server-side encryption.

2. Enable Server-Side Encryption:

- Use the AWS Management Console or AWS CLI to enable encryption.

sh

aws s3api put-bucket-encryption
    —bucket my-bucket
    —server-side-encryption-configuration
    '{"Rules":[{"ApplyServerSideEncryptionByDefault":
    {"SSEAlgorithm":"AES256"}}]}'

3. Publicly Accessible RDS Instances:

- **Vulnerability:** RDS instances that are publicly accessible.
- **Remediation:** Modify RDS instance settings to disable public access.

Step-by-Step Guide:

1. Identify Publicly Accessible RDS Instances:

- From the Prowler report, identify RDS instances with public access enabled.

2. Modify RDS Instance Settings:

- Use the AWS Management Console or AWS CLI to modify the RDS instance settings.

sh

aws rds modify-db-instance
  —db-instance-identifier mydbinstance
  —no-publicly-accessible

D.3 Verifying Remediation Effectiveness

After applying remediation steps, verifying that the vulnerabilities have been effectively mitigated is essential.

D.3.1 Running a Follow-Up Prowler Scan

Run a follow-up Prowler scan to verify the previously identified vulnerabilities have been resolved.

Step-by-Step Guide:

1. Run Prowler Scan:

- Execute Prowler again to perform a follow-up scan and generate a new report.

sh

./prowler -M csv

2. Review the Follow-Up Report:

- Open the new CSV report and check the status of the previously identified critical vulnerabilities.

D.3.2 Manual Verification

In addition to automated scans, manually verify that the remediation steps have been correctly applied.

Step-by-Step Guide:

1. Verify Security Group Rules:

- Check the security group rules in the AWS Management Console or using the AWS CLI to ensure they have been modified as intended.

```sh
aws ec2 describe-security-groups
  --group-ids sg-12345678
```

2. **Verify S3 Bucket Encryption:**

   - Check the encryption settings of the S3 buckets in the AWS Management Console or using the AWS CLI.

```sh
aws s3api get-bucket-encryption
  --bucket my-bucket
```

3. **Verify RDS Instance Settings:**

   - Check the RDS instance settings in the AWS Management Console or using the AWS CLI to ensure public access is disabled.

```sh
aws rds describe-db-instances
  --db-instance-identifier mydbinstance
```

D.3.3 Continuous Monitoring

Implement continuous monitoring to ensure that new vulnerabilities are promptly identified and remediated.

Step-by-Step Guide:

1. Set Up Automated Scans:

- Schedule regular Prowler scans using AWS Lambda and CloudWatch Events to monitor your environment continuously.

Example: Schedule a daily Prowler scan.

```sh
aws events put-rule
    —schedule-expression "rate(1 day)"
    —name ProwlerScanSchedule

aws lambda add-permission
    —function-name ProwlerScanFunction
    —statement-id ProwlerEventPermission
    —action 'lambda:InvokeFunction'
    —principal events.amazonaws.com
    —source-arn arn:aws:events:us-west-2:123456789012:rule/ProwlerScanSchedule

aws events put-targets
    —rule ProwlerScanSchedule
    —targets "Id"="1","Arn"="arn:aws:lambda:us-west-2:123456789012:function:ProwlerScanFunction"
```

2. Implement Alerts and Notifications:

- Configure alerts and notifications to notify your security team of critical findings.

CHAPTER 8: REMEDIATION AND RESPONSE

Example: Use Amazon SNS to send notifications.

sh

aws sns create-topic —name ProwlerAlerts

aws sns subscribe
   —topic-arn arn:aws:sns:us
   -west-2:123456789012:ProwlerAlerts
   —protocol email
   —notification-endpoint myemail@example.com

3. **Use Dashboards for Continuous Monitoring:**

- Set up dashboards in tools like Amazon QuickSight or Grafana to visualize security findings and track remediation status.

Example: Create a QuickSight dashboard to monitor Prowler scan results.

sh

aws quicksight create-dashboard
   —name ProwlerDashboard
   —source-entity "{

\"SourceTemplate\": {

\"DataSetReferences\": [

{

\"DataSetPlaceholder\": \"ProwlerDataSet\",

\"DataSetArn\": \"arn:aws:quicksight:us-west-2:123456789012:dataset/ProwlerDataSet\"

}

],

\"Arn\": \"arn:aws:quicksight:us-west-2:123456789012:template/ProwlerTemplate\"

}

}"

D.4 Conclusion

By following this hands-on exercise, you have learned how to use Prowler to identify critical vulnerabilities, apply appropriate remediation steps, and verify the effectiveness of your remediation efforts. Regular scanning, prompt remediation, and continuous monitoring are essential practices for maintaining a robust security posture in your AWS environment. As we move forward, we will explore additional strategies for integrating CSPM with DevOps practices to enhance security throughout the development lifecycle.

V

Advanced CSPM Strategies

Chapter 9: Integrating CSPM with DevOps

A. CSPM in CI/CD Pipelines

Integrating Cloud Security Posture Management (CSPM) into Continuous Integration and Continuous Deployment (CI/CD) pipelines is essential for maintaining a secure and compliant cloud environment throughout the software development lifecycle. This chapter provides a detailed guide on embedding CSPM practices into CI/CD pipelines to ensure that security is continuously assessed and enforced from development to production.

A.1 Importance of Integrating CSPM with CI/CD Pipelines

A.1.1 Shift-Left Security

Integrating CSPM into CI/CD pipelines shifts security to the left, embedding security checks earlier in the development process. This proactive approach helps identify and remediate vulnerabilities before they reach production.

Example: Running security scans on infrastructure-as-code (IaC) templates during the build process to catch misconfigurations early.

A.1.2 Continuous Security Assessment

Continuous integration of CSPM ensures that security assessments are conducted at every stage of the deployment pipeline. This continuous assessment helps maintain a secure posture even as code changes frequently.

Example: Automating security assessments of application code and cloud configurations every time a developer commits code.

A.1.3 Compliance Assurance

Automating compliance checks in CI/CD pipelines ensures that all deployments meet regulatory and organizational security standards. This continuous compliance helps avoid potential fines and maintains customer trust.

Example: Implementing automated checks for GDPR compliance during the deployment process.

A.2 Implementing CSPM in CI/CD Pipelines

A.2.1 Selecting CSPM Tools

Choose CSPM tools that integrate seamlessly with your CI/CD pipelines and support automated security assessments.

Popular CSPM Tools:

- **Prowler:** For AWS environments, provides security best practices and compliance checks.
- **Checkov:** For scanning Terraform, CloudFormation, Kubernetes, and other IaC files.
- **AWS Config:** Monitors and records AWS resource configurations.
- **Azure Policy:** Ensures Azure resources comply with organizational standards.

A.2.2 Integrating CSPM into the CI/CD Pipeline

Step-by-Step Guide:

1. Set Up CSPM Tooling:

- Ensure the CSPM tool is installed and configured in your CI/CD environment.

Example: Installing Prowler on a CI server.

sh

git clone https://github.com/prowler-cloud/prowler.git

cd prowler

2. Configure Pipeline Stages:

- Add CSPM checks as stages in your CI/CD pipeline to run security assessments at appropriate points.

Example: Integrating Prowler into a Jenkins pipeline.

groovy

pipeline {

agent any

stages {

stage('Checkout') {

steps {

git 'https://github.com/your-repo/your-app.git'

}

}

stage('Build') {

steps {

sh 'make build'

```
        }

    }

    stage('Test') {

        steps {

            sh 'make test'

        }

    }

    stage('Security Scan') {

        steps {

            dir('prowler') {

                sh './prowler -M json > prowler-results.json'

            }

        }

    }

    stage('Deploy') {

        steps {

            sh 'make deploy'
```

}

}

}

post {

always {

archiveArtifacts artifacts: 'prowler/prowler-results.json', allowEmptyArchive: true

}

}

}

3. Automate Remediation:

- Implement automated remediation for common security issues identified by CSPM tools.

Example: Using AWS Lambda to remediate insecure S3 bucket permissions detected by Prowler automatically.

python

import boto3

def lambda_handler(event, context):

```
s3 = boto3.client('s3')

for finding in event['findings']:

bucket_name = finding['resource']['id']

s3.put_bucket_acl(Bucket=bucket_name, ACL='private')
```

4. Set Up Notifications:

- Configure notifications to alert the development and security teams about security findings in the pipeline.

Example: Sending Prowler scan results to an SNS topic.

```sh
aws sns publish —topic-arn arn:aws:sns:us-west-2:123456789012:SecurityAlerts — message file://prowler-results.json
```

A.2.3 Continuous Monitoring and Feedback

Integrate continuous monitoring and feedback mechanisms to ensure that security assessments are up-to-date and actionable.

Step-by-Step Guide:

1. Continuous Monitoring:

- Use cloud-native monitoring tools to assess your deployed resources' security posture continuously.

Example: Enabling AWS Config rules to monitor resource configurations continuously.

sh

```
aws configservice put-config-rule
    —config-rule-name s3-bucket-public-read-prohibited
    —config-rule file://s3-bucket-public-read-prohibited.json
```

2. **Feedback Loops:**

- Establish feedback loops to ensure security findings are communicated to developers for remediation.

Example: Integrating Slack notifications for immediate feedback on security issues detected in the pipeline.

sh

```
aws sns create-topic —name SecurityFeedback

aws sns subscribe —topic-arn arn:aws:sns:us-west
    -2:123456789012:SecurityFeedback —protocol https
    —notification-endpoint https://hooks.slack.com/services
    /T00000/B00000/XXXXXXXXXXXXXXXXXXXXXXXX
```

A.2.4 Policy as Code

Implement policy as code to programmatically enforce security and compliance policies within the CI/CD pipeline.

Step-by-Step Guide:

1. Define Security Policies:

- Write security policies as code using tools like HashiCorp Sentinel, Open Policy Agent (OPA), or Azure Policy.

Example: Defining a Sentinel policy to enforce encryption on all Terraform-managed resources.

```hcl
policy "aws-s3-encryption" {

description = "Ensure all S3 buckets have encryption enabled"

enforcement_level = "mandatory"

policy = <

import "tfplan/v2" as tfplan

main = rule {

all tfplan.resources.aws_s3_bucket as _, bucket {
  bucket.applied_server_side_encryption_
```

configuration.rules[*].apply_server_side_encryption_by_default.sse_algorithm contains "AES256"

}

}

EOF

}

2. Integrate Policy Checks:

- Integrate policy checks into the CI/CD pipeline to enforce compliance before deployment.

Example: Adding a policy check stage in a GitLab CI pipeline.

```yaml
stages:

- build

- test

- policy-check

- deploy

policy-check:

stage: policy-check
```

script:

- sentinel apply -config=sentinel.hcl

A.2.5 Implementing Continuous Improvement

Ensure continuous improvement by regularly reviewing and updating CSPM practices in your CI/CD pipeline.

Step-by-Step Guide:

1. Regular Audits and Reviews:

- Conduct regular audits and reviews of your CI/CD pipeline to identify areas for improvement.

Example: Scheduling quarterly reviews of pipeline security checks and policies.

2. Update and Refine Security Policies:

- Update security policies to address new threats and changes in the cloud environment.

Example: Refining S3 bucket policies to incorporate new AWS best practices for data protection.

3. Training and Awareness:

- Provide ongoing training and awareness programs for developers and security teams to ensure they are aware of the latest security practices and tools.

Example: Conducting monthly security workshops to educate developers on secure coding practices and using CSPM tools.

A.3 Example: Integrating CSPM with a CI/CD Pipeline

Consider a practical example of integrating CSPM with a CI/CD pipeline using Jenkins and Prowler.

Step-by-Step Guide:

1. Set Up Jenkins Pipeline:

- Create a Jenkins pipeline with stages for checkout, build, test, security scan, and deploy.

Jenkinsfile:

groovy

pipeline {

agent any

stages {

stage('Checkout') {

steps {

```
git 'https://github.com/your-repo/your-app.git'

}

}

stage('Build') {

steps {

sh 'make build'

}

}

stage('Test') {

steps {

sh 'make test'

}

}

stage('Security Scan') {

steps {

dir('prowler') {

sh './prowler -M json > prowler-results.json'
```

```
            }

        }

    }

    stage('Deploy') {

        steps {

            sh 'make deploy'

        }

    }

}

post {

    always {

        archiveArtifacts artifacts: 'prowler/prowler-results.json',
            allowEmptyArchive: true

        script {

            def results = readFile('prowler/prowler-results.json')

            def findings = new groovy.json.JsonSlurper().parseText(results)

            if (findings.any { it.Severity == 'High' }) {
```

currentBuild.result = 'FAILURE'

mail to: 'security-team@example.com',

subject: "Build ${env.BUILD_NUMBER}
    failed due to high-severity security findings",

body: "Please review the attached Prowler report."

}

}

}

}

}

2. Run the Pipeline:

- Trigger the pipeline to perform all stages, including the Prowler security scan.

3. Review Results and Remediate:

- Review the Prowler scan results. If high-severity findings are detected, the pipeline will fail, and an email notification will be sent to the security team.

4. Implement Automated Remediation:

- Add Lambda functions or other automation tools to remediate common issues detected by Prowler.

5. Continuous Improvement:

- Regularly update the pipeline to incorporate new security checks and best practices.

A.4 Conclusion

Integrating CSPM into CI/CD pipelines ensures that security is continuously assessed and enforced throughout the software development lifecycle. Organizations can maintain a secure and compliant cloud environment by embedding security checkboxes, automating remediation, and implementing continuous monitoring and feedback early in the pr. Regular reviews and security policy and practice updates ensure continuous improvement and adaptation to evolving threats. We will explore additional advanced CSPM strategies to enhance cloud security as we move forward.

B. Ensuring Security in DevOps Practices

Integrating security into DevOps practices, often called DevSecOps, ensures that security is a continuous, integral part of the software development lifecycle. This chapter explores strategies and best practices for embedding security into DevOps processes, leveraging Cloud Security Posture Management (CSPM) tools, and fostering a culture of collaboration between development, operations, and security teams.

B.1 The Need for DevSecOps

B.1.1 Addressing Security Early

Embedding security into DevOps practices ensures that security vulnerabilities are identified and addressed early in the development lifecycle, reducing the risk of security breaches and costly fixes later.

Example: Running static application security testing (SAST) during the code commit phase to detect security issues before they are merged into the main branch.

B.1.2 Continuous Security

DevSecOps promotes continuous security, ensuring that security assessments and controls are applied consistently throughout the development, testing, deployment, and operational phases.

Example: Automating security compliance checks using tools like AWS Config or Azure Policy to ensure continuous adherence to security standards.

B.1.3 Collaboration and Shared Responsibility

DevSecOps fosters collaboration between development, operations, and security teams, promoting a shared responsibility for security across the entire organization.

Example: Establishing cross-functional teams that include developers, operations staff, and security professionals to collaborate on security initiatives.

B.2 Key Principles of DevSecOps

B.2.1 Shift-Left Security

Shift-left security involves integrating security checks early in the development process, allowing developers to identify and fix security issues as they code.

Example: Incorporating security tools like Checkmarx or SonarQube into the integrated development environment (IDE) to provide real-time feedback on security issues.

B.2.2 Automation

Automating security processes ensures consistency, reduces human error, and allows scalable security practices in fast-paced DevOps environments.

Example: Using CI/CD tools like Jenkins or GitLab CI to automate security scans and enforce security policies during the build and deployment processes.

B.2.3 Continuous Monitoring

Continuous monitoring involves assessing the security posture of applications and infrastructure to detect and respond to security incidents in real time.

Example: Implementing continuous monitoring tools like Datadog or Prometheus to collect and analyze security-related metrics and logs.

B.2.4 Policy as Code

Policy as code involves programmatically defining and enforcing security policies, ensuring that security controls are consistently applied and version-controlled.

Example: Using Open Policy Agent (OPA) to define and enforce security policies for Kubernetes deployments.

B.3 Implementing Security in DevOps Practices

B.3.1 Integrating Security Tools

Integrate security tools into the DevOps toolchain to automate security assessments and enforce security policies.

Step-by-Step Guide:

1. Select Security Tools:

- Choose security tools that integrate seamlessly with your DevOps processes and support automation.

Example Tools:

- **Static Application Security Testing (SAST):** Checkmarx, SonarQube
- **Dynamic Application Security Testing (DAST):** OWASP ZAP, Burp Suite
- **Container Security:** Aqua Security, Twistlock

2. Integrate with CI/CD Pipelines:

- Add security tools as stages in your CI/CD pipelines to perform automated security assessments.

Example: Adding a SAST stage in a Jenkins pipeline.

groovy

pipeline {

agent any

stages {

stage('Checkout') {

steps {

git 'https://github.com/your-repo/your-app.git'

```
        }

        }

        stage('Build') {

            steps {

                sh 'make build'

            }

        }

        stage('Test') {

            steps {

                sh 'make test'

            }

        }

        stage('SAST') {

            steps {

                sh 'checkmarx scan —project your-project
                    —branch ${env.BRANCH_NAME}'

            }
```

```
            }
                stage('DAST') {

            steps {

            sh 'zap-cli start && zap-cli quick-scan
                http://your-app-url'

            }

            }

            stage('Deploy') {

            steps {

            sh 'make deploy'

            }

            }

            }

            post {

            always {

            archiveArtifacts artifacts: 'zap-report.html',
                allowEmptyArchive: true

            archiveArtifacts artifacts: 'checkmarx-report.xml',
                allowEmptyArchive: true
```

}

}

}

3. Automate Policy Enforcement:

- Use tools to enforce security policies automatically in the CI/CD pipeline.

Example: Using Sentinel to enforce security policies on Terraform deployments.

hcl

policy "no-public-s3-buckets" {

description = "Ensure no S3 buckets are public"

enforcement_level = "mandatory"

policy = <

import "tfplan/v2" as tfplan

main = rule {

all tfplan.resources.aws_s3_bucket as _, bucket {

not bucket.applied_acl is "public-read" or bucket.applied_acl is "public-read-write"

}

}

EOF

}

B.3.2 Secure Coding Practices

Educate developers on secure coding practices and provide them with tools and resources to write secure code.

Step-by-Step Guide:

1. Provide Training:

- Offer regular training sessions and workshops on secure coding practices.

Example: Conducting OWASP Top 10 training sessions for developers.

2. Use Secure Coding Tools:

- Integrate secure coding tools into the development environment to provide real-time feedback on security issues.

Example: Integrating SonarQube into the IDE to highlight security issues as developers write code.

3. Implement Code Reviews:

- Establish a code review process that includes security checks to identify and address security issues before the code is merged.

Example: Requiring peer reviews for all code changes and using tools like GitHub Code Scanning to automate security checks.

B.3.3 Infrastructure as Code (IaC) Security

Ensure that infrastructure as code (IaC) templates are secure and compliant with security policies.

Step-by-Step Guide:

1. Scan IaC Templates:

- Use tools to scan IaC templates for security issues before they are applied.

Example: Using Checkov to scan Terraform templates for misconfigurations.

sh

checkov -d /path/to/terraform/code

2. Enforce IaC Policies:

- Define and enforce security policies for IaC using policy as code tools.

Example: Using OPA to enforce Kubernetes security policies.

```yaml
apiVersion: policy/v1
kind: PodSecurityPolicy
metadata:
  name: restricted
spec:
  privileged: false
  allowPrivilegeEscalation: false
  requiredDropCapabilities:
    - ALL
  volumes:
    - 'configMap'
    - 'emptyDir'
    - 'secret'
  hostNetwork: false
  hostIPC: false
  hostPID: false
```

runAsUser:

rule: 'MustRunAsNonRoot'

3. Automate IaC Deployment:

- Use CI/CD pipelines to automate the deployment of IaC, ensuring that security checks are performed as part of the deployment process.

Example: Adding a Terraform deployment stage in a GitLab CI pipeline.

```yaml
stages:
- plan
- apply

terraform_plan:
  stage: plan
  script:
    - terraform init
    - terraform plan -out=tfplan
  artifacts:
    paths:
```

- tfplan

terraform_apply:

stage: apply

script:

- terraform apply tfplan

when: manual

B.3.4 Continuous Monitoring and Incident Response

Implement continuous monitoring and incident response practices to detect and respond to real-time security incidents.

Step-by-Step Guide:

1. Set Up Monitoring Tools:

- Use monitoring tools to collect and analyze security-related metrics and logs.

Example: Using AWS CloudWatch and GuardDuty to monitor AWS resources.

sh

aws guardduty create-detector —enable

```
aws cloudwatch put-metric-alarm
  —alarm-name SecurityIncidents
  —metric-name GuardDutyFindings
  —namespace AWS/GuardDuty —statistic Sum
  —period 300 —threshold 1 —comparison-operator GreaterThanOrEqualToThreshold
  —evaluation-periods 1 —alarm-actions arn:aws:sns:us-west-2:123456789012:SecurityAlerts
```

2. **Implement Incident Response Plans:**

- Develop and implement incident response plans to handle security incidents effectively.

Example: Creating a playbook for responding to a data breach.

```markdown
# Data Breach Incident Response Playbook

## Detection
  - Identify and verify the breach through monitoring tools and logs.

## Containment
  - Isolate affected systems to prevent further data loss.

## Eradication
  - Remove the cause of the breach (e.g., malware, vulnerabilities).

## Recovery
  - Restore affected systems and verify their integrity.

## Post-Incident
  - Conduct a post-incident review and update security measures.
```

3. Automate Incident Response:

- Use automation to respond to common security incidents and reduce response time.

Example: Using AWS Lambda to remediate misconfigured security groups detected automatically by GuardDuty.

```python
import boto3

def lambda_handler(event, context):

    ec2 = boto3.client('ec2')

    for finding in event['detail']['findings']:

        group_id = finding['resource']['id']

        ec2.revoke_security_group_ingress(

            GroupId=group_id,

            IpPermissions=[

                {

                    'IpProtocol': 'tcp',

                    'FromPort': 22,

                    'ToPort': 22,
```

'IpRanges': [{'CidrIp': '0.0.0.0/0'}]

}

]

)

B.4 Best Practices for Ensuring Security in DevOps

B.4.1 Foster a Security-First Culture

Promote a culture of security within the organization by encouraging collaboration and shared responsibility for security among all teams.

Example: Hosting regular security awareness training and including security goals in performance evaluations.

B.4.2 Implement Continuous Security Training

Provide continuous security training for developers, operations, and security teams to keep them updated on the latest security threats and best practices.

Example: Offering access to online security courses and certifications for team members.

B.4.3 Use Metrics and KPIs

Track security metrics and key performance indicators (KPIs) to measure the effectiveness of security practices and identify areas for improvement.

Example: Monitoring the number of vulnerabilities detected and remediated in each release cycle.

B.4.4 Regularly Review and Update Security Practices

Regularly review and update security practices to ensure they remain effective and relevant in the face of evolving threats.

Example: Conducting quarterly security reviews and updating policies and procedures based on the latest threat intelligence.

B.4.5 Leverage Community and Industry Resources

By leveraging community and industry resources, stay informed about the latest security trends and best practices.

Example: Participating in security conferences, forums, and industry groups to exchange knowledge and learn from peers.

B.5 Conclusion

Ensuring security in DevOps practices requires a comprehensive approach to integrating security into every software development lifecycle phase. Organizations can maintain a secure and compliant cloud environment by adopting DevSecOps principles, automating security processes, and fostering a culture of collaboration and shared responsibility. Continuous improvement, regular training, and staying informed about the latest security trends are essential for effectively managing security in DevOps practices. We will explore additional advanced CSPM strategies to enhance cloud security as we move forward.

C. Hands-On Exercise: Integrating Prowler in CI/CD Pipelines

In this hands-on exercise, you will learn how to integrate Prowler, an open-source AWS security assessment tool, into your CI/CD pipelines using Jenkins or GitLab CI. This integration will enable you to automate security checks as part of your deployment process, ensuring that your AWS environment maintains a robust security posture.

C.1 Setting up Prowler Scans in Jenkins

C.1.1 Prerequisites

Before starting, ensure you have the following:

- Jenkins installed and configured.
- AWS CLI configured with necessary permissions.
- Prowler installed on the Jenkins server.

C.1.2 Installing Prowler

1. Clone the Prowler repository:

sh

```
git clone https://github.com/prowler-cloud/prowler.git
cd prowler
```

2. Install dependencies (if required):

sh

```
pip install -r requirements.txt
```

C.1.3 Configuring Jenkins Pipeline

1. Create a Jenkins Pipeline:

- Open your Jenkins dashboard.
- Create a new pipeline job.

2. Edit the Pipeline Script:

- Add the following pipeline script to integrate Prowler scans:

```groovy
pipeline {
    agent any
    environment {
        AWS_ACCESS_KEY_ID = credentials('aws-access-key-id')
        AWS_SECRET_ACCESS_KEY = credentials('aws-secret-access-key')
        AWS_DEFAULT_REGION = 'us-west-2'
    }
    stages {
        stage('Checkout') {
            steps {
                git 'https://github.com/your-repo/your-app.git'
            }
```

```
}

stage('Build') {

steps {

sh 'make build'

}

}

stage('Test') {

steps {

sh 'make test'

}

}

stage('Security Scan') {

steps {

dir('prowler') {

sh './prowler -M json > prowler-results.json'

}

}
```

```
}

stage('Deploy') {

steps {

sh 'make deploy'

}

}

}

post {

always {

archiveArtifacts artifacts: 'prowler/prowler-results.json',
   allowEmptyArchive: true

script {

def results = readFile('prowler/prowler-results.json')

def findings = new groovy.json.JsonSlurper().parseText(results)

if (findings.any { it.Severity == 'High' }) {

currentBuild.result = 'FAILURE'

mail to: 'security-team@example.com',
```

subject: "Build ${env.BUILD_NUMBER}
failed due to high-severity security findings",

body: "Please review the attached Prowler report."

}

}

}

}

}

3. Run the Pipeline:

- Save the pipeline script and trigger a build.
- Monitor the pipeline stages to ensure Prowler scans are executed, and results are archived.

C.2 Setting up Prowler Scans in GitLab CI

C.2.1 Prerequisites

Before starting, ensure you have the following:

- GitLab CI/CD configured.
- AWS CLI configured with necessary permissions.

- Prowler installed in the GitLab runner environment.

C.2.2 Installing Prowler

1. Clone the Prowler repository:

sh

git clone https://github.com/prowler-cloud/prowler.git

cd prowler

2. Install dependencies (if required):

sh

pip install -r requirements.txt

C.2.3 Configuring GitLab CI Pipeline

1. Create a '.gitlab-ci.yml' file in your repository root:

yaml

stages:

- build

- test

- security_scan

- deploy

variables:

AWS_ACCESS_KEY_ID: "your-aws-access-key-id"

AWS_SECRET_ACCESS_KEY: "your-aws-secret-access-key"

AWS_DEFAULT_REGION: "us-west-2"

build:

stage: build

script:

- make build

test:

stage: test

script:

- make test

security_scan:

stage: security_scan

script:

- git clone https://github.com/prowler-cloud/prowler.git

- cd prowler

- ./prowler -M json > prowler-results.json

artifacts:

paths:

- prowler/prowler-results.json

deploy:

stage: deploy

script:

- make deploy

only:

- master

2. **Run the Pipeline:**

- Commit and push the '.gitlab-ci.yml' file to your GitLab repository.
- Monitor the pipeline stages in GitLab CI to ensure Prowler scans are executed, and results are archived.

C.3 Automating Security Checks in the Deployment Process

Automating security checks in the deployment process ensures your application is secure and compliant before it goes live. Here's how to set up automated security checks:

C.3.1 Define Security Policies

Define security policies that need to be enforced during the deployment process. These can include encryption requirements, network configurations, and access controls.

Example: Ensuring all S3 buckets are encrypted.

C.3.2 Implement Policy as Code

Use policy as code tools like Open Policy Agent (OPA) or AWS Config rules to define and enforce security policies.

Example: Using OPA to enforce security policies for Kubernetes deployments.

yaml

apiVersion: policy/v1

kind: PodSecurityPolicy

```yaml
metadata:
  name: restricted
spec:
  privileged: false
  allowPrivilegeEscalation: false
  requiredDropCapabilities:
    - ALL
  volumes:
    - 'configMap'
    - 'emptyDir'
    - 'secret'
  hostNetwork: false
  hostIPC: false
  hostPID: false
  runAsUser:
    rule: 'MustRunAsNonRoot'
```

C.3.3 Automate Security Checks

Integrate security checks into your CI/CD pipeline to automate the enforcement of security policies.

Step-by-Step Guide:

1. Add Security Checks to the Pipeline:

    - Incorporate security checks as stages in your CI/CD pipeline.

Example: Adding security checks in Jenkins.

groovy

pipeline {

agent any

stages {

stage('Checkout') {

steps {

git 'https://github.com/your-repo/your-app.git'

}

}

stage('Build') {

```
steps {

sh 'make build'

}

}

stage('Test') {

steps {

sh 'make test'

}

}

stage('Security Scan') {

steps {

dir('prowler') {

sh './prowler -M json > prowler-results.json'

}

}

}

stage('Policy Check') {
```

```
steps {

  sh 'opa eval —input prowler-results.json —data policy.rego'

}

}

stage('Deploy') {

  steps {

    sh 'make deploy'

  }

}

}

post {

  always {

    archiveArtifacts artifacts: 'prowler/prowler-results.json',
      allowEmptyArchive: true

    script {

      def results = readFile('prowler/prowler-results.json')

      def findings = new groovy.json.JsonSlurper().parseText(results)
```

```
if (findings.any { it.Severity == 'High' }) {

currentBuild.result = 'FAILURE'

mail to: 'security-team@example.com',

subject: "Build ${env.BUILD_NUMBER}
  failed due to high-severity security findings",

body: "Please review the attached Prowler report."

}

}

}

}

}
```

2. Monitor and Review Results:

- Monitor the results of the security checks and review any findings to ensure compliance with security policies.

Example: Using GitLab CI to monitor security check results.

yaml

stages:

- build

- test

- security_scan

- policy_check

- deploy

security_scan:

stage: security_scan

script:

- git clone https://github.com/prowler-cloud/prowler.git

- cd prowler

- ./prowler -M json > prowler-results.json

artifacts:

paths:

- prowler/prowler-results.json

policy_check:

stage: policy_check

script:

- opa eval —input prowler-results.json —data policy.rego

only:

- master

C.4 Conclusion

Integrating Prowler into CI/CD pipelines in Jenkins or GitLab CI helps automate security checks, ensuring your AWS environment maintains a robust security posture throughout the development and deployment processes. Organizations can effectively embed security into their DevOps practices by defining security policies, implementing policy as code, and automating security checks. Continuous monitoring and review of security check results further enhance the security of the deployment process, leading to a more secure and compliant cloud environment. We will explore additional advanced CSPM strategies to enhance cloud security as we move forward.

Chapter 10: Multi-Cloud and Hybrid Environments

A. Managing Security Across Multiple Cloud Providers

Managing security across multiple cloud providers and hybrid environments presents unique challenges and opportunities. This chapter provides a comprehensive guide to implementing effective security strategies in these environments, ensuring consistent security policies, seamless integration, and robust monitoring and response capabilities.

A.1 Understanding Multi-Cloud and Hybrid Environments

A.1.1 Definitions

- **Multi-Cloud Environment:** Utilizes multiple cloud computing services from different providers (e.g., AWS, Azure, Google Cloud) to achieve greater flexibility, avoid vendor lock-in, and leverage the best services from each provider.
- **Hybrid Environment:** This combination of on-premises infrastructure and cloud services allows data and applications to be shared between

them. This approach enables organizations to maintain legacy systems while benefiting from cloud scalability and innovation.

A.1.2 Benefits

- **Resilience and Redundancy:** Distributing workloads across multiple cloud providers enhances resilience and redundancy, reducing the risk of downtime due to provider-specific issues.
- **Optimization and Flexibility:** Leveraging the strengths of different cloud providers allows organizations to optimize performance and cost-efficiency.
- **Avoiding Vendor Lock-In:** Using multiple providers reduces dependency on a single vendor, providing greater flexibility and bargaining power.

A.1.3 Challenges

- **Complexity:** Managing security across multiple platforms introduces configuration, monitoring, and policy enforcement complexity.
- **Consistency:** Ensuring consistent security policies and practices across diverse environments can be challenging.
- **Integration:** Seamlessly integrating security tools and practices across cloud providers and on-premises infrastructure requires careful planning and execution.

A.2 Security Best Practices for Multi-Cloud and Hybrid Environments

A.2.1 Unified Security Strategy

Develop a unified security strategy encompassing all cloud providers and on-premises infrastructure, ensuring consistent policies and practices.

Key Elements:

- **Centralized Policy Management:** Use centralized tools to define and enforce security policies across all environments.
- **Standardized Configuration:** Standardize security configurations to ensure consistency across cloud providers.

Example: Using Terraform to manage infrastructure as code (IaC) across AWS, Azure, and Google Cloud, ensuring consistent configuration and security policies.

A.2.2 Identity and Access Management (IAM)

Implement robust IAM practices to control access to resources across multiple environments.

Key Elements:

- **Single Sign-On (SSO):** Implement SSO to provide a unified authentication mechanism across all cloud providers.
- **Role-Based Access Control (RBAC):** Use RBAC to ensure users have

the minimum necessary permissions to perform their tasks.

Example: Using AWS IAM, Azure Active Directory, and Google Cloud IAM with SSO to manage user access across all environments.

A.2.3 Network Security

Implement network security measures to protect data and applications across multiple cloud providers.

Key Elements:

- **Virtual Private Cloud (VPC):** Use VPCs to isolate resources and control traffic flow within and between cloud environments.
- **Secure Connectivity:** Use VPNs or dedicated connections to connect on-premises infrastructure with cloud environments securely.

Example: Configuring VPCs in AWS, Virtual Networks in Azure, and VPCs in Google Cloud, and using AWS Direct Connect, Azure ExpressRoute, and Google Cloud Interconnect for secure connectivity.

A.2.4 Data Security

Ensure data is protected at rest and in transit across all environments.

Key Elements:

- **Encryption:** Encrypt data at rest and in transit using strong encryption algorithms.

- **Data Classification:** Classify data based on sensitivity and apply appropriate security controls.

Example: Using AWS KMS, Azure Key Vault, and Google Cloud KMS to manage encryption keys and encrypt data across all environments.

A.2.5 Monitoring and Logging

Implement comprehensive monitoring and logging to detect and respond to security incidents across multiple environments.

Key Elements:

- **Centralized Logging:** Aggregate logs from all cloud providers and on-premises infrastructure into a centralized logging system.
- **Continuous Monitoring:** Implement continuous monitoring to detect anomalies and potential security incidents.

Example: A combination of AWS CloudWatch and Google Cloud Monitoring can aggregate Azure Monitor logs into a centralized SIEM solution like Splunk or Elasticsearch.

A.2.6 Compliance and Governance

Ensure compliance with regulatory requirements and enforce governance policies across all environments.

Key Elements:

- **Compliance Automation:** Automated tools continuously monitor and enforce compliance with regulatory standards.
- **Policy as Code:** Implement governance policies as code to ensure consistency and automate enforcement.

Example: Using AWS Config, Azure Policy, and Google Cloud Asset Inventory to automate compliance checks and enforce governance policies.

A.3 Tools for Managing Security in Multi-Cloud and Hybrid Environments

A.3.1 Cloud Security Posture Management (CSPM) Tools

CSPM tools help manage security across multiple cloud providers by continuously monitoring cloud configurations and ensuring compliance with security policies.

Popular CSPM Tools:

- **Palo Alto Networks Prisma Cloud:** Provides comprehensive visibility and control over security and compliance across AWS, Azure, and Google Cloud.
- **Check Point CloudGuard:** Offers multi-cloud security management with automated compliance checks and threat prevention.
- **Aqua Security:** Provides security for containers and cloud-native applications across multiple cloud providers.

A.3.2 Security Information and Event Management (SIEM) Tools

SIEM tools aggregate and analyze logs from multiple sources to detect and respond to security incidents across diverse environments.

Popular SIEM Tools:

- **Splunk:** Offers robust log aggregation, real-time analysis, and automated response capabilities.
- **IBM QRadar:** Provides comprehensive threat detection and incident response across multi-cloud and hybrid environments.
- **Elastic SIEM:** An open-source solution that integrates with the Elastic Stack for centralized logging and monitoring.

A.3.3 Multi-Cloud Management Platforms

Multi-cloud management platforms provide a unified interface for managing resources, security, and compliance across multiple cloud providers.

Popular Platforms:

- **HashiCorp Terraform:** Enables consistent infrastructure as code (IaC) across multiple cloud providers.
- **Red Hat CloudForms:** Provides multi-cloud management with automated provisioning, governance, and policy enforcement.
- **VMware CloudHealth:** Offers cost management, security, and governance capabilities across AWS, Azure, and Google Cloud.

A.4 Implementing a Multi-Cloud Security Strategy

A.4.1 Develop a Security Framework

Develop a comprehensive security framework that outlines policies, procedures, and controls for managing security across multiple cloud providers.

Key Elements:

- **Risk Assessment:** Conduct a risk assessment to identify potential security risks and vulnerabilities in each cloud environment.
- **Security Policies:** Define security policies and standards for all cloud environments.
- **Security Controls:** Implement security controls to mitigate identified risks and enforce security policies.

Example: Developing a security framework based on industry standards such as NIST, ISO 27001, and CIS Benchmarks.

A.4.2 Implement Security Automation

Automate security processes to ensure consistency and reduce the potential for human error.

Key Elements:

- **Automated Provisioning:** Use infrastructure as code (IaC) to automate the provisioning and configuration of resources.
- **Automated Compliance Checks:** Implement automated compliance

checks to monitor and enforce security policies continuously.

Example: Using Terraform and AWS Config to automate the provisioning of compliant AWS resources.

A.4.3 Foster a Security-First Culture

Promote a security-first culture within the organization by providing training, resources, and support for security best practices.

Key Elements:

- **Training and Awareness:** Provide employees with regular training and awareness programs to promote security best practices.
- **Collaboration:** Foster collaboration between development, operations, and security teams to ensure security is integrated into all aspects of the organization.

Example: Conducting regular security workshops and hackathons to engage employees and promote a security-first mindset.

A.4.4 Continuous Improvement

Continuously review and improve security practices to adapt to threats and changing environments.

Key Elements:

- **Regular Audits:** Conduct regular security audits to identify gaps and

areas for improvement.
- **Incident Reviews:** Review security incidents to identify root causes and implement measures to prevent recurrence.

Example: Conducting quarterly security audits and post-incident reviews to improve the organization's security posture continuously.

A.5 Conclusion

Managing security across multiple cloud providers and hybrid environments requires a comprehensive, unified approach that ensures consistent security policies, seamless integration, and robust monitoring and response capabilities. Organizations can effectively secure their multi-cloud and hybrid environments by implementing best practices for identity and access management, network security, data security, and compliance. Leveraging CSPM, SIEM, and multi-cloud management tools further enhances the organization's ability to manage security across diverse environments. Continuous improvement and fostering a security-first culture are essential for maintaining a strong security posture in the face of evolving threats. We will explore additional advanced CSPM strategies to enhance cloud security as we move forward.

B. CSPM Strategies for Hybrid Cloud Setups

Managing security in hybrid cloud setups, which combine on-premises infrastructure with cloud services, presents unique challenges and opportunities. Cloud Security Posture Management (CSPM) strategies must be adapted to ensure comprehensive security across both environments. This chapter provides a detailed guide on implementing effective CSPM strategies for hybrid cloud setups, ensuring consistent security policies, seamless integration, and robust monitoring and response capabilities.

B.1 Understanding Hybrid Cloud Setups

B.1.1 Definition

A hybrid cloud setup combines on-premises infrastructure with public and/or private cloud services. This allows data and applications to be shared between on-premises systems and cloud environments, providing flexibility, scalability, and cost efficiency.

B.1.2 Benefits

- **Flexibility:** Hybrid clouds offer flexibility in choosing the optimal deployment environment for different workloads.
- **Scalability:** Organizations can scale resources on-demand using cloud services while maintaining control over critical data and applications on-premises.
- **Cost Efficiency:** Hybrid setups enable cost optimization by leveraging cloud resources for fluctuating workloads while using on-premises infrastructure for steady-state operations.

B.1.3 Challenges

- **Complexity:** Managing security across on-premises and cloud environments introduces complexity of configuration, monitoring, and policy enforcement.
- **Consistency:** Ensuring consistent security policies and practices across diverse environments can be challenging.
- **Integration:** Seamlessly integrating security tools and practices across different environments requires careful planning and execution.

B.2 Key CSPM Strategies for Hybrid Cloud Setups

B.2.1 Unified Security Policy Management

To ensure consistency, develop unified security policies that apply across both on-premises and cloud environments.

Key Elements:

- **Centralized Policy Repository:** Maintain a centralized repository of security policies that apply to all environments.
- **Standardized Policies:** Standardize security policies to ensure they can be uniformly enforced across on-premises and cloud setups.

Example: Using a centralized configuration management tool like Ansible or Puppet to apply consistent security policies across on-premises servers and cloud instances.

B.2.2 Integrated Identity and Access Management (IAM)

Implement integrated IAM solutions to manage access control across on-premises and cloud environments.

Key Elements:

- **Single Sign-On (SSO):** SSO solutions provide unified authentication and authorization across all environments.
- **Federated Identity Management:** Implement federated identity management to extend on-premises IAM to cloud services.

Example: Using Microsoft Azure Active Directory to provide SSO and federated identity management across on-premises applications and Azure services.

B.2.3 Secure Connectivity

Establish secure connectivity between on-premises infrastructure and cloud environments to protect data in transit.

Key Elements:

- **Virtual Private Networks (VPNs):** Use VPNs to create secure tunnels between on-premises and cloud environments.
- **Direct Connections:** Use dedicated connections like AWS Direct Connect or Azure ExpressRoute for secure and reliable connectivity.

Example: Configuring a VPN to securely connect an on-premises data center with an AWS VPC, ensuring encrypted communication between environments.

B.2.4 Consistent Configuration Management

Use configuration management tools to ensure consistent security configurations across all environments.

Key Elements:

- **Infrastructure as Code (IaC):** Use IaC tools to manage and automate the provisioning and configuration of infrastructure.
- **Automated Compliance Checks:** Implement automated compliance checks to ensure configurations adhere to security policies.

Example: Using Terraform to manage infrastructure configurations and enforce security policies across on-premises servers and cloud instances.

B.2.5 Comprehensive Monitoring and Logging

Implement comprehensive monitoring and logging to detect and respond to security incidents across hybrid environments.

Key Elements:

- **Centralized Logging:** Aggregate logs from on-premises and cloud environments into a centralized logging system.
- **Continuous Monitoring:** Implement continuous monitoring to detect anomalies and potential security incidents.

Example: A SIEM solution like Splunk aggregates and analyzes logs from on-premises servers and cloud services, providing a unified view of security events.

B.2.6 Data Security and Encryption

Ensure data security and encryption practices are consistent across all environments to protect data at rest and in transit.

Key Elements:

- **Encryption:** Encrypt data at rest and in transit using strong encryption algorithms.
- **Data Classification and Segmentation:** Classify data based on sensitivity and implement appropriate security controls.

Example: Using AWS KMS and on-premises HSMs to manage encryption keys and encrypt data across both environments.

B.3 Implementing CSPM in Hybrid Cloud Setups

B.3.1 Risk Assessment and Management

Conduct regular risk assessments to identify and manage security risks across hybrid environments.

Key Elements:

- **Threat Modeling:** Perform threat modeling to identify potential security threats and vulnerabilities.
- **Risk Mitigation:** Implement risk mitigation strategies to address identified risks.

Example: Using a risk assessment framework like NIST to identify and mitigate security risks in a hybrid cloud setup.

B.3.2 Policy as Code

Implement policy as code to enforce security and compliance policies across all environments programmatically.

Key Elements:

- **Define Policies:** Write security and compliance policies as code using tools like Open Policy Agent (OPA) or HashiCorp Sentinel.
- **Enforce Policies:** Use automated tools to enforce policies across both on-premises and cloud environments.

Example: Using OPA to define and enforce Kubernetes security policies across on-premises and cloud-based Kubernetes clusters.

B.3.3 Security Automation

Automate security processes to ensure consistency and reduce the potential for human error.

Key Elements:

- **Automated Provisioning:** IaC tools are used to automate the provisioning and configuration of secure infrastructure.
- **Automated Compliance Checks:** Implement automated compliance checks to monitor and enforce security policies continuously.

Example: Using Chef or Ansible to automate the provisioning and configuration of secure environments across both on-premises and cloud infrastructure.

B.3.4 Incident Response Planning

Develop and implement incident response plans that encompass both on-premises and cloud environments.

Key Elements:

- **Unified Incident Response Team:** Establish a unified incident response team with expertise in both on-premises and cloud security.
- **Integrated Response Procedures:** Develop integrated response procedures that address incidents across all environments.

Example: Creating a comprehensive incident response playbook that includes procedures for responding to security incidents in both on-premises data centers and cloud environments.

B.3.5 Continuous Improvement

Continuously review and improve security practices to adapt to evolving threats and changes in the hybrid environment.

Key Elements:

- **Regular Audits:** Conduct regular security audits to identify gaps and areas for improvement.
- **Post-Incident Reviews:** Review security incidents to identify root causes and implement measures to prevent recurrence.

Example: Conducting quarterly security audits and post-incident reviews to improve the organization's security posture continuously.

B.4 Tools for CSPM in Hybrid Cloud Setups

B.4.1 Cloud Security Posture Management (CSPM) Tools

CSPM tools help manage security across hybrid environments by continuously monitoring configurations and ensuring compliance with security policies.

Popular CSPM Tools:

- **Prisma Cloud:** Provides comprehensive visibility and control over security and compliance across on-premises and cloud environments.
- **Dome9 Arc:** Offers multi-cloud security management with automated compliance checks and threat prevention.
- **Aqua Security:** Provides security for containers and cloud-native applications across hybrid environments.

B.4.2 Security Information and Event Management (SIEM) Tools

SIEM tools aggregate and analyze logs from multiple sources to detect and respond to security incidents across hybrid environments.

Popular SIEM Tools:

- **Splunk:** Offers robust log aggregation, real-time analysis, and automated response capabilities.
- **IBM QRadar:** Provides comprehensive threat detection and incident response across hybrid environments.
- **Elastic SIEM:** An open-source solution that integrates with the Elastic Stack for centralized logging and monitoring.

B.4.3 Configuration Management Tools

Configuration management tools help ensure consistent security configurations across hybrid environments.

Popular Tools:

- **Terraform:** Enables consistent infrastructure as code (IaC) across on-premises and cloud environments.
- **Ansible:** Provides automated configuration management and compliance enforcement across hybrid environments.
- **Puppet:** Automates the provisioning and configuration of secure infrastructure across both on-premises and cloud environments.

B.5 Case Study: Implementing CSPM in a Hybrid Cloud Setup

Scenario: A financial services company with on-premises data centers and cloud services in AWS and Azure seeks to implement CSPM to ensure consistent security and compliance across all environments.

B.5.1 Develop a Unified Security Policy

The company develops a unified security policy that applies to both on-premises and cloud environments, ensuring consistent security practices.

B.5.2 Integrate IAM Solutions

The company implements Azure Active Directory to provide SSO and federated identity management across on-premises applications and cloud services in AWS and Azure.

B.5.3 Establish Secure Connectivity

The company configures VPNs to securely connect its on-premises data centers with AWS and Azure, ensuring encrypted communication between environments.

B.5.4 Implement Consistent Configuration Management

The company uses Terraform to manage infrastructure configurations and enforce security policies across both on-premises servers and cloud instances in AWS and Azure.

B.5.5 Deploy Comprehensive Monitoring and Logging

The company implements Splunk to aggregate and analyze logs from on-premises servers and cloud services, providing a unified view of security events.

B.5.6 Conduct Regular Risk Assessments

The company performs regular risk assessments using the NIST framework to identify and mitigate security risks across its hybrid environment.

B.5.7 Automate Security Processes

The company uses Ansible to automate the provisioning and configuration of secure environments across both on-premises and cloud infrastructure.

B.5.8 Develop an Integrated Incident Response Plan

The company creates a comprehensive incident response playbook that includes procedures for responding to security incidents in both on-premises data centers and cloud environments.

B.5.9 Continuously Improve Security Practices

The company conducts quarterly security audits and post-incident reviews to improve its security posture and adapt to evolving threats continuously.

B.6 Conclusion

Implementing effective CSPM strategies for hybrid cloud setups ensures comprehensive security across both on-premises and cloud environments. Organizations can maintain consistent security practices by developing unified security policies, integrating IAM solutions, establishing secure connectivity, and using configuration management tools. Leveraging CSPM and SIEM tools, automating security processes, and fostering a culture of continuous improvement further enhance the organization's ability to manage security in hybrid environments. We will explore additional advanced CSPM strategies to enhance cloud security as we move forward.

Chapter 11: Compliance and Regulatory Considerations

A. Understanding Industry-Specific Regulations

Compliance with industry-specific regulations ensures that cloud environments meet legal and security standards. This chapter provides a comprehensive guide to understanding and navigating various industry-specific regulations and outlines strategies for integrating compliance into Cloud Security Posture Management (CSPM) practices.

A.1 Overview of Industry-Specific Regulations

A.1.1 Importance of Compliance

Compliance with industry-specific regulations helps organizations avoid legal penalties, maintain customer trust, and protect sensitive data. It also ensures that security practices are aligned with industry standards, reducing the risk of data breaches and other security incidents.

A.1.2 Common Industry-Specific Regulations

Different industries are subject to regulations dictating specific security and privacy requirements. Below are some of the most common industry-specific regulations:

- **Healthcare:** Health Insurance Portability and Accountability Act (HIPAA)
- **Financial Services:** Payment Card Industry Data Security Standard (PCI DSS), Gramm-Leach-Bliley Act (GLBA)
- **Retail:** PCI DSS
- **Government:** Federal Risk and Authorization Management Program (FedRAMP), National Institute of Standards and Technology (NIST) frameworks
- **Education:** Family Educational Rights and Privacy Act (FERPA)

A.2 Key Industry-Specific Regulations

A.2.1 Health Insurance Portability and Accountability Act (HIPAA)

Overview:

HIPAA sets the standard for protecting sensitive patient data in the healthcare industry. Organizations that handle protected health information (PHI) must implement physical, network, and process security measures to ensure HIPAA compliance.

Key Requirements:

- **Privacy Rule:** Protects individuals' medical records and other personal health information.
- **Security Rule:** Sets standards for electronic PHI (ePHI) protection.
- **Breach Notification Rule:** This rule requires covered entities to notify affected individuals, the Secretary of Health and Human Services (HHS), and the media of a breach of unsecured PHI.

CSPM Strategies:

- **Data Encryption:** Encrypt ePHI at rest and in transit to protect data integrity and confidentiality.
- **Access Controls:** Implement strict access controls to ensure only authorized personnel can access ePHI.
- **Audit Trails:** Maintain detailed audit trails to track access to ePHI and detect potential security incidents.

A.2.2 Payment Card Industry Data Security Standard (PCI DSS)

Overview:

PCI DSS is a set of security standards to ensure that all companies that accept, process, store, or transmit credit card information maintain a secure environment.

Key Requirements:

- **Build and Maintain a Secure Network:** Install and maintain a firewall configuration to protect cardholder data.
- **Protect Cardholder Data:** Encrypt the transmission of cardholder data across open and public networks.

- **Maintain a Vulnerability Management Program:** Use and regularly update anti-virus software or programs.
- **Implement Strong Access Control Measures:** Restrict access to cardholder data by business need to know.
- **Regularly Monitor and Test Networks:** Track and monitor all access to network resources and cardholder data.

CSPM Strategies:

- **Network Segmentation:** To reduce the scope of PCI DSS compliance, segment the cardholder data environment (CDE) from the rest of the network.
- **Regular Scans and Assessments:** Conduct regular vulnerability scans and security assessments to identify and address security issues.
- **Access Management:** Implement robust access control measures, including multi-factor authentication (MFA) and least privilege access.

A.2.3 Federal Risk and Authorization Management Program (FedRAMP)

Overview:

FedRAMP provides a standardized approach to security assessment, authorization, and continuous monitoring for cloud products and services used by federal agencies.

Key Requirements:

- **Security Assessment:** Conduct a comprehensive security assessment of cloud service offerings.

- **Authorization:** Obtain authorization from the Joint Authorization Board (JAB) or an agency to operate cloud services.
- **Continuous Monitoring:** Implement continuous monitoring to ensure ongoing compliance with FedRAMP security requirements.

CSPM Strategies:

- **Security Documentation:** Maintain detailed security documentation, including system security plans (SSPs) and security assessment reports (SARs).
- **Automated Monitoring:** Automated tools monitor security controls and detect compliance issues continuously.
- **Incident Response:** Develop and test incident response plans to address security incidents and breaches quickly.

A.2.4 General Data Protection Regulation (GDPR)

Overview:

GDPR is a European Union (EU) regulation that addresses data protection and privacy for individuals within the EU and the European Economic Area (EEA) and the transfer of personal data outside these areas.

Key Requirements:

- **Data Protection by Design and Default:** Implement data protection measures from the design phase of projects.
- **Consent Management:** Obtain explicit consent from individuals before processing their personal data.
- **Data Subject Rights:** Respect data subject rights, including the right to

access, rectify, and delete personal data.
- **Breach Notification:** Notify the relevant supervisory authority and affected individuals in the event of a data breach.

CSPM Strategies:

- **Data Inventory and Mapping:** Maintain a detailed inventory of personal data and map data flows to ensure GDPR compliance.
- **Privacy Impact Assessments:** Conduct privacy impact assessments (PIAs) to identify and mitigate privacy risks.
- **Data Minimization and Anonymization:** Implement data minimization and anonymization techniques to reduce the risk of data breaches.

A.3 Integrating Compliance into CSPM Practices

A.3.1 Automating Compliance Checks

Automated tools are used to monitor and enforce compliance with regulations industry-specific continuously.

Key Elements:

- **Automated Scanning:** Implement automated scanning tools to identify compliance issues and security vulnerabilities.
- **Policy Enforcement:** Use policy as code to enforce compliance policies programmatically across cloud environments.

Example: Using AWS Config and AWS Security Hub to automate compliance checks and enforce HIPAA and PCI DSS security policies.

A.3.2 Continuous Monitoring and Reporting

Implement continuous monitoring and reporting to ensure ongoing compliance with regulatory requirements.

Key Elements:

- **Real-Time Monitoring:** Use real-time monitoring tools to detect and respond to compliance issues as they arise.
- **Regular Reporting:** Generate regular compliance reports to demonstrate adherence to regulatory standards.

Example: Azure Policy and Azure Security Center are used to monitor compliance with GDPR continuously and generate compliance reports for audits.

A.3.3 Training and Awareness

Provide regular training and awareness programs to ensure employees understand their roles and responsibilities in maintaining compliance.

Key Elements:

- **Compliance Training:** Offer training sessions on industry-specific regulations and compliance requirements.
- **Awareness Campaigns:** Conduct awareness campaigns to promote a culture of compliance within the organization.

Example: Providing annual HIPAA compliance training for healthcare employees and conducting regular phishing awareness campaigns.

A.3.4 Incident Response and Breach Notification

Develop and implement incident response plans that include breach notification procedures to ensure compliance with regulatory requirements.

Key Elements:

- **Incident Response Plan:** Develop a comprehensive incident response plan that outlines procedures for detecting, responding to, and recovering from security incidents.
- **Breach Notification:** Establish breach notification procedures to ensure timely communication with regulatory authorities and affected individuals.

Example: Creating a GDPR-compliant incident response plan that includes steps for notifying the relevant supervisory authority and affected individuals within 72 hours of a data breach.

A.4 Tools for Managing Compliance

A.4.1 Compliance Management Platforms

Compliance management platforms help organizations manage and automate compliance with industry-specific regulations.

Popular Tools:

- **OneTrust:** Provides tools for managing privacy, security, and third-party risk, helping organizations comply with GDPR, CCPA, and other

regulations.
- **TrustArc:** Offers compliance management solutions for GDPR, HIPAA, and other regulations, including assessments, monitoring, and reporting.
- **MetricStream:** Provides integrated risk management and compliance solutions for various industries, including financial services, healthcare, and manufacturing.

A.4.2 Cloud Provider Compliance Tools

Cloud providers offer built-in tools and services to help organizations achieve and maintain compliance with industry-specific regulations.

AWS:

- **AWS Config:** Tracks AWS resource configurations and compliance with internal policies and best practices.
- **AWS Security Hub:** Provides a comprehensive view of security alerts and compliance status across AWS accounts.

Azure:

- **Azure Policy:** Enforces organizational standards and assesses compliance at scale.
- **Azure Security Center:** Strengthens security posture and provides advanced threat protection across hybrid workloads.

Google Cloud:

- **Google Cloud Security Command Center (SCC):** Provides visibility into

security and compliance across Google Cloud assets.
- **Forseti Security:** An open-source security toolkit for Google Cloud Platform (GCP) that helps with compliance monitoring and enforcement.

A.5 Case Study: Achieving HIPAA Compliance in a Hybrid Cloud Environment

Scenario: A healthcare organization seeks HIPAA compliance using a hybrid cloud environment with on-premises servers and AWS cloud services.

A.5.1 Implement Data Encryption

The organization encrypts all ePHI at rest and in transit using AWS KMS for cloud data and on-premises HSMs for local data.

A.5.2 Enforce Access Controls

The organization implements strict access controls using AWS IAM and on-premises Active Directory to ensure that only authorized personnel can access ePHI.

A.5.3 Maintain Audit Trails

The organization uses AWS CloudTrail and on-premises logging tools to maintain detailed audit trails of all access to ePHI and detect potential security incidents.

A.5.4 Conduct Regular Risk Assessments

The organization performs regular risk assessments using the NIST framework to identify and mitigate security risks in both on-premises and cloud environments.

A.5.5 Automate Compliance Monitoring

The organization uses AWS Config and AWS Security Hub to automate compliance checks and continuously monitor adherence to HIPAA requirements.

A.5.6 Provide Employee Training

To promote a culture of compliance, the organization conducts annual HIPAA compliance training for all employees and regular security awareness campaigns.

CHAPTER 11: COMPLIANCE AND REGULATORY CONSIDERATIONS

A.6 Conclusion

Understanding and adhering to industry-specific regulations is essential for ensuring the security and compliance of cloud environments. Organizations can achieve and maintain compliance with regulatory requirements by implementing unified security policies, automating compliance checks, and leveraging compliance management tools. Continuous monitoring, training, and incident response planning enhance the organization's ability to manage compliance in cloud environments. We will explore additional advanced CSPM strategies to enhance cloud security as we move forward.

B. Using CSPM for Compliance Management

Cloud Security Posture Management (CSPM) tools ensure compliance with industry regulations and standards. They provide automated and continuous monitoring, assessment, and remediation capabilities that help organizations maintain compliance across diverse cloud environments. This chapter explores leveraging CSPM for compliance management, detailing strategies, tools, and best practices.

B.1 Importance of Compliance Management

B.1.1 Legal and Regulatory Requirements

Compliance with legal and regulatory requirements is essential to avoid fines, penalties, and legal action. Regulations such as GDPR, HIPAA, PCI DSS, and others mandate specific security measures and practices.

Example: GDPR requires organizations to implement appropriate technical and organizational measures to protect personal data, including encryption and access controls.

B.1.2 Protecting Sensitive Data

Compliance management helps protect sensitive data from breaches and unauthorized access, maintaining customer trust and safeguarding organizational reputation.

Example: HIPAA mandates the protection of electronic protected health information (ePHI) through administrative, physical, and technical safeguards.

B.1.3 Ensuring Business Continuity

Effective compliance management ensures business continuity by mitigating risks and preventing disruptions caused by non-compliance incidents.

Example: PCI DSS compliance helps prevent credit card fraud and data breaches, ensuring that businesses can continue to process payments securely.

B.2 Leveraging CSPM for Compliance Management

B.2.1 Continuous Monitoring and Assessment

CSPM tools provide continuous monitoring and assessment of cloud environments to ensure compliance with regulatory requirements.

Key Elements:

- **Real-Time Monitoring:** Continuously monitor cloud resources and configurations for compliance violations.
- **Automated Assessments:** Conduct automated assessments against regulatory benchmarks and standards.

Example: Using AWS Config to continuously monitor AWS resources for compliance with HIPAA requirements and automatically assess resource configurations.

B.2.2 Automated Remediation

CSPM tools can automatically remediate compliance issues by applying predefined policies and configurations.

Key Elements:

- **Policy Enforcement:** Enforce compliance policies automatically through predefined rules and configurations.
- **Self-Healing Systems:** Implement self-healing mechanisms that automatically correct non-compliant configurations.

Example: Using Azure Policy to automatically enforce encryption on all storage accounts and remediate any non-compliant resources.

B.2.3 Compliance Reporting

CSPM tools provide detailed compliance reports that help demonstrate adherence to regulatory requirements during audits and assessments.

Key Elements:

- **Audit Trails:** Maintain comprehensive audit trails of all compliance-related activities.
- **Compliance Dashboards:** Use dashboards to visualize compliance status and identify areas for improvement.

Example: Using Google Cloud Security Command Center (SCC) to generate compliance reports detailing data access and protection measures for GDPR.

B.2.4 Integration with DevOps

Integrate CSPM into DevOps processes to ensure compliance checks are performed throughout the software development lifecycle.

Key Elements:

- **CI/CD Integration:** Incorporate compliance checks into CI/CD pipelines to identify and remediate issues early.
- **Shift-Left Security:** Shift compliance checks to the left by integrating them into the development phase.

Example: Integrating Checkov into a Jenkins pipeline to scan Terraform templates for compliance with PCI DSS before deployment.

B.3 Implementing CSPM for Compliance Management

B.3.1 Selecting the Right CSPM Tool

Choose a CSPM tool that aligns with your organization's compliance requirements and cloud environment.

Key Criteria:

- **Regulatory Coverage:** Ensure the tool covers relevant regulations and standards.
- **Integration Capabilities:** Verify that the tool integrates with your existing cloud infrastructure and DevOps tools.
- **Automated Remediation:** Look for tools that offer automated remediation capabilities.

Popular CSPM Tools:

- **Prisma Cloud:** Provides comprehensive compliance management across multi-cloud environments.
- **AWS Security Hub:** Offers integrated security and compliance monitoring for AWS resources.
- **Azure Security Center:** Provides continuous assessment and compliance management for Azure environments.

B.3.2 Defining Compliance Policies

Define compliance policies that align with regulatory requirements and best practices.

Key Elements:

- **Regulatory Requirements:** Identify specific regulatory requirements relevant to your industry.
- **Internal Policies:** Develop internal policies that complement regulatory requirements and address organizational needs.
- **Policy Documentation:** Document policies clearly and ensure they are accessible to relevant stakeholders.

Example: Defining a policy for data encryption at rest and in transit to comply with GDPR and internal data protection standards.

B.3.3 Configuring CSPM Tools

Configure CSPM tools to enforce compliance policies and monitor cloud environments continuously.

Key Steps:

- **Policy Configuration:** Configure CSPM tools with your defined compliance policies.
- **Automated Checks:** Set up automated checks to continuously monitor and assess compliance.
- **Remediation Rules:** Define remediation rules to address non-compliant configurations automatically.

Example: Configuring AWS Config rules to monitor and enforce compliance with PCI DSS requirements for AWS resources.

B.3.4 Training and Awareness

Provide training and awareness programs to ensure that employees understand compliance requirements and how to use CSPM tools effectively.

Key Elements:

- **Compliance Training:** Offer regular training sessions on relevant regulations and compliance policies.
- **Tool Training:** Provide hands-on training for using CSPM tools and interpreting compliance reports.
- **Awareness Campaigns:** Conduct awareness campaigns to promote a culture of compliance within the organization.

Example: Conducting annual GDPR training for all employees and providing specific training on using Azure Security Center for compliance monitoring.

B.3.5 Continuous Improvement

Regularly review and update compliance policies and CSPM configurations to adapt to evolving regulations and organizational needs.

Key Elements:

- **Regular Audits:** Conduct regular audits to assess compliance and

identify areas for improvement.
- **Feedback Loops:** Establish feedback loops to refine and enhance compliance management practices continuously.
- **Regulatory Updates:** Stay informed about regulatory changes and update compliance policies and CSPM configurations accordingly.

Example: Conduct quarterly compliance audits and update CSPM tool configurations to reflect changes in HIPAA requirements.

B.4 Case Study: Using CSPM for PCI DSS Compliance

Scenario: A retail organization uses CSPM tools to achieve and maintain PCI DSS compliance for its multi-cloud environment.

B.4.1 Selecting a CSPM Tool

The organization selects Prisma Cloud for its comprehensive multi-cloud compliance management capabilities.

B.4.2 Defining Compliance Policies

The organization defines PCI DSS compliance policies, including requirements for network security, encryption, access controls, and monitoring.

B.4.3 Configuring Prisma Cloud

The organization configures Prisma Cloud to enforce PCI DSS policies, setting up automated checks and remediation rules for:

- **Firewall Configuration:** Ensuring proper firewall rules are in place to protect cardholder data.
- **Encryption:** Enforcing encryption for cardholder data at rest and in transit.
- **Access Controls:** Implementing strict access controls based on business need-to-know.

B.4.4 Training and Awareness

The organization provides PCI DSS compliance training for employees and specific training on using Prisma Cloud for compliance monitoring and reporting.

B.4.5 Continuous Improvement

The organization conducts regular PCI DSS audits, reviews Prisma Cloud compliance reports, and updates policies and configurations as needed.

Outcome: The organization successfully achieves and maintains PCI DSS compliance, ensuring cardholder data security across its multi-cloud environment.

B.5 Conclusion

Using CSPM for compliance management gives organizations the tools and capabilities to ensure continuous compliance with industry-specific regulations. Organizations can maintain a robust security posture and avoid regulatory penalties by leveraging CSPM for continuous monitoring, automated remediation, and compliance reporting. Integrating CSPM into DevOps processes, providing training and awareness, and continuously improving compliance practices further enhance the organization's ability to manage compliance effectively. We will explore additional advanced CSPM strategies to enhance cloud security as we move forward.

C. Generating Compliance Reports

Generating compliance reports ensures that your cloud environment adheres to regulatory requirements and internal security policies. These reports provide critical insights into the compliance status of your cloud resources, help identify non-compliant configurations, and offer documented evidence of compliance during audits. This section explores generating compliance reports using Cloud Security Posture Management (CSPM) tools and best practices for creating effective reports.

C.1 Importance of Compliance Reports

C.1.1 Demonstrating Compliance

Compliance reports are essential for demonstrating adherence to regulatory requirements and industry standards. They provide documented evidence of your organization's compliance posture, which is crucial during audits and assessments.

Example: Generating a HIPAA compliance report to show that all electronic Protected Health Information (ePHI) is encrypted and access is controlled.

C.1.2 Identifying Non-Compliance

Compliance reports help identify areas where your cloud environment does not meet regulatory requirements or internal policies. This allows for timely remediation of non-compliant configurations.

Example: Using a PCI DSS compliance report to identify unencrypted storage volumes and take corrective action.

C.1.3 Enhancing Security Posture

Regularly generating and reviewing compliance reports enhances your overall security posture by ensuring continuous monitoring and remediation of compliance issues.

Example: Generating monthly compliance reports to track and address security vulnerabilities and misconfigurations.

C.2 Using CSPM Tools to Generate Compliance Reports

C.2.1 Selecting a CSPM Tool

Choose a CSPM tool that supports the generation of compliance reports for your specific regulatory requirements and cloud environment.

Popular CSPM Tools:

- **AWS Security Hub:** Aggregates security findings and compliance checks for AWS environments.
- **Azure Security Center:** Provides continuous assessment and compliance reporting for Azure resources.
- **Google Cloud Security Command Center (SCC):** Offers security and compliance insights for Google Cloud resources.
- **Prisma Cloud:** Supports multi-cloud environments and provides comprehensive compliance reporting capabilities.

C.2.2 Configuring CSPM Tools for Compliance Reporting

Configure your CSPM tool to monitor your cloud environment and generate compliance reports continuously.

Key Steps:

1. **Define Compliance Policies:** Configure the CSPM tool with relevant compliance policies and standards (e.g., HIPAA, PCI DSS, GDPR).
2. **Set Up Continuous Monitoring:** Enable continuous monitoring to

assess resource configurations against defined policies automatically.

3. **Schedule Report Generation:** Schedule regular compliance report generation (e.g., daily, weekly, monthly) to ensure continuous visibility.

Example: Configuring AWS Security Hub to generate daily compliance reports for PCI DSS.

sh

aws securityhub enable-security-hub
  —enable-default-standards

aws securityhub create-insight
  —name "PCI DSS Compliance"
  —filters '{...}'
  —group-by-attribute "ResourceType"

C.2.3 Generating Compliance Reports

Generate compliance reports using your CSPM tool's reporting capabilities.

Example: Generating a compliance report in Azure Security Center.

1. **Navigate to Security Center:** Go to the Azure Security Center dashboard.
2. **Select Regulatory Compliance:** Click on the "Regulatory compliance" tab.
3. **Generate Report:** Select the desired compliance standard (e.g., PCI DSS) and generate the compliance report.

```sh
az security regulatory-compliance-assessment list
  --subscription
```

C.3 Best Practices for Generating Effective Compliance Reports

C.3.1 Define Clear Objectives

Clearly define the objectives of your compliance reports to ensure they meet the needs of stakeholders and regulatory requirements.

Key Elements:

- **Regulatory Requirements:** Identify the specific regulatory requirements that the report needs to address.
- **Stakeholder Needs:** Understand the needs of stakeholders, such as auditors, compliance officers, and executive management.

Example: Defining the objective of a PCI DSS compliance report to demonstrate encryption of cardholder data and access control measures.

C.3.2 Ensure Comprehensive Coverage

Ensure your compliance reports comprehensively cover all relevant resources and configurations in your cloud environment.

Key Elements:

- **Resource Inventory:** Maintain an up-to-date inventory of all cloud resources.
- **Policy Scope:** Define the scope of compliance policies to include all relevant resources and configurations.

Example: Including all storage accounts, databases, and virtual machines in a HIPAA compliance report to ensure comprehensive coverage of ePHI.

C.3.3 Use Standardized Formats

Use standardized formats for compliance reports to ensure consistency and facilitate easy interpretation by stakeholders.

Key Elements:

- **Report Templates:** Use predefined report templates that adhere to industry standards and best practices.
- **Consistent Structure:** Ensure that all reports follow a consistent structure, including sections for summary, findings, and recommendations.

Example: Using standardized PCI DSS report templates that include sections for firewall configurations, encryption status, and access controls.

C.3.4 Automate Report Generation

Automate the generation of compliance reports to ensure regular and timely reporting, reduce manual effort, and minimize errors.

Key Elements:

- **Scheduled Reports:** To maintain continuous visibility, schedule regular report generation (e.g., daily, weekly, monthly).
- **Automated Tools:** CSPM tools are used to automate report generation and distribution.

Example: Scheduling monthly GDPR compliance reports in Google Cloud SCC to ensure ongoing visibility into data protection measures.

C.3.5 Review and Validate Reports

Regularly review and validate compliance reports to ensure accuracy and address discrepancies or gaps.

Key Elements:

- **Review Process:** Establish a review process that involves key stakeholders, such as compliance officers and security analysts.
- **Validation Checks:** Perform validation checks to verify the accuracy and completeness of report data.

Example: Conducting quarterly reviews of HIPAA compliance reports with the organization's compliance team to ensure all ePHI is adequately protected.

C.4 Tools and Techniques for Effective Compliance Reporting

C.4.1 CSPM Tool Integration

Integrate CSPM tools with other security and compliance tools to enhance reporting capabilities and provide a comprehensive view of compliance status.

Example: Integrating AWS Security Hub with AWS Config and AWS CloudTrail to provide a unified view of compliance status and audit trails.

C.4.2 Custom Reporting Dashboards

Use custom reporting dashboards to visualize compliance data and provide actionable insights for stakeholders.

Example: Creating custom dashboards in Azure Security Center to visualize compliance status for various regulatory standards, such as PCI DSS and HIPAA.

C.4.3 Report Customization

Customize compliance reports to meet specific regulatory requirements and stakeholder needs, including tailored findings and recommendations.

Example: Customizing GDPR compliance reports in Prisma Cloud to include specific data protection measures and recommendations for improvement.

C.5 Case Study: Generating GDPR Compliance Reports with Google Cloud SCC

Scenario: A European retail company must generate GDPR compliance reports for its Google Cloud environment.

C.5.1 Configure Google Cloud SCC

The company continuously configures Google Cloud SCC to monitor its cloud resources for GDPR compliance.

1. **Enable SCC:** Enable Google Cloud SCC in the organization's Google Cloud environment.
2. **Define GDPR Policies:** Configure SCC with GDPR compliance policies to monitor data protection measures.

C.5.2 Schedule Regular Report Generation

The company schedules regular GDPR compliance report generation to ensure continuous visibility and adherence to regulatory requirements.

1. **Set Up Scheduled Reports:** Schedule monthly GDPR compliance reports in Google Cloud SCC.
2. **Automate Distribution:** Automate the distribution of reports to key stakeholders, including compliance officers and data protection officers.

CHAPTER 11: COMPLIANCE AND REGULATORY CONSIDERATIONS

C.5.3 Review and Validate Reports

The company establishes a review process to validate the accuracy and completeness of GDPR compliance reports.

1. **Conduct Quarterly Reviews:** Conduct quarterly reviews of GDPR compliance reports with the compliance team.
2. **Perform Validation Checks:** Perform validation checks to verify the accuracy of report data and address any discrepancies.

Outcome: The company successfully generates and reviews GDPR compliance reports, ensuring continuous adherence to data protection regulations and enhancing its overall security posture.

C.6 Conclusion

Generating compliance reports is critical for maintaining adherence to regulatory requirements and internal security policies. Organizations can ensure a robust compliance posture by leveraging CSPM tools for continuous monitoring, automated reporting, and compliance assessment. Implementing best practices for report generation, including defining clear objectives, ensuring comprehensive coverage, and automating report generation, further enhances the effectiveness of compliance management. Regularly reviewing and validating reports, integrating CSPM tools with other security solutions, and using custom reporting dashboards provide actionable insights for maintaining continuous compliance. We will explore additional advanced CSPM strategies to enhance cloud security as we move forward.

D. Hands-On Exercise: Compliance Reporting with Prowler

Prowler is an open-source tool designed to perform AWS security best practices assessments and compliance audits. This hands-on exercise will guide you through configuring compliance-specific checks using Prowler, generating compliance reports, and interpreting the results to ensure your AWS environment meets regulatory requirements.

D.1 Configuring Compliance-Specific Checks

D.1.1 Installing Prowler

Before configuring compliance-specific checks, you need to install Prowler on your system.

Steps to Install Prowler:

1. Clone the Prowler Repository:

sh

git clone https://github.com/prowler-cloud/prowler.git

cd prowler

2. Install Dependencies:

Ensure you have installed the necessary dependencies, such as AWS CLI and Python.

D.1.2 Setting Up AWS Credentials

Configure AWS credentials to allow Prowler to access your AWS environment. You can use the AWS CLI to configure your credentials.

sh

aws configure

Provide your AWS Access Key, Secret Access Key, and default region.

D.1.3 Configuring Compliance Checks

Prowler supports various compliance frameworks, including CIS benchmarks, PCI DSS, GDPR, and HIPAA. You can configure Prowler to run checks specific to these frameworks.

Example: Configuring Prowler for PCI DSS checks.

1. Run PCI DSS Checks:

sh

./prowler -g pci

2. Customizing Checks:

You can customize the checks by editing the configuration files in the 'checks' directory. For instance, you can modify the corresponding check files to focus on specific PCI DSS controls.

sh

vim checks/check_pci_3_2_1/3.2.1/1_1_1

Modify the script as per your requirements.

D.2 Generating and Interpreting Compliance Reports

D.2.1 Running Compliance Checks

Execute Prowler to run the configured compliance checks and generate reports.

Steps to Run Compliance Checks:

1. Execute Prowler with the Desired Compliance Group:

sh

./prowler -g pci -M json

This command runs PCI DSS compliance checks and generates a report in JSON format.

2. Generate Reports in Different Formats:

Prowler supports multiple report formats, including CSV, JSON, and HTML.

Example: Generating a CSV report.

sh

./prowler -g pci -M csv > pci_compliance_report.csv

D.2.2 Interpreting Compliance Reports

Once the compliance checks are complete, you need to interpret the results to understand the compliance status of your AWS environment.

Key Sections of the Report:

- **Check ID:** The unique identifier for each check.
- **Status:** The result of the check (e.g., PASS, FAIL).
- **Region:** The AWS region where the check was performed.
- **Resource ID:** The identifier of the resource that was checked.
- **Message:** Detailed information about the check and its result.

Steps to Interpret the Report:

1. Review the Overall Status:

Look at the overall pass/fail status to get a high-level understanding of your compliance posture.

2. Identify Failed Checks:

Focus on the failed checks to identify areas that require attention.

3. Analyze Detailed Messages:

Read the detailed messages for failed checks to understand the specific issues and recommended remediation steps.

Example: Interpreting a Sample PCI DSS Compliance Report

```sh
{

"ComplianceStatus": "FAIL",

"CheckID": "PCI.2.1",

"Region": "us-west-2",

"ResourceID": "sg-0a123b456c789de01",

"Message": "Security group sg-0a123b456c789de01 allows inbound traffic from 0.0.0.0/0 to port 22 (SSH)."
}
```

- **ComplianceStatus:** FAIL indicates non-compliance with the specified control.
- **CheckID:** PCI.2.1 corresponds to the specific PCI DSS control.
- **ResourceID:** sg-0a123b456c789de01 is the security group that failed the check.
- **Message:** Provides details about the issue—here, a security group allows unrestricted SSH access.

D.2.3 Remediation and Continuous Improvement

After interpreting the compliance reports, remediate any identified issues and continuously improve your compliance posture.

1. Prioritize Issues:

Prioritize the remediation efforts based on the severity and impact of the issues.

2. Implement Remediation:

Follow the recommended steps to fix the non-compliant configurations.

Example: Restricting SSH access to specific IP ranges in the security group.

sh

```
aws ec2 revoke-security-group-ingress
    —group-id sg-0a123b456c789de01
    —protocol tcp
    —port 22
    —cidr 0.0.0.0/0

aws ec2 authorize-security-group-ingress
    —group-id sg-0a123b456c789de01
    —protocol tcp
    —port 22
    —cidr 203.0.113.0/24
```

3. Re-run Compliance Checks:

After implementing remediation, re-run the compliance checks to ensure the issues have been resolved.

4. Automate and Schedule Reports:

Automate the compliance checks and schedule regular report generation to maintain continuous visibility and ensure ongoing compliance.

Example: Setting up a cron job to run Prowler daily and generate PCI DSS compliance reports.

```sh
0 0 * * * /path/to/prowler/prowler -g pci -M csv > /path/to/reports/pci_compliance_report_$(date +\%F).csv
```

D.3 Best Practices for Compliance Reporting with Prowler

D.3.1 Define Clear Compliance Objectives

Clearly define the compliance objectives for using Prowler to ensure the reports meet regulatory requirements and internal policies.

Example: Setting objectives for PCI DSS compliance to protect cardholder data and prevent data breaches.

D.3.2 Customize Checks for Your Environment

Customize Prowler checks to align with your specific compliance requirements and cloud environment.

Example: Modifying Prowler checks to include additional controls relevant to your industry.

D.3.3 Automate and Schedule Regular Reports

Automate the generation of compliance reports and schedule them regularly to ensure continuous monitoring.

Example: Setting up automated daily compliance checks and monthly detailed reports.

D.3.4 Review and Act on Reports

Regularly review compliance reports and take prompt action to remediate any identified issues.

Example: Review monthly HIPAA compliance reports and address issues related to ePHI protection.

D.3.5 Continuous Improvement

Improve your compliance posture by regularly updating your checks and configurations based on the latest regulatory requirements and best practices.

Example: Updating Prowler configurations to incorporate new PCI DSS requirements as they are released.

D.4 Conclusion

Using Prowler for compliance reporting efficiently and effectively ensures that your AWS environment meets regulatory requirements and internal security policies. You can maintain a robust compliance posture by configuring compliance-specific checks, generating detailed compliance reports, and interpreting the results. Regular review, automation, and continuous improvement are key to sustaining compliance and enhancing your overall security posture. As we continue to explore advanced CSPM strategies, incorporating tools like Prowler will be integral to achieving and maintaining compliance in complex cloud environments.

VI

Case Studies and Best Practices

Chapter 12: Real-World CSPM Implementations

A. Case Studies of Successful CSPM Deployments

Implementing Cloud Security Posture Management (CSPM) effectively can significantly enhance an organization's security posture and ensure compliance with regulatory requirements. This chapter presents real-world case studies of successful CSPM deployments, showcasing best practices and lessons learned from various industries.

A.1 Case Study: Financial Services Firm Achieving PCI DSS Compliance

A.1.1 Background

A leading financial services firm with a multi-cloud environment spanning AWS and Azure sought to achieve and maintain compliance with the Payment Card Industry Data Security Standard (PCI DSS). The firm handles sensitive payment card information and must ensure robust security measures across its infrastructure.

A.1.2 Challenges

- **Multi-Cloud Complexity:** Managing security and compliance across multiple cloud platforms.
- **Continuous Compliance:** Ensuring ongoing compliance with PCI DSS requirements.
- **Data Protection:** Protecting sensitive cardholder data from breaches and unauthorized access.

A.1.3 Solution

The firm deployed Prisma Cloud to manage its cloud security posture across AWS and Azure environments. Key steps included:

- **Policy Configuration:** Defining and implementing PCI DSS-specific policies within Prisma Cloud.
- **Continuous Monitoring:** Setting up continuous monitoring to detect and report compliance violations automatically.
- **Automated Remediation:** Leveraging Prisma Cloud's automated remediation capabilities to address non-compliant configurations.

A.1.4 Implementation Steps

1. **Initial Assessment:** Conducted a comprehensive assessment of existing cloud resources and configurations.
2. **Policy Definition:** Defined PCI DSS policies in Prisma Cloud, focusing on encryption, access controls, and network security.
3. **Deployment:** Deployed Prisma Cloud agents across all cloud environments to enable continuous monitoring.
4. **Automated Checks:** Configured automated compliance checks and set up alerts for policy violations.
5. **Remediation:** Implemented automated remediation workflows to address identified issues promptly.

A.1.5 Results

- **Improved Compliance:** Achieved and maintained PCI DSS compliance across multi-cloud environments.
- **Enhanced Security:** Strengthened overall security posture with continuous monitoring and automated remediation.
- **Operational Efficiency:** Reduced manual effort required for compliance management through automation.

A.2 Case Study: Healthcare Organization Ensuring HIPAA Compliance

A.2.1 Background

A large healthcare organization managing sensitive patient information must ensure compliance with the Health Insurance Portability and Accountability Act (HIPAA). The organization utilized AWS for its cloud infrastructure and required robust security measures to protect electronic Protected Health Information (ePHI).

A.2.2 Challenges

- **Data Protection:** Ensuring the confidentiality, integrity, and availability of ePHI.
- **Access Controls:** Implementing strict access controls to limit access to sensitive data.
- **Audit and Monitoring:** Maintaining detailed audit logs and continuous monitoring access to ePHI.

A.2.3 Solution

The healthcare organization deployed AWS Security Hub to manage its security posture and ensure HIPAA compliance. Key steps included:

- **Configuration Management:** Using AWS Config to monitor resource configurations and ensure compliance with HIPAA requirements.
- **Continuous Monitoring:** Enabling continuous monitoring of security configurations and access controls.
- **Compliance Reporting:** Generating detailed compliance reports to demonstrate adherence to HIPAA regulations.

A.2.4 Implementation Steps

1. **Initial Setup:** Enabled AWS Security Hub and integrated it with AWS Config for continuous monitoring.
2. **Policy Definition:** Defined HIPAA-specific policies, including encryption, access controls, and audit logging.
3. **Monitoring and Alerts:** Configured alerts for non-compliant configurations and security incidents.
4. **Automated Remediation:** Set up automated remediation for common compliance issues, such as unencrypted data stores.
5. **Compliance Reporting:** Generated regular compliance reports to track and demonstrate adherence to HIPAA requirements.

A.2.5 Results

- **HIPAA Compliance:** Achieved and maintained HIPAA compliance across AWS infrastructure.
- **Data Security:** Enhanced protection of ePHI with robust encryption and access controls.
- **Continuous Improvement:** Established a framework for monitoring and improving security posture.

A.3 Case Study: E-commerce Company Ensuring GDPR Compliance

A.3.1 Background

An e-commerce company operating in Europe must ensure compliance with the General Data Protection Regulation (GDPR). The company used Google Cloud Platform (GCP) for its cloud infrastructure and required comprehensive data protection measures.

A.3.2 Challenges

- **Data Privacy:** Ensuring the privacy and protection of customer data.
- **Regulatory Compliance:** Meeting GDPR data handling, processing, and storage requirements.
- **Incident Response:** Implementing effective incident response and breach notification procedures.

A.3.3 Solution

The e-commerce company deployed Google Cloud Security Command Center (SCC) to manage its security posture and ensure GDPR compliance. Key steps included:

- **Data Inventory:** Conducting a data inventory and mapping data flows to understand data usage.
- **Policy Enforcement:** Using SCC to enforce data protection policies, including encryption and access controls.
- **Continuous Monitoring:** Enabling continuous monitoring and alerts for policy violations and potential breaches.

CHAPTER 12: REAL-WORLD CSPM IMPLEMENTATIONS

A.3.4 Implementation Steps

1. **Initial Assessment:** Conducted a thorough assessment of data usage and compliance status.
2. **Data Protection Policies:** Defined GDPR-specific data protection policies in SCC.
3. **Monitoring and Alerts:** Configured SCC to monitor compliance and alert for policy violations.
4. **Incident Response:** Developed and tested incident response plans to ensure timely breach notifications.
5. **Compliance Reporting:** Generated regular compliance reports to demonstrate adherence to GDPR requirements.

A.3.5 Results

- **GDPR Compliance:** Achieved and maintained GDPR compliance across GCP infrastructure.
- **Enhanced Data Privacy:** Improved data privacy with strong encryption and access controls.
- **Effective Incident Response:** Implemented effective incident response procedures for GDPR compliance.

A.4 Lessons Learned and Best Practices

A.4.1 Define Clear Compliance Objectives

Clearly define compliance objectives and align them with regulatory requirements and business needs.

Example: Setting specific goals for PCI DSS compliance, such as encrypting all cardholder data and implementing strong access controls.

A.4.2 Leverage Automation

Use CSPM tools to automate compliance monitoring, reporting, and remediation to reduce manual effort and ensure continuous compliance.

Example: Automating compliance checks and remediation workflows in Prisma Cloud to address PCI DSS requirements.

A.4.3 Continuous Monitoring and Improvement

Implement continuous monitoring to detect and address compliance issues in real time and regularly review and update compliance policies and procedures.

Example: Using AWS Security Hub for continuous monitoring and regular reviews to ensure ongoing HIPAA compliance.

A.4.4 Comprehensive Training and Awareness

Provide comprehensive training and awareness programs to ensure all employees understand compliance requirements and their roles in maintaining compliance.

Example: Conducting regular GDPR training sessions for all employees and specific training on using Google Cloud SCC for compliance monitoring.

A.4.5 Regular Audits and Reviews

Conduct regular audits and reviews of compliance status to identify and address any gaps or weaknesses in the compliance posture.

Example: Performing quarterly compliance audits and using the results to improve security measures and processes.

A.5 Conclusion

Successful CSPM deployments significantly enhance an organization's security posture and ensure compliance with regulatory requirements. Organizations can achieve and maintain compliance across complex cloud environments by leveraging CSPM tools for continuous monitoring, automated remediation, and detailed compliance reporting. These case studies highlight the practical application of CSPM strategies and provide valuable insights for organizations seeking to enhance their cloud security and compliance efforts.

B. Lessons Learned from Industry Leaders

Implementing Cloud Security Posture Management (CSPM) is critical for ensuring security and compliance in cloud environments. This section highlights key lessons from industry leaders who have successfully deployed CSPM solutions. By examining their experiences, we can derive best practices and strategies for enhancing security and compliance in various cloud setups.

B.1 Key Lessons from Successful CSPM Implementations

B.1.1 Establish Clear Objectives and Scope

Lesson: Defining clear objectives and scope is essential for the success of CSPM initiatives. This involves understanding the specific compliance requirements, security goals, and business needs.

Example: A global financial institution clearly defined its objective to achieve PCI DSS compliance across its multi-cloud environment, which included AWS and Azure. This clarity helped in selecting appropriate CSPM tools and setting up relevant policies.

Best Practice: Conduct a thorough assessment of regulatory requirements and internal security policies to establish clear objectives and scope for CSPM deployment.

B.1.2 Invest in Automation for Continuous Monitoring and Remediation

Lesson: Automation is key to managing complex cloud environments and ensuring continuous compliance. Automated monitoring and remediation reduce the risk of human error and enhance operational efficiency.

Example: A healthcare organization used AWS Config and AWS Security Hub to automate the monitoring and remediation of HIPAA compliance issues. This approach significantly reduced manual effort and improved response times to potential security incidents.

Best Practice: Leverage CSPM tools that offer robust automation capabilities for continuous monitoring, assessment, and remediation of compliance and security issues.

B.1.3 Foster a Culture of Security and Compliance

Lesson: Successful CSPM implementation requires a culture prioritizing security and compliance. This involves continuous education and engagement of all stakeholders, from executives to developers.

Example: An e-commerce company implemented regular security training and awareness programs to ensure all employees understood GDPR requirements and their role in maintaining compliance. This cultural shift led to better adherence to security policies and practices.

Best Practice: Establish ongoing training and awareness programs to foster a culture of security and compliance within the organization.

B.1.4 Integrate CSPM with DevOps Processes

Lesson: Integrating CSPM with DevOps processes ensures that security and compliance are embedded throughout the software development lifecycle. This approach, known as DevSecOps, helps in early detection and remediation of issues.

Example: A technology firm integrated CSPM tools like Checkov into its CI/CD pipelines to automatically scan infrastructure-as-code (IaC) templates for compliance with industry standards. This integration helped catch and fix compliance issues before deployment.

Best Practice: Incorporate CSPM checks into DevOps workflows to ensure continuous security and compliance from development through deployment.

B.1.5 Regularly Review and Update Policies

Lesson: Cloud environments and regulatory requirements are dynamic, necessitating regular reviews and updates of security and compliance policies. This ensures that the organization remains compliant and secure over time.

Example: A large manufacturing company reviewed its CSPM policies and configurations quarterly to align with the latest industry standards and regulatory changes. This proactive approach helped maintain a strong security posture.

Best Practice: Schedule regular reviews and updates of CSPM policies and configurations to keep pace with evolving regulatory requirements and security threats.

B.2 Conclusion

Lessons learned from industry leaders highlight the importance of clear objectives, automation, cultural integration, DevSecOps practices, and regular reviews in successful CSPM implementations. By adopting these best practices, organizations can enhance their security posture, achieve continuous compliance, and effectively manage the complexities of modern cloud environments. These insights from real-world implementations provide a roadmap for organizations seeking to optimize their CSPM strategies and ensure robust cloud security and compliance.

Chapter 13: Best Practices for CSPM

A. Establishing a Security-First Culture

Establishing a security-first culture is essential for the successful implementation and ongoing effectiveness of Cloud Security Posture Management (CSPM). A security-first culture ensures that security considerations are embedded in every organization's operations, from development and deployment to daily business activities. This chapter explores best practices for fostering a security-first culture within an organization.

A.1 Importance of a Security-First Culture

A.1.1 Enhancing Security Posture

A security-first culture helps enhance an organization's overall security posture by ensuring security is a top priority in all activities. This leads to more robust and resilient security practices.

Example: Development teams prioritize secure coding practices and regularly review and update security controls, resulting in fewer vulnerabilities in the deployed applications.

A.1.2 Ensuring Compliance

A security-first culture ensures consistent compliance with regulatory requirements and industry standards, reducing the risk of non-compliance and the associated penalties.

Example: Regular training and awareness programs on GDPR compliance help ensure all employees understand their responsibilities in protecting personal data.

A.1.3 Building Customer Trust

Organizations that strongly commit to security can build and maintain customer trust. Customers are likelier to do business with companies that take data protection seriously.

Example: Publicly sharing security certifications and compliance achievements can reassure customers of the organization's commitment to protecting their data.

A.2 Strategies for Establishing a Security-First Culture

A.2.1 Executive Leadership and Commitment

Leadership commitment is crucial for establishing and maintaining a security-first culture. Executives must prioritize security and demonstrate their commitment through actions and resources.

Key Actions:

- **Allocate Resources:** Ensure sufficient resources are allocated to security initiatives, including budget, personnel, and tools.
- **Set Expectations:** Communicate the importance of security to all employees and set expectations for security practices.
- **Lead by Example:** Executives should follow security best practices and participate in security initiatives.

Example: The CEO regularly discusses security topics in company meetings and supports investments in advanced security tools and training programs.

A.2.2 Comprehensive Training and Awareness Programs

Regular training and awareness programs are essential for educating employees about security best practices, policies, and procedures. These programs should be tailored to different roles within the organization.

Key Components:

- **Onboarding Training:** Security training will be included in the onboarding process for new employees.
- **Role-Specific Training:** Provide specialized training for different roles,

such as developers, IT staff, and management.
- **Regular Refreshers:** Conduct refresher courses to update employees on the latest security threats and practices.
- **Phishing Simulations:** Use phishing simulations to educate employees on recognizing and responding to phishing attacks.

Example: Conducting quarterly security workshops for developers on secure coding practices and annual training sessions for all employees on recognizing phishing attempts.

A.2.3 Clear Security Policies and Procedures

Develop and maintain comprehensive security policies and procedures that outline expected behaviors and practices. Ensure that these documents are easily accessible to all employees.

Key Elements:

- **Policy Documentation:** Document security policies and procedures clearly and concisely.
- **Accessibility:** Make security policies and procedures accessible through an internal knowledge base or intranet.
- **Regular Updates:** Regularly review and update security policies to reflect changes in the threat landscape and regulatory requirements.

Example: Creating an internal security policy portal where employees can easily access the latest security policies, procedures, and guidelines.

A.2.4 Integration of Security into Development Processes

Integrating security into the development process, often called DevSecOps, ensures that security is considered at every stage of the software development lifecycle.

Key Practices:

- **Secure Coding Standards:** Implement secure coding standards and guidelines for developers.
- **Automated Security Testing:** Integrate automated security testing tools into the CI/CD pipeline to identify and remediate vulnerabilities early.
- **Code Reviews:** Conduct regular code reviews focusing on security to identify and address potential issues.
- **Threat Modeling:** During the design phase, threat modeling is performed to identify and mitigate potential security risks.

Example: Implementing a CI/CD pipeline that includes automated static and dynamic security testing tools to catch vulnerabilities before code is deployed to production.

A.2.5 Continuous Monitoring and Improvement

Continuous monitoring and improvement are critical for maintaining a strong security posture. This involves regularly assessing security controls, monitoring for threats, and making necessary improvements.

Key Practices:

- **Continuous Monitoring:** Implement real-time tools to detect and respond to security incidents.
- **Regular Audits:** Conduct security audits and assessments to identify gaps and areas for improvement.
- **Feedback Loops:** Establish feedback loops to incorporate lessons learned from incidents and audits into security practices.
- **Incident Response Drills:** Conduct regular incident response drills to ensure readiness for potential security incidents.

Example: Using a Security Information and Event Management (SIEM) system to monitor security events continuously and conduct bi-annual incident response drills.

A.2.6 Foster Collaboration Across Teams

Collaboration across different teams, such as development, operations, and security, ensures that security is a shared responsibility and that all stakeholders are involved in maintaining a secure environment.

Key Practices:

- **Cross-Functional Teams:** Create cross-functional teams that include members from development, operations, and security to work on security initiatives.
- **Regular Communication:** Establish regular communication channels, such as security stand-ups or weekly meetings, to discuss security topics and share updates.
- **Shared Goals:** Set shared security goals and metrics to encourage collaboration and collective ownership of security responsibilities.

Example: Establishing a DevSecOps team that includes development, operations, and security representatives to collaborate on securing the CI/CD pipeline.

A.3 Measuring the Success of a Security-First Culture

A.3.1 Key Performance Indicators (KPIs)

Define and track key performance indicators (KPIs) to measure the success of your security-first culture. KPIs should be aligned with your security objectives and provide insights into the effectiveness of your initiatives.

Example KPIs:

- **Incident Response Time:** Measure the average time to detect, respond to, and remediate security incidents.
- **Compliance Metrics:** Track compliance with internal security policies and regulatory requirements.
- **Employee Training Participation:** Monitor security training programs' participation rate and completion.
- **Vulnerability Metrics:** Track the number and severity of vulnerabilities identified and remediated.

Example: Tracking the average incident response time and aiming to reduce it by 20% over the next year.

A.3.2 Employee Feedback and Surveys

Gather feedback from employees regularly through surveys and informal discussions to assess the effectiveness of security initiatives and identify areas for improvement.

Key Questions:

- **Training Effectiveness:** Are the security training programs effective and relevant?
- **Policy Clarity:** Are security policies and procedures clear and easy to follow?
- **Support and Resources:** Do employees feel they have the necessary support and resources to follow security best practices?

Example: Conducting an annual security culture survey to gather feedback on training programs, policy clarity, and overall security awareness.

A.3.3 Incident Analysis and Reporting

Analyze security incidents and near-misses to identify root causes, trends, and areas for improvement. Use this analysis to enhance security practices and prevent future incidents.

Key Practices:

- **Root Cause Analysis:** Perform root cause analysis for each incident to understand what went wrong and how it can be prevented.
- **Trend Analysis:** Identify trends in security incidents to address systemic issues and improve overall security posture.

- **Reporting and Communication:** Report incident analysis findings to relevant stakeholders regularly and use them to inform security strategy and practices.

Example: Analyzing security incidents over the past year to identify common root causes and implementing targeted training to address these issues.

A.4 Conclusion

Establishing a security-first culture is crucial for successfully implementing CSPM and maintaining a robust security posture in cloud environments. By securing leadership commitment, providing comprehensive training, integrating security into development processes, fostering collaboration, and continuously monitoring and improving security practices, organizations can create a culture where security is a shared responsibility and a top priority. Measuring the success of these initiatives through KPIs, employee feedback, and incident analysis ensures that the organization remains vigilant and proactive in addressing security challenges. Adopting these best practices will enhance cloud security and achieve continuous compliance as we move forward.

B. Continuous Improvement and Adaptation

In the rapidly evolving cloud security landscape, continuous improvement and adaptation are essential for maintaining a robust security posture. This chapter explores the strategies and practices for fostering a culture of continuous improvement and adaptation in Cloud Security Posture Management (CSPM), ensuring security measures evolve in response to emerging threats and changing regulatory requirements.

B.1 Importance of Continuous Improvement and Adaptation

B.1.1 Addressing Emerging Threats

Cyber threats constantly evolve, with new vulnerabilities and attack vectors emerging regularly. Continuous improvement ensures that security measures are updated to address these evolving threats effectively.

Example: Regularly updating security policies and practices to protect against the latest ransomware tactics and phishing schemes.

B.1.2 Keeping Up with Regulatory Changes

Regulatory requirements and industry standards frequently change to address new security challenges and protect sensitive data. Continuous adaptation ensures ongoing compliance with these evolving requirements.

Example: Adapting data protection policies to comply with updates to the General Data Protection Regulation (GDPR) and the California Consumer Privacy Act (CCPA).

B.1.3 Enhancing Security Posture

Continuous improvement fosters a proactive approach to security, helping organizations identify and mitigate potential risks before they become significant issues.

Example: Implementing regular security assessments and adopting new security technologies to strengthen security posture.

B.2 Strategies for Continuous Improvement in CSPM

B.2.1 Regular Security Assessments and Audits

Conducting regular security assessments and audits helps identify vulnerabilities and areas for improvement. These assessments should be thorough and encompass all aspects of the cloud environment.

Key Practices:

- **Vulnerability Scanning:** Regularly scan cloud resources for vulnerabilities and misconfigurations.
- **Penetration Testing:** Perform periodic penetration testing to simulate attacks and identify weaknesses.
- **Compliance Audits:** Conduct regular audits to ensure adherence to regulatory requirements and internal policies.

Example: Scheduling quarterly vulnerability scans and annual penetration tests to assess the security posture and identify areas for improvement.

B.2.2 Implementing Feedback Loops

Establishing feedback loops ensures that lessons learned from security incidents, assessments, and audits are integrated into security practices and policies.

Key Practices:

- **Post-Incident Reviews:** Conduct post-incident reviews to analyze security incidents and identify root causes.
- **Continuous Feedback:** Collect feedback from security teams, developers, and other stakeholders to inform security practices.
- **Policy Updates:** Regularly update security policies and procedures based on feedback and lessons learned.

Example: Conducting a post-incident review after a security breach to identify security control gaps and update incident response procedures accordingly.

B.2.3 Embracing Automation and AI

Leveraging automation and artificial intelligence (AI) can enhance continuous improvement by providing real-time insights and automating repetitive security tasks.

Key Practices:

- **Automated Monitoring:** Implement automated monitoring tools to assess the security posture and detect anomalies continuously.
- **AI-Powered Analytics:** Use AI and machine learning to analyze security

data and identify patterns and trends.
- **Automated Remediation:** Deploy automated remediation workflows to address common security issues and reduce response times.

Example: Using AI-powered threat detection tools to analyze network traffic and detect unusual patterns indicative of a potential attack.

B.2.4 Continuous Training and Education

Ongoing training and education ensure employees stay informed about the latest security threats and best practices, fostering a security-aware culture.

Key Practices:

- **Regular Training Sessions:** Offer regular training sessions on emerging threats, security best practices, and regulatory changes.
- **Certifications and Courses:** Encourage employees to pursue security certifications and participate in relevant courses.
- **Security Awareness Programs:** Implement security awareness programs to educate employees about recognizing and responding to security threats.

Example: Provide monthly training sessions on new security threats and best practices and encourage employees to obtain certifications such as Certified Information Systems Security Professional (CISSP).

B.3 Adapting to Changing Regulatory Requirements

B.3.1 Staying Informed About Regulatory Changes

Keeping abreast of changes in regulatory requirements is crucial for maintaining compliance. Organizations should have processes in place to monitor and interpret regulatory updates.

Key Practices:

- **Regulatory Monitoring:** Subscribe to regulatory news feeds, join industry groups, and participate in compliance forums.
- **Legal Consultation:** Regularly consult with legal experts to understand the implications of regulatory changes.
- **Internal Reviews:** Conduct internal reviews to assess the impact of regulatory updates on existing policies and practices.

Example: Monitoring updates to GDPR and CCPA regulations and consulting with legal experts to ensure compliance with new data protection requirements.

B.3.2 Implementing Policy Changes

Adapting security and compliance policies to reflect regulatory changes is essential for ongoing compliance. This involves updating documentation, procedures, and controls.

Key Practices:

- **Policy Review:** Regularly review and update security and compliance policies to align with regulatory changes.
- **Documentation Updates:** Ensure all relevant documentation is updated to reflect new requirements.
- **Training and Communication:** Communicate policy changes to all employees and provide training on new requirements.

Example: Updating data handling and privacy policies to comply with new provisions in GDPR and conducting training sessions to inform employees about these changes.

B.3.3 Conducting Impact Assessments

Conducting impact assessments helps organizations understand the implications of regulatory changes and plan appropriate responses.

Key Practices:

- **Risk Assessments:** Evaluate the risks associated with non-compliance and the potential impact on the organization.
- **Gap Analysis:** Perform gap analysis to identify areas where current practices fall short of new regulatory requirements.
- **Implementation Planning:** Develop and implement plans to address identified gaps and ensure compliance.

Example: Conducting a GDPR impact assessment to identify compliance gaps and implementing a remediation plan to address these gaps.

B.4 Tools and Technologies for Continuous Improvement

B.4.1 Security Information and Event Management (SIEM)

SIEM tools provide real-time monitoring, detection, and response capabilities, enabling continuous improvement through data-driven insights.

Key Features:

- **Real-Time Monitoring:** Monitor security events in real-time to detect and respond to threats.
- **Log Management:** Collect and analyze logs from various sources to identify patterns and anomalies.
- **Incident Response:** Automate incident response workflows to streamline the remediation process.

Example: Implementing a SIEM solution like Splunk to monitor security events and automate the response to detected threats.

B.4.2 Threat Intelligence Platforms

Threat intelligence platforms provide actionable insights into emerging threats, helping organizations stay ahead of potential attacks.

Key Features:

- **Threat Analysis:** Analyze threat data to identify trends and patterns.
- **Threat Feeds:** Integrate threat feeds from various sources to stay informed about new vulnerabilities and attack vectors.

- **Automated Threat Hunting:** Automated tools proactively hunt for environmental threats.

Example: Using a threat intelligence platform like ThreatConnect to gather and analyze threat data and inform security strategies.

B.4.3 Continuous Integration/Continuous Deployment (CI/CD) Tools

Integrating security into CI/CD pipelines ensures that security checks are performed continuously throughout the development lifecycle.

Key Features:

- **Automated Testing:** Automate security testing to identify and remediate vulnerabilities early.
- **Policy Enforcement:** Enforce security policies at each CI/CD pipeline stage.
- **Continuous Monitoring:** Monitor code changes and deployments for compliance with security standards.

Example: Implementing a CI/CD tool like Jenkins with integrated security testing tools to automate the security assessment of code changes.

B.5 Case Study: Continuous Improvement in CSPM

B.5.1 Background

A global technology company with a diverse cloud infrastructure must continuously improve its security posture and adapt to changing regulatory requirements. The company deployed CSPM tools across its AWS, Azure, and Google Cloud environments.

B.5.2 Strategies Implemented

1. Regular Security Assessments:

- Conducted quarterly vulnerability scans and annual penetration tests.
- Performed continuous compliance audits to ensure adherence to regulatory requirements.

2. Feedback Loops:

- Established post-incident review processes to analyze security incidents and identify root causes.
- Regularly collected feedback from security teams and developers to inform policy updates.

3. Automation and AI:

- Implemented automated monitoring and remediation workflows using AI-powered tools.
- Deployed machine learning algorithms to analyze security data and detect anomalies.

4. Training and Education:

- Provided ongoing training sessions on emerging threats and best practices.
- Encouraged employees to obtain security certifications and participate in relevant courses.

5. Adapting to Regulatory Changes:

- Monitored regulatory updates and conducted impact assessments.
- Updated security and compliance policies to reflect new regulatory requirements.
- Conducted internal reviews to ensure compliance with updated regulations.

B.5.3 Results

- **Enhanced Security Posture:** Improved security posture through continuous monitoring, automated remediation, and regular assessments.
- **Regulatory Compliance:** Maintained compliance with evolving regulatory requirements, reducing the risk of non-compliance penalties.
- **Proactive Threat Detection:** Enhanced threat detection capabilities using AI-powered analytics and automated threat hunting.
- **Informed Workforce:** Fostered a security-aware culture through continuous training and education, leading to better adherence to security practices.

B.6 Conclusion

Continuous improvement and adaptation are essential for maintaining a robust security posture in the dynamic landscape of cloud security. Organizations can effectively manage their cloud security posture by implementing regular security assessments, establishing feedback loops, leveraging automation and AI, providing continuous training, and staying informed about regulatory changes. These strategies, supported by appropriate tools and technologies, ensure that security measures evolve in response to emerging threats and regulatory requirements, maintaining a strong and proactive security stance. As organizations adopt cloud technologies, embracing continuous improvement and adaptation will be key to sustaining long-term security and compliance.

C. Keeping Up with Evolving Threats

In the dynamic landscape of cloud security, threats are continually evolving, making it essential for organizations to stay ahead by proactively updating their Cloud Security Posture Management (CSPM) strategies. This chapter delves into best practices for keeping up with evolving threats, ensuring that security measures remain robust and effective.

C.1 Importance of Staying Ahead of Evolving Threats

C.1.1 Protecting Sensitive Data

Evolving threats pose significant risks to sensitive data, including intellectual property, customer information, and financial records. Staying ahead of these threats helps prevent data breaches and protect organizational assets.

Example: Regularly updating encryption protocols to protect sensitive customer data from new decryption techniques.

C.1.2 Ensuring Business Continuity

Emerging threats can disrupt business operations, leading to downtime and financial loss. Proactive threat management ensures business continuity by mitigating risks before they impact operations.

Example: Implementing advanced threat detection systems to identify and neutralize ransomware attacks, minimizing downtime quickly.

C.1.3 Maintaining Compliance

Compliance requirements often evolve in response to new threats. Keeping up with these changes ensures that organizations remain compliant with regulations and avoid penalties.

Example: Adapting data protection measures to comply with new provisions in the GDPR or CCPA in response to emerging privacy concerns.

C.2 Strategies for Keeping Up with Evolving Threats

C.2.1 Continuous Threat Monitoring

Continuous threat monitoring involves the real-time analysis of network traffic, system logs, and other data sources to detect and respond to threats as they emerge.

Key Practices:

- **Real-Time Analytics:** Implement real-time analytics tools to monitor suspicious activity and anomalies.
- **Threat Intelligence Feeds:** Integrate threat intelligence feeds to stay informed about the latest threats and vulnerabilities.
- **Automated Alerts:** Set up automated alerts to immediately notify security teams of potential threats.

Example: Using a SIEM system like Splunk to monitor network traffic and generate alerts for anomalous behavior continuously.

C.2.2 Leveraging Threat Intelligence

Threat intelligence provides actionable insights into emerging threats, helping organizations proactively defend against potential attacks.

Key Practices:

- **Threat Intelligence Platforms:** Utilize platforms that aggregate and analyze threat data from multiple sources.

- **Collaboration and Sharing:** Participate in threat intelligence sharing communities to gain insights from other organizations and industry experts.
- **Actionable Insights:** Translate threat intelligence into actionable security measures, such as updating firewall rules or patching vulnerabilities.

Example: Leveraging a threat intelligence platform like ThreatConnect to gather and analyze threat data and use this information to update security controls.

C.2.3 Regular Security Training and Drills

Regular training and drills ensure that employees are aware of the latest threats and know how to respond effectively.

Key Practices:

- **Security Awareness Programs:** Conduct ongoing security awareness programs to educate employees about emerging threats.
- **Incident Response Drills:** Perform regular incident response drills to test the effectiveness of response plans and improve readiness.
- **Role-Specific Training:** Provide specialized training tailored to the specific responsibilities of different roles, such as developers, IT staff, and executives.

Example: Conducting quarterly phishing simulation exercises to train employees on recognizing and responding to phishing attacks.

C.2.4 Implementing Advanced Security Technologies

Adopting advanced security technologies helps organizations stay ahead of sophisticated threats and enhance their overall security posture.

Key Technologies:

- **AI and Machine Learning:** Use AI and machine learning to detect and respond to threats in real time, identifying patterns and anomalies that traditional methods might miss.
- **Behavioral Analytics:** Implement behavioral analytics to monitor user and entity behavior and detect deviations that may indicate a threat.
- **Endpoint Detection and Response (EDR):** Deploy EDR solutions to provide real-time endpoint monitoring and response capabilities.

Example: Using an AI-powered EDR solution like CrowdStrike to detect and respond to endpoint threats in real time.

C.2.5 Regular Security Assessments and Penetration Testing

Regular security assessments and penetration testing help identify vulnerabilities and weaknesses that emerging threats could exploit.

Key Practices:

- **Vulnerability Scanning:** Conduct regular vulnerability scans to identify and remediate security gaps.
- **Penetration Testing:** Perform periodic penetration tests to simulate attacks and uncover potential vulnerabilities.
- **Security Audits:** Conduct comprehensive security audits to assess

existing controls' effectiveness and identify areas for improvement.

Example: Scheduling bi-annual penetration tests to evaluate the security posture and implement necessary improvements.

C.3 Adapting to New Threats and Technologies

C.3.1 Agile Security Policies

Adopting agile security policies allows organizations to quickly adapt to new threats and incorporate emerging technologies into their security framework.

Key Practices:

- **Flexible Policies:** Develop security policies that can be easily updated to address new threats and technologies.
- **Continuous Review:** Regularly review and update security policies to reflect changes in the threat landscape.
- **Cross-Functional Collaboration:** Foster collaboration between security teams and other departments to ensure policies remain relevant and effective.

Example: Implement a policy review rating process incorporating feedback from security teams, developers, and legal experts to ensure policies stay current.

C.3.2 Proactive Threat Hunting

Proactive threat hunting involves actively searching for threats within the network rather than relying solely on automated detection tools.

Key Practices:

- **Dedicated Threat Hunting Teams:** Establish dedicated teams responsible for proactive threat hunting.
- **Advanced Analytics:** Use advanced analytics and threat intelligence to guide threat-hunting activities.
- **Continuous Improvement:** Regularly update threat-hunting techniques and tools based on the latest threat intelligence and attack trends.

Example: Deploying a threat-hunting team using behavioral analytics and intelligence to identify and mitigate advanced persistent threats (APTs).

C.3.3 Embracing Zero Trust Architecture

Zero Trust Architecture (ZTA) is a security model that assumes no implicit trust, even within the network perimeter, and requires continuous verification of user and device identities.

Key Practices:

- **Identity Verification:** Implement strong identity verification measures, such as multi-factor authentication (MFA) and single sign-on (SSO).
- **Least Privilege Access:** Enforce the principle of least privilege, grant-

ing users and devices only the access necessary for their roles.
- **Micro-Segmentation:** Use micro-segmentation to isolate network segments and limit the lateral movement of threats.

Example: Adopting a Zero Trust model that requires MFA for all users and micro-segments of the network to protect sensitive data and applications.

C.3.4 Continuous Learning and Adaptation

Fostering a continuous learning and adaptation culture ensures that security teams stay informed about the latest threats and technologies.

Key Practices:

- **Ongoing Education:** Encourage security professionals to pursue ongoing education and certifications in emerging technologies and threat landscapes.
- **Knowledge Sharing:** Promote knowledge sharing within the organization through regular meetings, workshops, and collaborative platforms.
- **Industry Engagement:** Participate in industry conferences, forums, and working groups to stay informed about the latest developments in cloud security.

Example: Encouraging security team members to attend industry conferences like Black Hat and DEF CON and to share insights with the broader team.

C.4 Case Study: Adapting to Evolving Threats with CSPM

C.4.1 Background

A multinational retail company faced increasing cyber threats as it expanded its online presence and adopted a multi-cloud strategy. The company needed to stay ahead of evolving threats and protect its customer data and intellectual property.

C.4.2 Strategies Implemented

1. Continuous Threat Monitoring:

- Implemented a SIEM solution to monitor network traffic and detect anomalies continuously.
- Integrated threat intelligence feeds to stay informed about the latest threats.

2. Advanced Security Technologies:

- Deployed AI-powered behavioral analytics to detect unusual user activity.
- Implemented an EDR solution to provide real-time monitoring and response for endpoints.

3. Regular Security Assessments:

- Conducted quarterly vulnerability scans and annual penetration tests.
- Performed regular compliance audits to ensure adherence to regulatory

requirements.

4. Proactive Threat Hunting:

- Established a dedicated threat-hunting team to actively search for threats within the network.
- Used advanced analytics and threat intelligence to guide threat-hunting activities.

5. Zero Trust Architecture:

- Adopted a Zero Trust model, requiring MFA for all users and implementing micro-segmentation to protect sensitive data.

C.4.3 Results

- **Enhanced Threat Detection:** Continuous monitoring and advanced analytics improved threat detection capabilities.
- **Proactive Defense:** Identified and mitigated potential threats before they could cause significant damage.
- **Improved Compliance:** Maintained compliance with evolving regulatory requirements through regular audits and policy updates.
- **Resilient Security Posture:** Established a robust security posture that adapted to new threats and technologies.

C.5 Conclusion

Staying ahead of evolving threats is critical for maintaining a robust cloud security posture. Organizations can proactively address emerging threats by implementing continuous threat monitoring, leveraging threat intelligence, adopting advanced security technologies, and fostering a continuous learning and adaptation culture. Agile security policies, proactive threat hunting, and the adoption of Zero Trust Architecture further enhance an organization's ability to defend against sophisticated attacks. These strategies, supported by regular security assessments and a commitment to ongoing education, ensure that security measures remain effective in the face of an ever-changing threat landscape. As organizations continue to embrace cloud technologies, these best practices will be essential for sustaining long-term security and compliance.

VII

Conclusion

Chapter 14: The Future of CSPM

A. Emerging Trends in Cloud Security

As cloud computing continues to evolve, so do its threats and challenges. Several emerging trends in cloud computing shape security posture management (CSPM) security, the future of cloud. This chapter explores these trends and their implications for organizations seeking to enhance their cloud security posture.

A.1 Increasing Adoption of Multi-Cloud and Hybrid Cloud Environments

A.1.1 Challenges of Multi-Cloud and Hybrid Environments

Organizations adopting multi-cloud and hybrid cloud strategies to leverage the best services from different providers and avoid vendor lock-in face new security challenges. These include managing disparate security controls, ensuring consistent policies across environments, and maintaining visibility into complex infrastructures.

Key Considerations:

- **Unified Security Policies:** Develop and enforce unified security policies that apply consistently across all cloud environments.
- **Integrated Monitoring:** Implement integrated monitoring solutions that provide visibility into multi-cloud and hybrid environments.
- **Cross-Platform Compliance:** Ensure compliance with regulatory requirements across different cloud platforms.

Example: Using a CSPM solution like Prisma Cloud to manage security policies and monitor compliance across AWS, Azure, and Google Cloud.

A.1.2 CSPM Solutions for Multi-Cloud and Hybrid Environments

Future CSPM solutions will increasingly focus on supporting multi-cloud and hybrid environments, providing unified security management and seamless integration with various cloud platforms.

Emerging Features:

- **Cross-Cloud Visibility:** Enhanced visibility into security posture across multiple cloud providers.
- **Automated Policy Enforcement:** Automated enforcement of security policies and compliance requirements across diverse environments.
- **Advanced Analytics:** Advanced analytics is used to detect and respond to threats in multi-cloud and hybrid setups.

Example: Implementing a multi-cloud CSPM solution that offers a centralized dashboard for monitoring security posture and compliance across all cloud environments.

A.2 Integration of Artificial Intelligence and Machine Learning

A.2.1 Enhancing Threat Detection and Response

Artificial Intelligence (AI) and Machine Learning (ML) transform cloud security by enhancing threat detection and response capabilities. These technologies enable the analysis of vast amounts of data to identify patterns and anomalies that may indicate security threats.

Key Benefits:

- **Real-Time Analysis:** AI and ML can analyze data in real-time to detect threats faster and more accurately.
- **Behavioral Analytics:** These technologies can identify unusual behaviors and activities that may signal an insider threat or a compromised account.
- **Automated Responses:** AI-driven systems can automate responses to detected threats, reducing response times and minimizing the impact of security incidents.

Example: Using an AI-powered CSPM tool that detects anomalies in network traffic and automatically isolates compromised resources to prevent further damage.

A.2.2 Predictive Security Measures

AI and ML can also predict potential security threats based on historical data and trends, allowing organizations to address vulnerabilities proactively before they are exploited.

Emerging Features:

- **Predictive Analytics:** Leveraging historical data to predict and preempt potential security threats.
- **Adaptive Security:** Implementing adaptive security measures that dynamically adjust based on the current threat landscape.

Example: Deploying an ML-driven CSPM tool that predicts likely attack vectors and suggests proactive security measures to mitigate risks.

A.3 Zero Trust Architecture (ZTA)

A.3.1 The Rise of Zero Trust

Zero Trust Architecture (ZTA) is gaining traction as a robust security model that assumes no implicit trust and requires continuous verification of user and device identities. This model addresses the limitations of traditional perimeter-based security approaches.

Key Principles:

- **Least Privilege Access:** Granting users and devices only the access necessary for their roles.
- **Continuous Verification:** Continuously verifying the identities of users and devices, regardless of their location.
- **Micro-Segmentation:** Segmenting networks to limit the lateral movement of threats and contain breaches.

Example: Implementing Zero-Trust policies that require all users to have multi-factor authentication (MFA) and enforce micro-segmentation to protect sensitive data.

A.3.2 CSPM and Zero Trust

Future CSPM solutions will integrate Zero Trust principles to enhance cloud security. These solutions will provide tools to implement and manage Zero Trust policies effectively.

Emerging Features:

- **Identity and Access Management:** Enhanced identity and access management capabilities that support Zero Trust principles.
- **Network Segmentation:** Tools to implement and manage network segmentation and micro-segmentation.
- **Continuous Compliance:** Continuous monitoring and compliance checks to ensure adherence to Zero Trust policies.

Example: Using a CSPM solution that integrates with identity management systems to enforce Zero Trust policies across cloud environments.

A.4 DevSecOps Integration

A.4.1 Embedding Security in DevOps

DevSecOps aims to integrate security into every phase of the software development lifecycle, from planning and development to deployment and operations. This approach ensures that security is a continuous and shared responsibility.

Key Benefits:

- **Early Detection:** Identifying and addressing security issues early in the development process.
- **Automated Security Testing:** Integrating automated security testing into CI/CD pipelines to catch vulnerabilities before deployment.
- **Collaborative Culture:** Fostering a collaborative culture where security, development, and operations teams work together seamlessly.

Example: Implementing security checks in CI/CD pipelines using tools like Checkov to scan infrastructure-as-code (IaC) templates for vulnerabilities.

A.4.2 CSPM and DevSecOps

Future CSPM solutions will support DevSecOps practices by providing tools and integrations to incorporate security into development workflows seamlessly.

Emerging Features:

- **CI/CD Integrations:** Integrations with CI/CD tools to automate security checks and enforce policies during development.
- **Shift-Left Security:** Tools to shift security considerations to the earliest stages of the development lifecycle.
- **Collaboration Platforms:** Platforms that support collaboration between security, development, and operations teams.

Example: Using a CSPM tool that integrates with Jenkins and GitLab to automate security scans and enforce compliance during the build and deployment processes.

A.5 Enhanced Compliance and Governance

A.5.1 Evolving Regulatory Landscape

The regulatory landscape for cloud security is continually evolving, with new laws and standards being introduced to address emerging threats and protect sensitive data. Organizations must adapt to these changes to remain compliant.

Key Considerations:

- **Dynamic Compliance:** Adapting to new and changing regulatory requirements promptly.
- **Automated Compliance Monitoring:** Implementing automated compliance monitoring to ensure continuous adherence to regulatory standards.
- **Comprehensive Audits:** Conducting comprehensive audits to identify compliance gaps and implement corrective measures.

Example: A CSPM solution automatically monitors compliance with new data protection regulations, such as the California Privacy Rights Act (CPRA).

A.5.2 Future CSPM Solutions for Compliance

Future CSPM solutions will offer enhanced features to help organizations manage compliance and governance more effectively.

Emerging Features:

- **Regulatory Updates:** Tools that provide real-time updates on regulatory changes and their implications.
- **Compliance Dashboards:** Comprehensive dashboards that offer real-time visibility into compliance status across cloud environments.
- **Automated Reporting:** Automated reporting tools that generate compliance reports for audits and assessments.

Example: Implementing a CSPM tool that provides a compliance dashboard with real-time updates on adherence to various regulatory frameworks.

A.6 Conclusion

The future of CSPM is shaped by several emerging trends that will enhance cloud security and compliance. As organizations increasingly adopt multi-cloud and hybrid environments, CSPM solutions will evolve to provide unified security management and visibility across diverse platforms. Integrating AI and machine learning will revolutionize threat detection and response, enabling proactive and predictive security measures. Zero Trust Architecture will become a cornerstone of cloud security, ensuring continuous verification and least privilege access. DevSecOps practices will embed security into every development lifecycle phase, fostering a culture of collaboration and shared responsibility. Enhanced compliance and governance features will help organizations navigate the evolving regulatory landscape and maintain robust security postures.

By staying informed about these emerging trends and adopting innovative CSPM solutions, organizations can effectively manage their cloud security posture and protect against evolving threats. Embracing continuous improvement and adaptation will be key to sustaining long-term security and compliance in the ever-changing world of cloud computing.

B. The Role of AI and Machine Learning in CSPM

As cloud environments become increasingly complex and threats continue to evolve, Artificial Intelligence (AI) and Machine Learning (ML) are playing a pivotal role in advancing Cloud Security Posture Management (CSPM). These technologies provide new threat detection, response, and security management capabilities. This chapter explores how AI and ML are transforming CSPM and what the future holds for these technologies in cloud security.

B.1 Enhancing Threat Detection and Response

B.1.1 Real-Time Threat Detection

AI and ML enable real-time threat detection by analyzing vast data to identify patterns and anomalies indicative of security threats. Unlike traditional rule-based systems, AI/ML models can learn from historical data and adapt to new threats.

Key Features:

- **Anomaly Detection:** AI models can identify unusual behaviors that may indicate a security breach, such as unexpected data access patterns or abnormal network traffic.
- **Behavioral Analysis:** ML algorithms can analyze user and entity behavior over time, creating profiles that help detect deviations from normal behavior.

Example: Implementing an AI-powered anomaly detection system that flags unusual login times or locations, potentially indicating compromised credentials.

B.1.2 Predictive Analytics

Predictive analytics uses AI/ML to forecast potential security threats based on historical data and trends. This proactive approach helps organizations anticipate and mitigate risks before they materialize.

Key Features:

- **Risk Prediction:** AI models can predict the likelihood of security incidents based on historical patterns and current indicators.
- **Proactive Measures:** Based on predictive insights, organizations can implement proactive security measures, such as preemptive patching or increased monitoring.

Example: Using ML to analyze past security incidents and predict potential future attacks, allowing the security team to reinforce defenses accordingly.

B.1.3 Automated Incident Response

AI and ML can automate various aspects of incident response, reducing the time and effort required to mitigate security incidents. Automated responses can contain threats quickly, minimizing their impact on the organization.

Key Features:

- **Immediate Actions:** AI-driven systems can automatically isolate compromised resources, block malicious IP addresses, or apply security patches.
- **Orchestration:** ML models can coordinate responses across multiple systems and platforms, ensuring comprehensive incident management.

Example: Deploying an AI-driven incident response platform that automatically quarantines affected endpoints upon detecting a malware infection.

B.2 Improving Compliance and Governance

B.2.1 Automated Compliance Monitoring

AI and ML enhance compliance monitoring by continuously analyzing cloud environments to ensure adherence to regulatory requirements and internal policies. Automated compliance checks ensure that security configurations remain consistent and up-to-date.

Key Features:

- **Continuous Auditing:** AI models can perform ongoing compliance audits, identifying deviations from established standards in real time.
- **Policy Enforcement:** ML algorithms can enforce compliance policies automatically, ensuring that cloud resources remain within the defined security parameters.

Example: Implementing an AI-based compliance tool that continuously monitors and enforces GDPR requirements across cloud environments.

B.2.2 Intelligent Reporting

AI and ML can generate intelligent compliance reports that provide deeper insights into an organization's security posture. These reports can highlight trends, identify recurring issues, and suggest areas for improvement.

Key Features:

- **Advanced Analytics:** AI-driven analytics can uncover patterns and correlations in compliance data, providing actionable insights.
- **Customizable Reports:** ML models can tailor reports to specific regulatory frameworks, business needs, or stakeholder preferences.

Example: Using AI to generate compliance reports that show current compliance status and predict potential future compliance risks based on trends.

B.3 Enhancing Security Operations

B.3.1 Security Automation and Orchestration

AI and ML streamline security operations through automation and orchestration, reducing the workload on security teams and improving operational efficiency.

Key Features:

- **Task Automation:** AI can automate routine security tasks, such as log analysis, threat hunting, and vulnerability scanning.

- **Incident Orchestration:** ML-driven orchestration platforms can coordinate complex incident response activities across different tools and teams.

Example: Deploying an ML-powered security orchestration platform that automatically triggers response workflows based on detected threats.

B.3.2 Adaptive Security Posture

AI and ML enable adaptive security postures that evolve in response to changing threat landscapes. These technologies can dynamically adjust security controls based on real-time threat intelligence and environmental changes.

Key Features:

- **Dynamic Configuration:** AI models can automatically adjust security configurations, such as firewall rules or access controls, in response to emerging threats.
- **Self-Learning Systems:** ML algorithms can continuously learn from new data, improving their ability to detect and respond to threats over time.

Example: Implementing an AI-driven firewall that dynamically updates its rules based on real-time threat intelligence feeds.

B.4 Future Trends in AI and ML for CSPM

B.4.1 Integration with DevSecOps

Integrating AI and ML with DevSecOps practices will enhance the security of development pipelines by automating security testing and compliance checks.

Key Features:

- **Automated Code Analysis:** AI models can analyze code for vulnerabilities during development, providing developers with immediate feedback.
- **CI/CD Integration:** ML algorithms can integrate with CI/CD tools to enforce security policies and conduct compliance checks throughout the development lifecycle.

Example: Using an AI-driven code analysis tool that scans code for vulnerabilities during each commit and provides recommendations for remediation.

B.4.2 Enhanced Threat Intelligence Platforms

Future threat intelligence platforms will leverage AI and ML to provide more comprehensive and actionable threat insights, enabling organizations to stay ahead of evolving threats.

Key Features:

- **Global Threat Correlation:** AI can correlate threat data from multiple sources globally, identifying widespread attack patterns and emerging threats.

- **Automated Threat Sharing:** ML-driven platforms can automatically share threat intelligence with trusted partners and industry groups, enhancing collective defense efforts.

Example: Implementing an AI-powered threat intelligence platform aggregating data from various sources and providing real-time alerts on emerging threats.

B.4.3 Advanced Behavioral Analytics

Behavioral analytics will become more sophisticated with AI and ML, providing deeper insights into user and entity behavior to detect insider threats and advanced persistent threats (APTs).

Key Features:

- **User Behavior Analysis:** AI models can create detailed user behavior profiles and detect deviations that may indicate malicious activity.
- **Entity Behavior Analysis:** ML algorithms can monitor the behavior of devices, applications, and other entities, identifying anomalies that could signify a security threat.

Example: Deploying an AI-based behavioral analytics tool that detects insider threats by monitoring deviations from typical user behavior patterns.

B.5 Conclusion

Integrating AI and ML into CSPM represents a significant advancement in cloud security. These technologies enhance threat detection and response, improve compliance monitoring and reporting, streamline security operations, and enable adaptive security postures. As AI and ML evolve, they will play an increasingly critical role in protecting cloud environments from sophisticated and emerging threats.

Organizations that adopt AI and ML-driven CSPM solutions will be better equipped to navigate the complexities of cloud security, maintain compliance, and stay ahead of evolving threats. By leveraging these advanced technologies, they can achieve a proactive and resilient security posture, ensuring the protection of their digital assets in the ever-changing landscape of cloud computing.

C. Preparing for Future Challenges

As cloud environments evolve and expand, the challenges of maintaining a robust security posture also increase. To effectively prepare for future challenges in Cloud Security Posture Management (CSPM), organizations must adopt forward-thinking strategies and continuously adapt to emerging threats and technological advancements. This chapter outlines key strategies and best practices for preparing for future challenges in CSPM.

C.1 Anticipating Emerging Threats

C.1.1 Staying Informed on Threat Trends

Keeping abreast of the latest threat trends is crucial for anticipating and mitigating emerging security risks. Regularly consuming threat intelligence reports, participating in security forums, and engaging with the cybersecurity community can provide valuable insights.

Key Practices:

- **Threat Intelligence Feeds:** Subscribe to threat intelligence feeds and integrate them into your CSPM solution to receive real-time updates on new threats.
- **Industry Collaboration:** Participate in industry-specific security groups and forums to share and receive information about emerging threats.
- **Continuous Learning:** Encourage security teams to attend conferences, webinars, and training sessions to stay updated on the latest threat trends.

Example: Leveraging threat intelligence platforms like Recorded Future or ThreatConnect to stay informed about new vulnerabilities and attack vectors relevant to your industry.

C.1.2 Advanced Threat Detection Techniques

Adopting advanced threat detection techniques, such as behavioral analytics and anomaly detection, can help identify sophisticated threats that traditional methods might miss.

Key Practices:

- **Behavioral Analytics:** Use behavioral analytics to establish baselines of normal activity and detect deviations that may indicate malicious behavior.
- **Anomaly Detection:** Implement anomaly detection systems that leverage machine learning to identify unusual patterns in network

traffic, user behavior, and system activity.
- **Honeypots and Deception:** Deploy honeypots and other deception technologies to detect and analyze attacker behavior.

Example: Implementing a machine learning-based anomaly detection system that flags unusual data access patterns, which could indicate a potential insider threat.

C.2 Adapting to Regulatory Changes

C.2.1 Proactive Compliance Management

Proactively managing compliance involves staying ahead of regulatory changes and implementing policies and controls to meet new requirements before they become mandatory.

Key Practices:

- **Regulatory Monitoring:** Regularly monitor updates from regulatory bodies and industry standards organizations to stay informed about upcoming changes.
- **Impact Assessments:** Conduct impact assessments to understand how regulatory changes affect your organization and plan necessary adjustments.
- **Policy Updates:** Continuously update security policies and procedures to align with new regulatory requirements.

Example: Using a CSPM solution that provides real-time updates on regulatory changes and suggests policy adjustments to maintain compliance.

C.2.2 Automating Compliance Processes

Automation can significantly reduce the burden of compliance management by continuously monitoring and enforcing regulatory requirements across cloud environments.

Key Practices:

- **Automated Audits:** Implement automated auditing tools that continuously assess compliance with relevant regulations and standards.
- **Policy as Code:** Use policy as code to define and enforce compliance policies programmatically, ensuring consistent application across all cloud resources.
- **Automated Reporting:** Generate automated compliance reports to provide real-time insights into your compliance status and streamline audit processes.

Example: Deploying a CSPM tool that automatically audits cloud configurations against frameworks like GDPR, HIPAA, and PCI DSS and generates compliance reports.

C.3 Leveraging Advanced Technologies

C.3.1 Embracing AI and Machine Learning

AI and machine learning are revolutionizing CSPM by enhancing threat detection, automating responses, and providing deeper insights into security data.

Key Practices:

- **AI-Powered Threat Detection:** Use AI to analyze large datasets and detect threats that traditional methods might miss.
- **Machine Learning Models:** Develop and train machine learning models to identify patterns and predict potential security incidents.
- **Automated Incident Response:** Implement AI-driven solutions that automatically contain and mitigate threats.

Example: Using an AI-powered CSPM platform that detects anomalies in user behavior and automatically triggers incident response workflows to contain potential breaches.

C.3.2 Integrating with DevSecOps

Integrating CSPM with DevSecOps practices ensures that security is embedded throughout the development lifecycle, from initial design to deployment and beyond.

Key Practices:

- **Security Testing in CI/CD:** Integrate security testing tools into CI/CD pipelines to catch vulnerabilities early in development.
- **Shift-Left Security:** Implement shift-left practices to address security issues at the earliest stages of development, reducing the cost and complexity of remediation.
- **Collaboration Tools:** Use collaboration tools to facilitate communication and coordination between development, operations, and security teams.

Example: Implementing a DevSecOps pipeline that includes static and dynamic application security testing (SAST and DAST) to ensure secure code deployment.

C.4 Enhancing Security Posture Management

C.4.1 Continuous Monitoring and Improvement

Continuous monitoring and improvement are essential for maintaining a robust security posture in the face of evolving threats and changing environments.

Key Practices:

- **Real-Time Monitoring:** Implement real-time monitoring solutions to continuously assess the security posture and detect incidents as they occur.
- **Feedback Loops:** Establish feedback loops to incorporate lessons learned from incidents and audits into ongoing security practices.
- **Regular Assessments:** Conduct security assessments, including vulnerability scans, penetration tests, and compliance audits, to identify and address gaps.

Example: Using a SIEM solution that provides real-time monitoring and integrates with CSPM tools to offer comprehensive visibility into security posture.

C.4.2 Incident Response and Recovery

Effective incident response and recovery capabilities are crucial for minimizing the impact of security incidents and ensuring rapid restoration of normal operations.

Key Practices:

- **Incident Response Plan:** Develop and maintain an incident response plan that outlines roles, responsibilities, and procedures for responding to security incidents.
- **Regular Drills:** Conduct incident response drills to test the plan's effectiveness and ensure readiness.
- **Recovery Procedures:** Establish and test recovery procedures to quickly restore systems and data following an incident.

Example: Implementing an incident response platform that automates key response tasks and coordinates actions across teams, ensuring a swift and effective response.

C.5 Building a Security-First Culture

C.5.1 Promoting Security Awareness

Building a security-first culture requires promoting security awareness across the organization and ensuring all employees understand their role in maintaining security.

Key Practices:

- **Training Programs:** Offer regular training programs on security best practices, emerging threats, and compliance requirements.
- **Awareness Campaigns:** Conduct security awareness campaigns to reinforce the importance of security and encourage proactive behavior.
- **Phishing Simulations:** Run phishing simulations to educate employees on recognizing and responding to phishing attempts.

Example: Developing a comprehensive security awareness program that includes monthly training sessions, regular email updates, and phishing simulation exercises.

C.5.2 Fostering Collaboration

Collaboration between security, development, and operations teams ensures that security is integrated into every organization's activities.

Key Practices:

- **Cross-Functional Teams:** Create cross-functional teams that include members from security, development, and operations to work on security initiatives.
- **Regular Meetings:** Hold meetings to discuss security topics, share updates, and address concerns.
- **Shared Goals:** Set shared security goals and metrics to promote collective ownership of security responsibilities.

Example: Establishing a DevSecOps team that meets weekly to discuss security issues, review progress, and plan future initiatives.

C.6 Conclusion

Preparing for future challenges in CSPM requires a proactive and adaptive approach. Organizations can effectively navigate the complexities of cloud security by anticipating emerging threats, adapting to regulatory changes, leveraging advanced technologies, enhancing security posture management, and building a security-first culture. These strategies and best practices will enable organizations to stay ahead of evolving threats, maintain compliance, and ensure the security and integrity of their cloud environments. As the landscape of cloud computing continues to evolve, a commitment to continuous improvement and adaptation will be key to sustaining long-term security and success.

VIII

Appendices

Appendix A: Glossary of Terms

A

Access Control

A security technique that regulates who or what can view or use resources in a computing environment. It ensures that only authorized users can access specific resources.

AI (Artificial Intelligence)

The simulation of human intelligence processes by machines, especially computer systems. These processes include learning, reasoning, and self-correction.

Anomaly Detection

The process of identifying data points, events, or observations that significantly deviate from the norm in a dataset often indicates potential security threats.

API (Application Programming Interface)

A set of protocols, routines, and tools for building software and applications specifies how software components should interact.

Attack Vector

A path or means by which a hacker gains access to a computer or network server to deliver a payload or malicious outcome.

B

Behavioral Analytics

A technology that uses machine learning to analyze patterns in user behavior to detect anomalies that may indicate security threats.

Breach

An incident where data is accessed without authorization. It is often used to refer to security incidents where sensitive, protected, or confidential data is copied, transmitted, viewed, stolen, or used by an individual unauthorized to do so.

C

Cloud Computing

The delivery of different services through the Internet, including data storage, servers, databases, networking, and software.

Cloud Security Posture Management (CSPM)

Tools and processes designed to monitor and manage cloud security and compliance continuously. CSPM identifies and remediates risks and misconfigurations across cloud environments.

Compliance

Adherence to standards, regulations, and laws that govern data security, privacy, and management.

Continuous Integration/Continuous Deployment (CI/CD)

A method to frequently deliver apps to customers by introducing automation into the stages of app development. The main concepts attributed to CI/CD are continuous integration, continuous deployment, and continuous delivery.

Cyber Threat

A malicious act that seeks to damage data, steal data, or disrupt digital life in general. It can come from various sources, including hackers, terrorist groups, hostile nation-states, criminal organizations, and insiders.

D

Data Breach

An incident where information is stolen or taken from a system without the knowledge or authorization of the system's owner.

DevSecOps

A methodology that integrates security practices within the DevOps process. It aims to automate core security tasks by embedding security controls and processes early in the DevOps workflow.

E

Encryption

Converting information or data into a code, especially to prevent unauthorized access.

Endpoint Detection and Response (EDR)

A cybersecurity technology that addresses the need for continuous monitoring and response to advanced threats. EDR solutions provide visibility into endpoint activities and help detect and respond to security incidents.

G

GDPR (General Data Protection Regulation)

EU law regulations on data protection and privacy for all individuals within the European Union and the European Economic Area also address transferring personal data outside the EU and EEA areas.

H

Honeypot

A security mechanism set to detect, deflect, or, in some manner, counteract attempts at unauthorized use of information systems. It consists of a computer, data, or network site that appears to be part of a network but is isolated and monitored.

I

IAM (Identity and Access Management)

A framework of policies and technologies for ensuring that the right individuals access the right resources at the right times for the right reasons.

Incident Response

The approach taken by an organization to prepare for, detect, contain, and recover from a data breach or cyberattack.

Insider Threat

A security risk that originates from within the targeted organization. It typically involves a current or former employee or business associate accessing inside information concerning the organization's security practices, data, and computer systems.

L

Least Privilege

A principle that dictates that users should be granted the minimum levels of access – or permissions – needed to perform their job functions.

M

Machine Learning (ML)

ML is a subset of artificial intelligence (AI) that enables systems to learn and improve from experience without being explicitly programmed. ML algorithms use statistical methods to identify patterns in data.

N

Network Segmentation

The practice of dividing a network into smaller segments, or subnets, to improve performance and security. Each subnet can be isolated and protected from the others.

P

Penetration Testing

A method of evaluating the security of a computer system or network by simulating an attack from a malicious source. The process involves identifying and exploiting vulnerabilities to determine how far an attacker could go.

Phishing

A type of cyber-attack where attackers send fraudulent messages designed to trick a human victim into revealing sensitive information or deploying malicious software, such as ransomware.

Predictive Analytics

Statistics, data mining, and machine learning techniques analyze current and historical data and make predictions about future events.

R

Real-Time Monitoring

The continuous, automated process of collecting and analyzing data to detect and respond to security incidents as they occur.

Risk Assessment

Identifying and analyzing relevant risks to achieving an organization's objectives form a basis for determining how the risks should be managed.

S

Security Information and Event Management (SIEM)

A set of complex technologies brought together to provide a holistic view of an organization's information technology (IT) security. SIEM systems aggregate and analyze activity from many different resources across an IT infrastructure.

Security Posture

The overall security status of an organization's software and hardware resources, network information, and security processes and services.

Shift-Left Security

The practice of performing security tests earlier in the software development lifecycle rather than waiting until the end of the process. This approach aims to identify and fix security issues early, reducing the cost and effort of remediation.

T

Threat Intelligence

Information about threats and threat actors that helps mitigate harmful events in cyberspace. It involves collecting and analyzing data about potential or current attacks that threaten an organization.

V

Vulnerability

A weakness or flaw in a system, network, or application that an attacker could exploit to gain unauthorized access or perform unauthorized actions.

Vulnerability Scanning

The process of identifying, quantifying, and prioritizing (or ranking) the vulnerabilities in a system.

Z

Zero Trust Architecture (ZTA)

A security concept centered around the belief that organizations should not automatically trust anything inside or outside their perimeters and must verify everything trying to connect to their systems before granting access.

Appendix B: CSPM Tool Comparison Matrix

Choosing the right Cloud Security Posture Management (CSPM) tool ensures robust security and compliance across cloud environments. This comparison matrix provides a detailed analysis of several leading CSPM tools, highlighting their features, strengths, and suitability for different use cases.

Key Criteria for Comparison

1. **Supported Cloud Platforms:** Which cloud platforms does the tool support (AWS, Azure, Google Cloud, multi-cloud)?
2. **Core Features:** What are the core features of the tool (compliance monitoring, threat detection, automated remediation, etc.)?
3. **Integration Capabilities:** How well does the tool integrate with other security and DevOps tools?
4. **User Interface and Reporting:** Is the tool user-friendly, and does it provide comprehensive reporting capabilities?
5. **Automation:** To what extent does the tool support automation of security tasks and compliance checks?
6. **Pricing:** What is the pricing model (subscription, pay-as-you-go, etc.)?

CSPM Tool Comparison Matrix

Feature/Tool	Prisma Cloud	AWS Security Hub	Azure Security Center	Google Cloud Security Command Center (SCC)	Dome9 (Check Point)	Orca Security
Supported Cloud Platforms	AWS, Azure, GCP, multi-cloud	AWS	Azure	GCP	AWS, Azure, GCP	AWS, Azure, GCP
Compliance Monitoring	Yes	Yes	Yes	Yes	Yes	Yes
Threat Detection	Yes	Yes	Yes	Yes	Yes	Yes
Automated Remediation	Yes	Yes	Yes	Yes	Yes	Yes
Integration Capabilities	High	Medium	Medium	Medium	High	High
User Interface	User-friendly	Integrated with AWS console	Integrated with Azure console	Integrated with GCP console	User-friendly	User-friendly
Reporting	Comprehensive	Basic	Comprehensive	Comprehensive	Comprehensive	Comprehensive
Automation	High	Medium	High	Medium	High	High
Pricing	Subscription	Pay-as-you-go	Pay-as-you-go	Pay-as-you-go	Subscription	Subscription

Detailed Analysis

Prisma Cloud (by Palo Alto Networks)

Supported Cloud Platforms: AWS, Azure, Google Cloud, multi-cloud

Core Features:

- **Compliance Monitoring:** Supports various compliance frameworks (CIS, GDPR, HIPAA, PCI DSS).
- **Threat Detection:** Uses machine learning for advanced threat detection.
- **Automated Remediation:** Provides automated remediation workflows.
- **Integration Capabilities:** Integrates with various DevOps and security tools, including SIEMs, SOARs, and CI/CD pipelines.
- **User Interface and Reporting:** Offers a user-friendly interface with comprehensive reporting capabilities.
- **Automation:** High level of automation for security tasks and compliance checks.
- **Pricing:** Subscription-based model.

Strengths:

- Extensive multi-cloud support.
- Advanced threat detection and remediation capabilities.
- Strong integration with other security and DevOps tools.

Suitability: Best for organizations with complex, multi-cloud environments seeking comprehensive security and compliance management.

AWS Security Hub

Supported Cloud Platforms: AWS

Core Features:

- **Compliance Monitoring:** Integrates with AWS Config to provide compliance monitoring for AWS resources.
- **Threat Detection:** Aggregates findings from various AWS services (GuardDuty, Inspector, Macie).
- **Automated Remediation:** Limited automated remediation capabilities, primarily through integration with AWS Lambda.
- **Integration Capabilities:** Integrates with other AWS services with limited integration with third-party tools.
- **User Interface and Reporting:** Integrated with the AWS Management Console, offering basic reporting features.
- **Automation:** Medium level of automation, mainly through AWS-native services.
- **Pricing:** Pay-as-you-go model.

Strengths:

- Seamless integration with other AWS services.
- Centralized view of security findings within the AWS ecosystem.

Suitability: Ideal for organizations primarily using AWS and looking for a native solution integrated with existing AWS services.

Azure Security Center

Supported Cloud Platforms: Azure

Core Features:

- **Compliance Monitoring:** Provides continuous compliance assessments for Azure resources.
- **Threat Detection:** Advanced threat detection using Microsoft Defender.
- **Automated Remediation:** High level of automated remediation through Azure Policy and Logic Apps.
- **Integration Capabilities:** Integrates with Azure services and supports integration with third-party tools.
- **User Interface and Reporting:** Integrated with the Azure portal, offering comprehensive reporting features.
- **Automation:** High level of automation for security tasks and compliance checks.
- **Pricing:** Pay-as-you-go model.

Strengths:

- Deep integration with Azure services.
- Strong compliance and threat detection capabilities.

Suitability: Best for organizations using Azure that require integrated security management and compliance monitoring.

Google Cloud Security Command Center (SCC)

Supported Cloud Platforms: Google Cloud

Core Features:

- **Compliance Monitoring:** Monitors compliance with Google Cloud best practices and regulatory requirements.
- **Threat Detection:** Uses Google Cloud-native threat detection services.
- **Automated Remediation:** Limited automated remediation capabilities, primarily through integration with Cloud Functions.
- **Integration Capabilities:** Integrates with Google Cloud services, but limited third-party integrations.
- **User Interface and Reporting:** Integrated with the Google Cloud Console, offering comprehensive reporting features.
- **Automation:** Medium level of automation, mainly through Google Cloud-native services.
- **Pricing:** Pay-as-you-go model.

Strengths:

- Seamless integration with Google Cloud services.
- Comprehensive compliance and threat detection features within Google Cloud.

Suitability: Ideal for organizations using Google Cloud and seeking integrated security management and compliance monitoring.

Dome9 (by Check Point)

Supported Cloud Platforms: AWS, Azure, Google Cloud

Core Features:

- **Compliance Monitoring:** Supports multiple compliance frameworks and continuous assessments.
- **Threat Detection:** Provides advanced threat detection capabilities.

- **Automated Remediation:** High level of automated remediation through custom scripts and policies.
- **Integration Capabilities:** Strong integration with other security tools and platforms.
- **User Interface and Reporting:** User-friendly interface with comprehensive reporting features.
- **Automation:** High level of automation for security tasks and compliance checks.
- **Pricing:** Subscription-based model.

Strengths:

- Extensive support for multi-cloud environments.
- Advanced automation and remediation capabilities.

Suitability: Best for organizations with multi-cloud strategies looking for robust security and compliance management.

Orca Security

Supported Cloud Platforms: AWS, Azure, Google Cloud

Core Features:

- **Compliance Monitoring:** Provides continuous compliance assessments and supports multiple frameworks.
- **Threat Detection:** Uses deep cloud asset visibility for comprehensive threat detection.
- **Automated Remediation:** High level of automated remediation capabilities.
- **Integration Capabilities:** Strong integration with various DevOps and security tools.
- **User Interface and Reporting:** Offers a user-friendly interface with

detailed reporting features.
- **Automation:** High level of automation for security tasks and compliance checks.
- **Pricing:** Subscription-based model.

Strengths:

- Comprehensive visibility across cloud environments.
- Advanced threat detection and remediation features.

Suitability: Ideal for organizations seeking deep visibility and robust security management across multiple cloud platforms.

Conclusion

Selecting the right CSPM tool depends on your organization's needs, cloud environment, and security requirements. This comparison matrix provides a detailed overview of the leading CSPM tools, helping you make an informed decision based on key features, integration capabilities, and overall suitability for your use case. Choosing the right CSPM solution can enhance your cloud security posture, ensure compliance, and protect your critical assets against evolving threats.

Appendix C: Additional Resources and Reading

This appendix provides a curated list of additional resources and recommended reading for those looking to deepen their understanding of cloud security posture management (CSPM) and enhance their expertise in cloud security. These resources cover various topics, from fundamental concepts to advanced practices, and are intended to support continuous learning and professional development.

Books

1. "Cloud Security and Privacy: An Enterprise Perspective on Risks and Compliance" by Tim Mather, Subra Kumaraswamy, and Shahed Latif

This book offers a comprehensive overview of cloud security and privacy issues, with practical risk management and compliance advice.

2. "Architecting the Cloud: Design Decisions for Cloud Computing Service Models (SaaS, PaaS, and IaaS)" by Michael J. Kavis

A detailed guide on cloud architecture, exploring different service models and their security implications.

3. "Mastering Cloud Security" by Kris Hermans

This book provides in-depth coverage of cloud security principles, strategies, and technologies, making it an excellent resource for security professionals.

4. **"Zero Trust Networks: Building Secure Systems in Untrusted Networks" by Evan Gilman and Doug Barth**

An essential read on the Zero Trust security model, offering practical guidance on implementing Zero Trust principles in cloud environments.

5. **"The DevOps Handbook: How to Create World-Class Agility, Reliability, & Security in Technology Organizations" by Gene Kim, Patrick Debois, John Willis, and Jez Humble**

While not exclusively about cloud security, this book covers DevSecOps practices crucial for integrating security into cloud operations.

Research Papers and Articles

1. **"The NIST Definition of Cloud Computing" by Peter Mell and Timothy Grance**

This seminal paper provides the foundational definition of cloud computing and its essential characteristics, service models, and deployment models.

2. **"Cloud Computing Security: From Single to Multi-Clouds" by Imran Razzak**

A research paper that explores security challenges and solutions in single-cloud and multi-cloud environments.

3. **"CSPM for Multi-Cloud Environments: Challenges and Solutions" by SANS Institute**

This whitepaper discusses the unique challenges of managing security posture in multi-cloud environments and offers practical solutions.

4. "The State of Cloud Security: 2023" by CSA (Cloud Security Alliance)

An annual report that provides insights into current cloud security trends, emerging threats, and best practices based on industry surveys.

5. "Machine Learning in Cybersecurity: A Comprehensive Survey" by IEEE

A detailed survey paper that explores the applications of machine learning in cybersecurity, including threat detection and response.

Online Courses and Tutorials

1. Coursera: "Cloud Security" by University of Maryland

A comprehensive course that covers key concepts and practices in cloud security, including risk management, compliance, and security architectures.

2. Udemy: "AWS Security Fundamentals"

This course introduces AWS security services and best practices for securing AWS environments.

3. LinkedIn Learning: "Cloud Security Architecture for CISOs"

A course designed for security leaders, focusing on building and managing secure cloud architectures.

4. Pluralsight: "Azure Security Engineer: Implement Advanced Network

Security"

A course that covers advanced network security topics in Azure, including secure network architectures and threat protection.

5. Google Cloud Training: "Security in Google Cloud Platform"

Google Cloud's training program focuses on security services and best practices for securing GCP environments.

Industry Reports and Guides

1. Gartner: "Magic Quadrant for Cloud Infrastructure and Platform Services"

An annual report that evaluates the leading cloud service providers and their security capabilities.

A comprehensive analysis of the top cloud workload security solutions, including their strengths and weaknesses.

3. CSA (Cloud Security Alliance): "Cloud Controls Matrix (CCM)"

A cybersecurity control framework for cloud computing, providing a detailed set of controls to manage cloud security risks.

4. OWASP: "Top Ten Cloud Security Risks"

A guide that outlines the top ten security risks in cloud environments and provides recommendations for mitigating these risks.

5. NIST: "Special Publication 800-53: Security and Privacy Controls for

Federal Information Systems and Organizations"

A catalog of security and privacy controls for federal information systems, widely used as a benchmark for security practices.

Blogs and Websites

1. Cloud Security Alliance Blog

The CSA blog offers regular updates, expert insights, and practical advice on various aspects of cloud security.

2. Dark Reading: Cloud Security

A dedicated section of Dark Reading that covers the latest news, research, and analysis on cloud security trends and threats.

3. AWS Security Blog

Amazon Web Services' official blog on cloud security features best practices, case studies, and updates on AWS security services.

4. Azure Security Blog

Microsoft Azure's official blog provides insights, tips, and updates on securing Azure environments.

5. Google Cloud Security Blog

Google Cloud's official security blog offers articles on security best practices, new features, and threat intelligence.

Professional Organizations and Certifications

1. (ISC)²: Certified Cloud Security Professional (CCSP)

A globally recognized certification that validates advanced skills and knowledge in cloud security.

2. Cloud Security Alliance (CSA)

An organization dedicated to defining and raising awareness of best practices to help ensure secure cloud computing.

3. ISACA: Certified Information Systems Auditor (CISA)

A certification that focuses on auditing, control, and assurance, relevant for assessing cloud security postures.

4. SANS Institute

A leading cybersecurity training and certification organization offers courses and certifications related to cloud security.

5. CompTIA Cloud+

A certification that validates the skills and expertise needed to secure and manage cloud technologies.

Appendix D: Templates and Checklists

Effective Cloud Security Posture Management (CSPM) requires careful planning, consistent execution, and regular assessment. This appendix provides a collection of templates and checklists to help streamline the management and assessment of cloud security practices. These resources are designed to ensure that all necessary steps are taken to secure cloud environments and maintain compliance with relevant standards and regulations.

D.1 Security Policy Template

Purpose: To define the organization's policies and procedures for managing cloud security and ensuring compliance.

Scope: This policy applies to all employees, contractors, and third-party users who access or manage the organization's cloud resources.

Cloud Security Policy

1. **Introduction**
   1.1 Purpose
   1.2 Scope
   1.3 Objectives

2. Roles and Responsibilities
   2.1 Security Team
   2.2 IT Department
   2.3 Employees
   2.4 Third-Party Vendors

3. Access Control
   3.1 User Authentication
   3.2 Multi-Factor Authentication (MFA)
   3.3 Role-Based Access Control (RBAC)

4. Data Protection
   4.1 Data Encryption
   4.2 Data Backup and Recovery
   4.3 Data Classification and Handling

5. Incident Response
   5.1 Incident Detection and Reporting
   5.2 Incident Response Plan
   5.3 Post-Incident Review

6. Compliance and Auditing
   6.1 Compliance Requirements
   6.2 Regular Audits
   6.3 Record Keeping

7. Security Training and Awareness
   7.1 Employee Training Programs
   7.2 Security Awareness Campaigns

8. Continuous Improvement
   8.1 Monitoring and Evaluation
   8.2 Policy Review and Update

APPENDIX D: TEMPLATES AND CHECKLISTS

9. **Approval and Review**
    9.1 Policy Approval
    9.2 Review Cycle

D.2 Risk Assessment Checklist

Purpose: To systematically identify and evaluate potential risks to cloud security and determine appropriate mitigation strategies.

Cloud Security Risk Assessment Checklist

1. Asset Identification
- ☐ Identify all cloud assets (e.g., data, applications, services).
- ☐ Classify assets based on their criticality and sensitivity.

2. Threat Identification
- ☐ Identify potential internal threats (e.g., insider threats).
- ☐ Identify potential external threats (e.g., cyber-attacks, natural disasters).

3. Vulnerability Assessment
- ☐ Conduct vulnerability scans on cloud resources.
- ☐ Review previous security incidents and known vulnerabilities.

4. Risk Analysis
- ☐ Evaluate the likelihood of each threat exploiting a vulnerability.
- ☐ Assess the potential impact of each risk on the organization.

5. Risk Mitigation
- ☐ Develop and implement risk mitigation strategies.
- ☐ Assign responsibilities for risk management activities.

6. Risk Monitoring
- [ ] Establish procedures for continuous monitoring of identified risks.
- [ ] Regularly review and update risk assessments.

D.3 Compliance Checklist

Purpose: To ensure that the organization adheres to relevant regulatory requirements and industry standards for cloud security.

Cloud Security Compliance Checklist

1. General Compliance
- [ ] Review and understand applicable regulations and standards (e.g., GDPR, HIPAA, PCI DSS).
- [ ] Ensure all cloud policies align with regulatory requirements.

2. Data Protection
- [ ] Implement data encryption for data at rest and in transit.
- [ ] Establish data retention and deletion policies.

3. Access Control
- [ ] Enforce strong authentication mechanisms, including MFA.
- [ ] Implement RBAC to restrict access based on user roles.

4. Incident Response
- [ ] Develop an incident response plan and ensure it includes regulatory reporting requirements.
- [ ] Conduct regular incident response drills.

5. Auditing and Monitoring
- [ ] Enable logging and monitoring of cloud activities.

☐ Conduct regular compliance audits and reviews.

6. Documentation
☐ Maintain documentation of compliance efforts, including policies, procedures, and audit reports.

☐ Ensure documentation is updated regularly and accessible to relevant stakeholders.

D.4 Incident Response Plan Template

Purpose: To outline the procedures and responsibilities for responding to security incidents in a cloud environment.

Incident Response Plan

1. Introduction
    1.1 Purpose
    1.2 Scope
    1.3 Objectives

2. Incident Response Team
    2.1 Roles and Responsibilities
    2.2 Contact Information

3. Incident Detection and Reporting
    3.1 Incident Detection Methods
    3.2 Incident Reporting Procedures

4. Incident Classification
    4.1 Severity Levels
    4.2 Classification Criteria

5. Incident Response Procedures
    5.1 Initial Response
    5.2 Containment
    5.3 Eradication
    5.4 Recovery

6. Communication and Coordination
    6.1 Internal Communication
    6.2 External Communication

7. Post-Incident Activities
    7.1 Post-Incident Review
    7.2 Lessons Learned
    7.3 Incident Documentation

8. Plan Testing and Maintenance
    8.1 Regular Testing
    8.2 Plan Review and Updates

9. Approval and Review
    9.1 Plan Approval
    9.2 Review Cycle

D.5 Cloud Security Audit Checklist

Purpose: To systematically evaluate the security posture of the organization's cloud environment and identify areas for improvement.

Cloud Security Audit Checklist

1. Organizational Security

☐ Review cloud security policies and procedures.
☐ Verify roles and responsibilities for cloud security management.

2. Access Control
☐ Check the implementation of authentication mechanisms, including MFA.
☐ Review access control policies and RBAC configurations.

3. Data Protection
☐ Verify data encryption methods for data at rest and in transit.
☐ Assess data backup and recovery processes.

4. Network Security
☐ Evaluate network security controls, including firewalls and security groups.
☐ Check the implementation of network segmentation.

5. Compliance and Governance
☐ Review compliance with relevant regulations and standards.
☐ Verify the effectiveness of compliance monitoring tools.

6. Incident Response
☐ Assess the incident response plan and procedures.
☐ Verify the execution of regular incident response drills.

7. Continuous Monitoring
☐ Check the implementation of continuous monitoring tools and processes.
☐ Review logging and alerting mechanisms.

8. Vulnerability Management
☐ Evaluate the vulnerability management program, including scanning and patching processes.

☐ Review the remediation of identified vulnerabilities.

9. Physical Security

☐ Verify the physical security measures for data centers and other critical infrastructure.

☐ Check access controls for physical facilities.

10. Documentation

☐ Ensure all security-related documentation is complete and up to date.

☐ Verify the availability of audit logs and compliance records.

About the Author

Edgardo Fernandez Climent, an accomplished IT leader with over two decades of experience, has significantly contributed to infrastructure, networks, and cybersecurity. His exceptional leadership skills and strategic vision have positioned him as a prominent figure in the industry. After graduating with honors in Computer Information Systems, Edgardo pursued an MBA and a Master's in Management Information Systems, further enhancing his expertise. He also holds several industry certifications, such as PMP, ITIL4, and Security+, demonstrating his commitment to professional development and staying at the forefront of industry standards.

Edgardo has consistently demonstrated his ability to lead organizations through complex technological transformations throughout his career. His deep understanding of emerging technologies and industry trends has enabled him to develop and implement innovative strategies that drive business growth and ensure technological resilience. Edgardo's leadership in navigating the ever-changing landscape of cybersecurity has been instrumental in safeguarding organizations against the evolving threats of the digital world.

As a visionary leader, Edgardo is known for his ability to inspire and motivate teams to achieve excellence. He fosters a culture of continuous learning and encourages his team members to embrace new technologies and develop their skills. Edgardo's commitment to mentoring and developing the next generation of IT leaders has profoundly impacted the industry as he shares his knowledge and experiences to empower others to succeed.

Edgardo's leadership style is characterized by his ability to build strong relationships, promote collaboration, and drive results. He has a proven track record of successfully leading cross-functional teams and aligning IT initiatives with business objectives. His strategic thinking and technical expertise have enabled him to develop and execute transformative initiatives that have delivered significant value to the organizations he has served.

Today, as a highly sought-after consultant in the IT industry, Edgardo continues to shape the technological landscape. His leadership and expertise are highly valued by organizations seeking to drive innovation, optimize their IT infrastructure, and strengthen their cybersecurity posture. Edgardo's journey is a testament to the power of visionary leadership, continuous learning, and a relentless pursuit of excellence in the ever-evolving field of information technology.

You can connect with me on:
- https://fernandezcliment.com
- https://twitter.com/efernandezclime
- https://www.facebook.com/edgardo.fernandez.climent
- https://amazon.com/author/efernandezcliment

Subscribe to my newsletter:
- https://fernandezcliment.com/join-our-mail-list

Also by Edgardo Fernandez Climent

Cloud Security Strategies: Protecting Data in the Digital Age

"Cloud Security Strategies: Protecting Data in the Digital Age" is an essential guide for IT professionals, security specialists, and business leaders navigating the complex landscape of cloud computing security. This comprehensive book offers a deep dive into the critical aspects of securing cloud environments, from foundational concepts to advanced strategies.

Written by an experienced cloud security expert, this book provides:

In-depth analysis of cloud security challenges across various service models (IaaS, PaaS, SaaS)

Best practices for designing secure cloud architectures and implementing robust security controls

Practical guidance on addressing misconfigurations and vulnerabilities in cloud environments

Strategies for real-time monitoring, incident response, and continuous improvement in cloud security

Readers will gain valuable insights into:

Identity and access management in the cloud

Data encryption and protection strategies

Network security in distributed environments

Compliance and regulatory considerations for cloud adoption

Emerging threats and future trends in cloud security

With real-world case studies, detailed technical explanations, and actionable advice, this book equips professionals with the knowledge and tools to safeguard their organizations' assets in the cloud. Whether you're new to cloud security or looking to enhance your expertise, "Cloud Security Strategies" provides the comprehensive guidance you need to protect your data in today's digital landscape confidently.

This book is an indispensable resource in the rapidly evolving field of cloud security. It is perfect for IT managers, security professionals, cloud architects, and anyone responsible for securing cloud infrastructure.

Multicloud Mastery: Architecting Success in the Age of Digital Transformation

Dive into the complex world of multicloud architectures with this comprehensive guide, tailored for IT professionals navigating the evolving landscape of cloud computing. Written by a seasoned practitioner with extensive experience in multicloud implementations, this book offers a deep dive into the strategies, best practices, and cutting-edge technologies that drive successful multicloud adoptions.

Key features include:

- In-depth exploration of multicloud architectures, from basic concepts to advanced implementations

- Practical strategies for seamless integration, security, and compliance across multiple cloud providers

- Case studies showcasing successful multicloud deployments and lessons learned from failures

- Detailed guidelines for cost optimization, performance tuning, and efficient resource management in multicloud environments

- Insights into emerging trends and future developments in multicloud technologies

- Comprehensive appendices covering everything from glossary terms to sample policies and cost calculation worksheets

Whether you're an IT manager considering a multicloud strategy, a cloud architect looking to optimize existing multicloud environments, or a developer aiming to leverage the full potential of diverse cloud services, this book provides the knowledge and tools you need to succeed.

Equip yourself with the expertise to architect, implement, and manage robust multicloud solutions. Stay ahead of the curve in the rapidly evolving world of cloud computing with "Mastering Multicloud" - your definitive guide to harnessing the power of multiple clouds for unparalleled flexibility, scalability, and innovation.

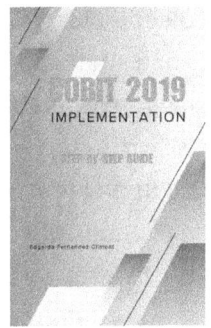

COBIT 2019 Implementation: A Step-by-Step Guide

"COBIT 2019 Implementation: A Step-by-Step Guide" is the ultimate companion for organizations embarking on implementing COBIT, the globally recognized IT governance and management framework. This comprehensive guide, written by a renowned expert in the field, provides a clear and practical roadmap for implementing COBIT, from understanding its core principles and components to tailoring and applying its processes and practices to specific organizational needs and contexts.

The book covers all phases of the COBIT implementation lifecycle, including:

- Assessing the current state of IT governance and management practices

- Setting objectives and scoping the implementation

- Building a high-performing implementation team

- Designing and implementing COBIT processes and controls

- Measuring and monitoring process performance and maturity

- Driving continuous improvement and optimization of IT capabilities and services

The book contains best practices, practical tools, and templates, including assessment checklists and process design templates. It also provides in-depth coverage of advanced topics such as integrating COBIT with other frameworks and standards, scaling COBIT for large and complex organizations, and applying COBIT to emerging technologies and business models.

Whether you are an IT professional, executive, or stakeholder looking to optimize your IT governance and management practices or a student or researcher seeking to deepen your knowledge of COBIT and its application, this book is an essential resource. With its clear and concise writing style, practical focus, and comprehensive coverage, "COBIT 2019 Implementation: A Step-by-Step Guide" is the definitive guide to implementing COBIT and driving greater value, efficiency, and agility from your IT investments and activities.

AIOps: Revolutionizing IT Operations with Artificial Intelligence

"AIOps: Revolutionizing IT Operations with Artificial Intelligence" is a must-read for IT professionals looking to leverage the transformative power of AI and machine learning in IT operations. This comprehensive guide demystifies the concepts, technologies, and best practices behind AIOps, enabling readers to implement intelligent automation, predictive analytics, and data-driven decision-making in their organizations.

The book begins by introducing the fundamental principles and components of AIOps, including data ingestion, anomaly detection, root cause analysis, and automated remediation. It then delves into real-world use cases and applications, showcasing how AIOps can revolutionize incident management, performance optimization, capacity planning, and user experience.

Readers will learn how to build and train AI models, integrate AIOps with existing IT processes and tools, and establish governance frameworks for responsible and ethical AI deployment. The book also explores the organizational and cultural aspects of AIOps adoption, providing strategies for change management, skill development, and continuous improvement.

Through practical examples, case studies, and expert insights, this book empowers IT professionals to harness the full potential of AIOps and drive digital transformation in their organizations. Whether you are an IT manager, system administrator, or data scientist, this book provides the knowledge and guidance needed to succeed in AI-driven IT operations.

AI-Powered Cybersecurity: The Promise and Perils of Generative AI

"AI-Powered Cybersecurity: The Promise and Perils of Generative AI" is a must-read for IT professionals seeking to understand and harness the power of GenAI in cybersecurity. This book explores GenAI's applications, benefits, and challenges in various cybersecurity domains, including threat detection, incident response, vulnerability management, and more.

The author, a practitioner with extensive experience in cybersecurity, AI, and GenAI, provides a balanced perspective on the potential of these technologies while also addressing critical concerns such as bias, explainability, and accountability. Through real-world case studies and practical insights, readers will learn how to effectively implement GenAI in their cybersecurity strategies and navigate AI-powered security's ethical and societal implications.

Whether you are a seasoned cybersecurity professional or an IT leader looking to stay ahead of the curve, this book will equip you with the knowledge and tools to make informed decisions about GenAI in your organization. Join the forefront of the cybersecurity revolution and discover how Generative AI is shaping the future of digital defense.

www.ingramcontent.com/pod-product-compliance
Lightning Source LLC
Chambersburg PA
CBHW071909210526
45479CB00002B/346